How People Change

The Norton Series on Interpersonal Neurobiology
Louis Cozolino, PhD, Series Editor
Allan N. Schore, PhD, Series Editor, 2007–2014
Daniel J. Siegel, MD, Founding Editor

The field of mental health is in a tremendously exciting period of growth and conceptual reorganization. Independent findings from a variety of scientific endeavors are converging in an interdisciplinary view of the mind and mental well-being. An interpersonal neurobiology of human development enables us to understand that the structure and function of the mind and brain are shaped by experiences, especially those involving emotional relationships.

The Norton Series on Interpersonal Neurobiology provides cutting-edge, multidisciplinary views that further our understanding of the complex neurobiology of the human mind. By drawing on a wide range of traditionally independent fields of research—such as neurobiology, genetics, memory, attachment, complex systems, anthropology, and evolutionary psychology—these texts offer mental health professionals a review and synthesis of scientific findings often inaccessible to clinicians. The books advance our understanding of human experience by finding the unity of knowledge, or consilience, that emerges with the translation of findings from numerous domains of study into a common language and conceptual framework. The series integrates the best of modern science with the healing art of psychotherapy.

A Norton Professional Book

How People Change:
Relationships and Neuroplasticity
in Psychotherapy

Edited by
MARION SOLOMON
and
DANIEL J. SIEGEL

W. W. Norton & Company
Independent Publishers Since 1923
New York • London

Note to Readers: Standards of clinical practice and protocol change over time, and no technique or recommendation is guaranteed to be safe or effective in all circumstances. This volume is intended as a general information resource for professionals practicing in the field of psychotherapy and mental health; it is not a substitute for appropriate training, peer review, and/or clinical supervision. Neither the publisher nor the author(s) can guarantee the complete accuracy, efficacy, or appropriateness of any particular recommendation in every respect.

For information about permission to reproduce selections from this book, write to
Permissions, W. W. Norton & Company, Inc., 500 Fifth Avenue, New York, NY 10110

For information about special discounts for bulk purchases, please contact
W. W. Norton Special Sales at specialsales@wwnorton.com or 800-233-4830

Manufacturing by Berryville Graphics
Production Manager: Christine Critelli

Library of Congress Cataloging-in-Publication Data

Names: Solomon, Marion Fried, editor. | Siegel, Daniel J., 1957-- editor.
Title: How people change : relationships and neuroplasticity in psychotherapy /
[edited by] Marion Solomon, Daniel J. Siegel.
Description: First edition. | New York : W.W. Norton & Company, [2017] | Series:
The Norton series on interpersonal neurobiology | Series: A Norton professional book |
Includes bibliographical references and index.
Identifiers: LCCN 2016039534 | ISBN 9780393711769 (hardcover)
Subjects: LCSH: Behavior therapy. | Psychotherapy. | Neuroplasticity. | Change (Psychology)
Classification: LCC RC489.B4 H624 2017 | DDC 616.89/142—dc23 LC record
available at https://lccn.loc.gov/2016039534

W. W. Norton & Company, Inc., 500 Fifth Avenue, New York, NY 10110
www.wwnorton.com

W. W. Norton & Company Ltd., 15 Carlisle Street, London W1D 3BS

1 2 3 4 5 6 7 8 9 0

To my children, Bonnie and Glenn, from whom I have learned so much, and my husband, Matthew, whose love and support makes all things possible.
—MFS

To Caroline, My In-House Healer
—DJS

Contents

Introduction

Marion Solomon and Daniel J. Siegel

WELCOME TO THE world of how we help the mind grow. We are psychotherapists, the editors and contributors of this book, who have found a
range of practices and approaches that help guide the growth of individuals, couples, and families toward well-being. As with any edited
text, you will find in these pages differing styles of writing and clinical practice that reflect each author's life experience as well as unique
understanding and articulation of the process of change that underlies
therapeutic work. One of the benefits of reading a multiauthored text
such as this is the compact offering of diverse presentations that illuminate a wide range of distinct strategies to support the growth of others
toward health and resilience. In this brief introduction, we (Marion
and Dan) offer you a synthetic overview of what you have in store. It is
our hope that within the wide range of explorations, you'll find something that touches you in a deep way, establishes an orientation across
a range of approaches, and perhaps inspires you to pursue the writings
of some of these authors in more depth in the future.

Psychotherapy is both an art and a science. Your experience as a
therapist will be shaped by a myriad of factors, from your own tem-
perament and upbringing to your style of learning and belief systems

regarding the nature of reality. It's no wonder there are so many unique approaches in the field of mental health! Even more, each person is unique, and not every approach to therapy works for everyone. For these reasons, we are excited to offer these introductory essays that sample a range of approaches and give you the chance to feel for yourself, in your own reading experience, how they relate to you and how they might work for different people with whom you work.

In our first chapter, Phillip M. Bromberg explores the important role that the experience of the therapist plays in joining with the inner life of the person in therapy. This chapter powerfully illuminates the notion of "self-states" and the ways in which each of us—therapist and client/patient alike—are created moment by moment in our interactions with others, and by the fantasies and memories that shape how our minds unfold in the present. This emerging process is central to the experience of both connection and transformation. Bromberg invites us to consider the deep ways in which this joining between two people shapes the process of change, and how we as therapists can participate fully to help facilitate this growth.

In the second chapter, Louis Cozolino and Vanessa Davis build on Bromberg's notion of the central role of our own inner experience in reflecting on the role of evolution in how our social brains have transformed across the generations. Exploring a range of emotions and their role in our inner and interpersonal lives, Cozolino and Davis illuminate the nature of shame and how this powerful state of self-dejection can influence not only our clients' life experiences, but even our own as therapists. In this way, these authors suggest that we view our relationships, both to others and to ourselves, as central to the healing process.

In Chapter 3, Margaret Wilkinson offers a broad view of the process of change, taking us deeply into the layers and circuitry in the brain to address how our relational connections may shape the way the brain changes in response to experience. We are offered a sophisticated review of how the field of neuroplasticity can reveal how therapeutic experiences may alter not only the synaptic connections linking neurons in a range of crucial circuits, but how myelin formation and the epigenetic regulation of gene expression can be molded by what we go through in life. Such neuroplastic responses can shape how traumatic experience may affect us; and the same neuroplasticity can hold hope—at any age—for how therapy may facilitate the process of long-lasting change.

In the fourth chapter, Pat Ogden invites us to explore the ways in which the focus of attention on the body's sensations and movements can be a primary component of the process of change. This powerful illumination of the ways in which going beneath and beyond words to push the boundaries of our windows of tolerance enables us to see how therapy is not simply a matter of being with clients/patients, but of helping them experience uncomfortable edges of their capacities and then move beyond those edges for deep change. Because focusing attention in this particular way streams energy patterns into awareness, therapists can greatly advance their work by utilizing this important source of our mental lives to further help clients/patients constructively change understandable but unwanted past adaptations.

Peter Levine then takes us on a journey into the question of *what is emotion* in Chapter 5, clarifying the differences and overlapping connections among bodily sensations, subjective feelings, and expressed emotion. By exploring the role of the body—its physiological responses, motor movements, and neural processes—in our emotional lives, Levine offers us helpful insights that widen our view of how therapy may help those with emotional dysregulation to achieve more harmonious states. This chapter further highlights Ogden's emphasis on how our usual focus on words needs to be deeply expanded to allow the non-worded world of the body and our states of mind to become a central focus in the process of change.

In Chapter 6, Russell Meares widens this view by exploring the importance of our connections with each other early in life to establish an integrated sense of self. Exploring the work of William James and Hughlings Jackson from the 19th century, Meares then offers insights from his own work on neural functioning in those with borderline personality. A take-home message from this chapter is that who we become is derived from how we've been a part of a relational connection, initially derived from what Colwyn Trevarthen has called "proto-conversations." The importance of this chapter to our foundational theoretical stance is to identify in principle how therapy may utilize such connections to help facilitate the growth of a more integrated self.

Daniel Hughes, in Chapter 7, offers insightful clinical vignettes involving work with children that enable us to dive deeply into the central role of a therapist's sense of wonder and empathy in creating the fabric of the therapeutic relationship at the heart of healing. Within these dialogues of exploration, children's narratives of who they are in the world and how they relate to others and to themselves are brought into a coherent state within the supportive explorations of therapists' caring curiosity. This relational connection is the pathway for helping children develop a sense of security and resilience in life.

In Chapter 8, psychoanalyst Martha Starks delves into the mathematical model of complex adaptive systems and explores the need, as Pat Ogden noted, of moving systems toward edges of functionality in order to promote growth. This chapter highlights the author's model of internal change, through classic psychoanalytic notions of id, ego, and superego, as well as pointing out the overlap of these insights with interpersonal subjective experience as well as relational interactions that cultivate change. From Bromberg to Stark, we are offered a wide range of ways of viewing the importance of the inner world and its interface with our connections with others. Ultimately, letting go of unhelpful patterns and adapting new strategies of growth are how these internal, experiential, and relational processes are again proposed to facilitate the change process.

In Chapter 9, Stan Tatkin clarifies this overlap further with his psychobiological approach to couple work, emphasizing the ways in which a therapist can place pressure on the system of a couple to both reveal and transform places that are stuck in their functioning. By exploring the nature of attachment, neural functioning, and relational regulation of affect, this approach further demonstrates the message of this book of how a therapist can utilize many levels of understanding from science to inform clinical strategies for change. Harnessing the power of long-term neural change, new levels of co-regulation, sufficiently repeated, can become embedded not only in behavioral change within the couple, but also in likely neural changes in the individuals themselves. *Inter* and *inner* become part of one unfolding process within psychotherapy.

In Marion Solomon's Chapter 10, we delve further into couple work, looking deeply at three cases to examine how defenses against attachment challenges from childhood can form the basis for the troubles of a couple in their present experiences and how to help each individual within the couple move toward a more flexible way of relating. In this chapter, we again see how understanding various neuroplastic responses of brain systems can help a therapist see how to move beyond engrained memory representations into new and more health-promoting ways of interacting. Here, too, *inner* and *inter* become the focus of therapeutic work.

In Bonnie Goldstein and Dan Siegel's final chapter, group therapy is explored with an aim to reveal how the process of communication within groups reflects the various ways individuals may have come to live a restricted life of isolation. The group setting can help facilitate ways of joining, of "feeling felt" by other members of the group, so that this unhealthful isolation can give rise to a more integrated way of being a linked yet differentiated person. The process of integration itself—the linkage of differentiated parts—can be seen as the fundamental mechanism of health and resilience. Here, this process of integration is illuminated and enhanced in the group setting.

There you have it: nearly a dozen ways to explore the process of change in psychotherapy. One link connecting each of these chapters, as we've seen, is the blending of the *inner* and the *inter* focus of the therapeutic work. In many ways, this balance of the inner and the interacting is itself a form of linking differentiated elements of our human reality, of cultivating more integration in the lives of those for whom we care in our professional work. There are many ways to catalyze integration, and these chapters may reveal the wide swath of strategies that help create the optimal internal and interactive regulation at the heart of change and the creation of well-being. We hope that this wide selection of authors and approaches will find a resonance with your own experiences and offer a jumping-off point from which you can dive more deeply into these varied and insightful approaches to healing and growth. Enjoy!

How People Change

1

Psychotherapy as the Growth of Wholeness

The Negotiation of Individuality and Otherness

Philip M. Bromberg

My one regret in life is that I am not someone else.
—Attributed to Woody Allen

We may still tremble, the fear of doing wretchedly may linger, but we grow. Flashes of inspiration come to guide the soul. In nature there is no outside.
When we are cast from a group or a condition we have still the companionship of all that is.
—Theodore Dreiser, *Jennie Gerhardt*

LIKE MOST EPIGRAPHS, those above were chosen for their implicit relevance to the perspective that organizes what is to follow. For me, it is their relevance to the power of the patient/therapist *relationship* as the medium through which a conceptual subtitle becomes a personal

17

experience—The Negotiation of Individuality and Otherness. Some-times, however, epigraphs seem to have a mind of their own, as did mine. They insisted in *participating* in the writing of the chapter, not just introducing it and then politely disappearing. In the following section, you are about to see what I mean.

Unbidden

I've never before used an epigraph in this way, much less *two*. Nor-mally, after choosing an epigraph that appeals to me, I then forget about it and concentrate on writing. But in composing this chapter, I wasn't able to do that, and as I wrote, I couldn't keep myself from returning to the epigraphs as if they were beckoning me—almost as if I kept reading and rereading them, they would somehow *show* me the meaning of my irrational behavior. In fact they did, but not in a nice, self-contained, rational way. What I received was not a "meaning" but a feeling of strangely pleasurable surrender to something new that was even *more* unbidden: The *words* of these two epigraphs, my reason for choosing them, kept changing *experientially* in unexpectedly personal ways while I was writing. Their words, the thing that *carries* the mean-ing in an epigraph, gradually became part of a previously unimaginable *relationship* with a human being I am imagining saying them.

I, of course, ask myself if this might be similar to what takes place while I am being a therapist—that the words of the stranger called "patient" *begin* as more real than the person who speaks them—and that the mean-ing of the words evolves as part of my growing relationship with the person speaking them. My answer is that it did feel *very* similar, and I am offering the opinion that, like the relational evolution of my epigraphs, the dyadic evolution we call "psychotherapy" *begins* as an unimaginable relationship that becomes increasingly imaginable because the author of the words, through the continuity of the relationship, is becoming real in new ways as shifting self-states revisit "old" things.

As I began to write this chapter, I first experienced my epigraphs only through the lens that led me to *choose* them; they seemed to *rep-resent* a polarity of self-experience in dealing with the challenge of liv-ing life, and they also seemed to *evoke* the complexity of meaning with regard to the concept of "change."

In the *first* epigraph, the concept of change is evoked as a *fantasy*—the fantasy of being "someone else." In the *second* epigraph, the idea of change is transmuted into "growth." It is relationally transmuted through the *evolution of fantasy into imagination*.[1] In the psychoanalytic relationship, the evolution takes place as an *interpersonal/relational* phenomenon in which the negotiation of selfhood and otherness transmutes the concept of change into the experiential paradox I call "staying the same while changing" (Bromberg, 1998e). In this spirit—get ready for the "unbidden."

The First Epigraph

There were quite a few revisits! In my *initial* ones I could *"imagine* hearing" the dissociated not-me voice of a self-state who is speaking *about* who he feels he *really* is—a person without hope. These first revisits were sort of "Ho-hum" because I wasn't able, affectively, to experience him speaking *from* that self-state. But I could at least *imagine hearing* him say that he truly wishes he were "someone else." I also could "imagine hearing" him confessing that he wraps this in humor—humor designed simultaneously to *express* its truth (i.e., his *"one* regret") while *masking* it in the fact that because he is actually *saying* it, he is unlikely to mean it. I then had the *thought* that he cannot "change" who he feels he *really* is, because for him it is the truth about who he feels he will *always* be. That thought led to another, and *this* one was *more* unbidden. "If he should enter psychotherapy," I said to myself, "it will not be with the hope that *change* means *growth*, but with the possibility that he might at least make the most of the fantasy of being a *different* self—someone else." I then said to myself, a bit self-consciously and only *partly* with humor, "He's not even real and you're already looking at him as a potential referral." As I said these words to myself, I *ended* my first revisit. But my epigraph wasn't yet through with *me*.

There was something about *hearing myself* say that line that enabled me to *continue* the unbidden "madness" of my revisits to the epigraph even though I kept telling myself, "Enough is enough." I am pretty sure the main source of my willingness was that even *while* I was saying, "He's not even real and you're already looking at him as a potential referral," I could feel that my own use of humor was at that moment close enough to his that I knew "enough *wasn't* enough."

So I return! What happens is different but not totally. I am trying less hard to "figure him out" *conceptually* through the words of the epigraph. And without knowing why, I am now feeling *personally engaged with* him as a human being. I am with a person who, in giving up hope, found a way of bearing his internal state of nonending aloneness. I am feeling *bad* for him. But strangely, I am also feeling bad for *myself*. I'm feeling *deprived*. Once again comes the thought that none of this is based in reality—but this time it *feels* like just "words."

I'm then aware of an unbidden *emotion*, and I recall that I had been vaguely aware of it in my *first* revisits but that it didn't feel *personal*. Even though I had known it was mine, it didn't feel like *me*. This time it is unpleasant, and I tell myself that it's about feeling *deprived*. I say, "I'm now able to feel close to him and know that *he* can't feel it." The unbidden emotion gets even bigger. With mixed feelings I recognize what it is: *loneliness!* Suddenly I'm not sure that my closeness to him is authentic. My *loneliness* is taking up all the space, and it does not feel like unreciprocated closeness to him. It is a *not unfamiliar* pain. With increasingly greater certainty, I recognize the experience as one I have from time to time with certain patients: the loneliness of being *with* such an internally alone person and feeling the helplessness of it.

As I began to recognize the affective source of my loneliness, the *recognition* becomes exciting because I am now feeling *authentically* close and I can experience the difference. Even though *he* can't experience it because he has given up hope, he doesn't have the power to deprive *me* of it. Through my *loneliness* I could feel close to the person I am *with*— close to the person who has *given up hope*. But in order for it to happen, I had to surrender myself to the reality of *my unbidden self-awareness* in a relationship with a stranger—in this case a stranger, who, one might *realistically* say, isn't even "real."

If this had taken place as part of a "real reality" in which I *had* been his therapist, could I have found a way to help the two of us *use* it by sharing my experience of it and inviting him to do the same? I think so, but what matters most to me here is not whether our relationship was one-sided, whether his existence was real or imaginary, or that it was derived from an epigraph. The experience I share with you is created by something affectively *alive* between myself and an "other" that *became* alive despite its uncertainty. What took place for *me* during my "revisiting" led to an affective recognition that the person I was "with," in addition to his living with an *unshareable* state of hopeless aloneness, might also be alive to a therapist whose loneliness in being with him *is* potentially sharable and could lead somewhere unforeseen because of its *joint* uncertainty. In my being able to feel the *personal* excitement of what was taking place, I knew that I wanted to share with my readers that I not only could experience this person as a "difficult patient," but also could experience a deepening awareness of something I already "knew": that I *enjoy* working with difficult patients such as him.

The Second Epigraph

I began by discussing my choice of these *two* epigraphs as representing a *conceptual* polarity with regard to how I *think* about things. In the *second* epigraph, what I could not anticipate was that the *experiential* polarity that emerged during my relationship with the speaker would be personally discrepant with the *conceptual* polarity of the words. The quotation from Dreiser's novel at first seemed like a windfall. I imagined it as the voice of a person who feels secure in the internal experience of *hope*, and who can speak passionately about *wholeness* as a gift that *transcends* the pain of struggling with life's challenges. *Hope* is presented not as a place that one finally "arrives at" but as the lifelong challenge it truly is. I continue to love the epigraph; what I feel toward the *speaker*, however, is unexpected.

It was a bit startling to find that the quality of my relational experience during the course of my revisits, though in one way reprising my revisits to the first epigraph, did so in *reverse*.[2] My relationship with him did *not deepen the meaning* of my initial assumption that the speaker is someone for whom individuality already includes "self–otherness" and thereby allows this person to live life with "the companionship of all that is." It *challenges* my assumption. As I begin to feel more affectively related to Dreiser's speaker, I find myself thinking that if I were to have a relationship with this person as a *patient*, I might initially feel admiration but would soon be fighting against my own cautiousness and perhaps boredom.

"What an odd thing to feel," said I, once again. "Those wonderful *words* represent a perspective on growth that I totally share—and it is so beautifully expressed." *So* beautifully expressed that, even in the earliest revisits, I can recall wondering why the person who spoke these words would ever *need* anything he doesn't already possess.

Yet, something in the revisits makes me now think the opposite—as well as feel shut out from direct *experience* of what I'm thinking. Why? Unlike the revisits to the first epigraph, I am not coming to feel personally close to the speaker at *any* point. No unbidden affect, no evolution in the relationship. Only my *thinking* is changing. I am wondering whether his magnificent prose and seemingly personal insight might be an *alternate* version of the use of humor by the creator of the first epigraph. Oh, hell! If true, it would make this person, *too*, a difficult patient. But I'm also aware that if I were his therapist in "real reality," the *felt* difficulty would be different in a way that was upsetting to me. Even though I didn't at all enjoy recognizing it, I had a strong sense that it would likely take longer and be more arduous for a relationship to develop in which I would be contributing my own *genuine* aliveness. It would be hard for me to *enjoy* being with him. It is the kind of insight that has an immediately "personal" downside as well as the potential for a more satisfying and enduring upside.

The upside, as with the speaker in the first epigraph, was a heightening of *personal* awareness, but with this speaker, it was, in an even *more* personal way, also the downside. What was most vivid was not about *him*, but my recognition that the "me" as analyst/therapist had feelings about him as "patient" that I didn't like looking at explicitly—in this instance, reminding me that my ability to enjoy *being* with a patient "like him" does not come as easily. I realized that although in one way I was blaming him for failing to be the "good" patient I thought I was getting, the hard part for me to accept was that I was blaming him for being who, in my eyes, he *is*. The person I am feeling myself to be at that moment is most definitely a "not-me."

But, happily, what made it less painful was the unbidden (and uncharacteristic) appearance of a *conceptual* revisit to something that I had offered in a piece of writing 20 years ago (Bromberg, 1998a)—an idea that we might do well to abandon the concept of "difficult patient" and replace it with "difficult dyad." I am pretty sure if he and I had been in my *office* as patient and analyst/therapist during the first few visits of an initial consultation, I would have been *less quickly* aware of my dissociative self-protection that was provided by the conveniently insightful use of a less critical *concept*—as you will see later in the chapter when you experience it in action with an actual patient.

State-Sharing and Self–Otherness

Having now introduced you to how my mind works, I am ready to begin what I suppose could be called the "chapter proper." The foundational perspective that shapes my thinking is enriched by, and, in an ever-expanding way, *intertwined* with Allan Schore's groundbreaking contributions to the fields of both psychotherapy and neuroscience—particularly some of his major work during the past two decades (1994, 2003a, 2003b, 2011, 2012). As you read, you will see that in addition to the key importance of affect regulation and dysregulation, both Allan and I place special emphasis on the *phenomenon and concept* of "state-sharing" (Schore, 2003a, 2011, 2012)—that is, the right-brain to right-brain communication process through which each person's states of mind are known to the other *implicitly.*

The interface between my own thinking and his, when linked to the centrality we each place of the *mind–brain–body* interface, provides the core context that I believe will allow psychoanalysis as *psychotherapy* to become most *genuinely* therapeutic. My wish to *start* with our twosome is not quite as unselfish as it might appear because it allows my experience of its *shared* pleasure to then recede enough for me to equally enjoy the *individual* pleasure of meandering around on my *own*—which I shall be doing before long.

All in all, I will be reflecting on how the *human relationship* between patient and analyst/therapist enables an individual self to *heal* and simultaneously co-creates a dynamic link between *healing and growth* that allows the *relationship* to evolve into a source of *sustained* growth that most justifies the name *psychotherapy*. Let me restate this last sentence in terms of the idea that people *change*—the broad concept that organizes the *book's* overarching coherence. I will not be trying to elucidate *how* they change, because I have *trouble* using the word change when applied to people. I will instead be devoting my efforts to thinking about what makes psychotherapy *possible*. With any given patient, no matter how much we value our *concepts*, the "answer" to what makes psychotherapy therapeutic is for me not definable as a concept. It is a relational *experience* that is shaped by two specific people, and what makes it therapeutic is its *uncertainty*—the very thing that makes it conceptually indefinable. I am especially referring to the experience I call "safe surprises" (Bromberg, 2006a, pp. 10, 23, 95–99, 198–199) that take place *between* the two individuals as they are struggling with relational uncertainty—and "hanging in" anyway, more or less *together*.

In addition to his *scientific* contribution, Allan Schore's interpersonal/relational *sensibility* as *both* a neurobiologist and clinician has been a major force in rebuilding a bridge between psychotherapy and psycho-analysis. The body of his work has systematically provided evidence that personality growth is *interpersonal/relational* at the mind and body levels. One objective in this chapter is to show *how* the phenomenon of state-sharing allows the extraordinary phenomenon of *self-state commun-ion* to take place *in a way* that allows both partners to include their own and the other's subjectivities *within* their individual perceptual contexts of what takes place between them in their ongoing relationship.

This current *era* also happens to be one in which two remarka-ble things have happened simultaneously: *quantum physics* has lost its self-consciousness about accepting the existence of things seemingly impossible at the same time that the *psychoanalytic* focus of attention has shifted from the idea of an "encapsulated mind" to openly explor-ing the *nature of self*. This concurrence, though not by design, certainly plays a role in why *data* have been accumulating so rapidly, indicating that mental functioning is *inherently* relational, and especially so in the link between minds. One consequence is that as we are perceiving the *scope* of the link between minds, it often feels so staggering that it gen-erates the word uncanny[3]—*just because it is.*

I mention this because I believe that no theory of psychoanalysis is relevant unless the praxis upon which its psychotherapeutic relevance depends *delivers surprises*—and in continuing to expand the surprises, furthers the discovery of new human capacities that are even more *uncanny.*

State-Sharing, Dissociation, and Enactment

As Schore puts it in describing the dissociative communication process that links state-sharing and psychotherapy: "Dynamically fluctuating moment-to-moment state-sharing represents an *organized dialogue occurring within milliseconds*, and acts as an *interactive* matrix in which both partners match states and then simultaneously adjust their social attention, stim-ulation, and accelerating arousal in response to their partner's signals" (2003a, p. 96, emphasis added). The relationship between dissociation and right-brain to right-brain state-sharing has a complex interface with the therapeutic process that Schore (2003b) writes about as the *paradox-ical dual role of dissociation*. He offers the view that the use of dissociation as a last-resort defensive strategy represents the greatest *counterforce* to effective psychotherapeutic treatment, while paradoxically serving on its *behalf* as a communication process. It allows *right-brain to right-brain state-sharing* to endow the patient–therapist relationship, through *enactment*, with the power to use *itself* as an interpersonal/relational medium that weakens the role of dissociation as a *counterforce* to self-growth. In other words, in its function as a nonconscious *communication* process, dissociation opens the way to *enactment*, which I believe is the *most* powerful therapeutic context of state-sharing—the coexistence in two *people* of differing versions of "reality"—the realities of their *relationship*, and the realities held by one's own states and those of the other. State-sharing is thus *more* than the sharing of the states themselves. It underwrites the sharing of affectively organized "truths" that have been *dissociatively unshareable* and thus unknowable to either person *in the way the mind of the other* experiences them. This is why it plays such a *singularly* robust role in the processing of enactments. By the analyst/therapist's sharing of his or her experience as it takes place with the client/patient, without having to first be conceptually "certain" of what it means, the patient–analyst relationship is allowed to become what psychotherapy is all about: facilitating the negotiation between self and other as it is played out for patient and analyst/therapist, with another *person* and between other *parts* of each of their selves.

I further suggest that the inability to negotiate otherness "out there in the world" is most frequently a result of the capacity having *already* been sacrificed in its *internal* role of negotiating otherness between one's own self-states—and that this in turn has compromised the person's capacity to be fully him- or herself in the world with a reasonable degree of affective safety. To successfully negotiate self-state differences with those of other *people*, there must be enough internal self-state *coherence* and enough capacity for *internal conflict* to bear the inevitable collisions between the subjectivities of one's *own* self-states.

Affect Tolerance From a Self-State Perspective

In his book *The Science of the Art of Psychotherapy*, Schore (2012, pp. 91–92) establishes that therapeutic effectiveness depends on the patient's being able to reexperience dysregulating affect in *affectively tolerable doses*. In agreement with Pat Ogden (Ogden, Pain, Minton, & Fisher, 2005), he links the neuroscience element (the fact that the affect-focused work occurs at the *edges* of the regulatory boundaries of the windows of affect tolerance) with my formulation that the therapeutic relationship "must feel safe but not perfectly safe. If it were even possible for the relationship to be perfectly safe, which it is not, there would be no potential for 'safe-surprises' because it would never be surprising that the analyst/therapist was not behaving, as expected, like a bad early object" (Bromberg 2006a, p. 95).

What makes this link especially important, Schore (2012, p. 92) goes on to say, is that when the mind is experienced from a self-state perspective, what we call *windows of affect tolerance* are *state-dependent* and not, as we have long believed, capable of being assessed simply by the degree of dysregulation taking place *without* knowing more about the particular self-state of the person that is most prominent in the relationship at that moment. Ignoring the state-dependence of affect tolerance leaves an analyst/therapist no means of confronting a phenomenon in which, as Schore discusses, the right brain's self-states have a *wide range* of arousal tolerance to support the unique, nonconscious psychobiological functions of each state. The term affective safety thereby refers to *an individualized range of tolerance for different self-states*. It is this fact about the meaning of "arousal tolerance," Shore adds (p. 92), that dovetails especially powerfully with my assertion that "the phenomenon of dissociation as a defense against self-destabilization . . . has its greatest relevance during enactments, a mode of clinical engagement that requires [a therapist's] closest attunement to the unacknowledged affective shifts in his [or her] own and the patient's self-states" (Bromberg, 2006a, p. 6).

Collisions, Safety, and Authenticity

Here is where I begin meandering around and ruminating about different things more or less on my *own*, among them the meaning of the words *safe and authentic* from a self-state perspective. We already know that affective safety is a key element in what makes psychotherapy a *healing* process as well as a growth process—a healing process that is identifiable in a patient's increasing ability to distinguish *safe surprises* from potential *trauma*. But in examining what enables the patient–therapist relationship called psychoanalysis to be *most* genuinely effective as psychotherapy, both words invite being reconsidered from a *self-state* perspective with regard to the issue of whether we know to *whom* they refer.

Relational Authenticity

In a pioneering article written over 40 years ago, Edgar Levenson (1974) stated that the meaning of intimacy has undergone great change in the patient–analyst relationship. In Levenson's words, it has come to denote *"a very ambiguous felt state*, difficult to formulate and, even more confusing, undergoing a continuous shift in its meaning" (p. 359). Levenson argued that the reality of this ever-shifting context of relational meaning demands a redefinition of what makes psychoanalysis therapeutic:

> Authentic therapy begins by admitting the *chaos*, plowing ahead, falling on one's face, listening for the feedback, and delineating the patterns of interaction as they emerge from one's mutual *experience*. A *feeling* of intimacy, an intense *personal* commitment, may emerge at the most stormy or unpleasant moments. *One risks one's own identity in every real therapy.* That's enough basis for *authentic* relationship. (Levenson, 1974, pp. 368–369, emphasis added)

Ah! But is the idea of an authentic *relationship* in itself enough of a basis for psychotherapeutic growth to take place? Levenson believes that the answer is yes, and so do I, but only when looked at from a self-state and dissociation perspective. Without this perspective, the recognition of who *feels* the authenticity and who *doesn't* is confusing and difficult to deal with in the here and now. This issue, in fact, makes it *especially* clarifying as to why I believe that psychoanalysis as psychotherapy is the utilization of an ever-shifting *self-state context*. As the basis for an ongoing "safe but not too safe" negotiation of individuality and otherness, it is *this* that allows *paradox* to exist—"self–otherness" without being "someone else."

From my point of view, what makes an analyst/therapist's response to a patient feel "authentic" is how closely it matches *an individual self-state's* experience of its own "me-ness." Each self-state in a person has its reason for existing as the "me" it is, and will not rewrite its personal reality simply to suit an analyst/therapist's "belief system" about what defines *personality* growth. *There is no way that a self-state narrative of "who I am" ever changes directly; it cannot be cognitively edited and replaced by a better, more "adaptive" one.* Only a change in here-and-now *perceptual* reality can alter the self-state reality that defines the patient's internal world at a given moment, and this process requires an enacted collision of *personal* subjectivities between patient and therapist.

This is why the analyst/therapist's open *struggle* with his or her uncertainty plays as much of a role in the therapeutic process as an "analytic stance" based on either empathy or cognitive clarity derived through "understanding." Each self-state comes to attain a relational clarity about its *personal* significance that gradually alleviates the patient's previously held sense of entitlement about who he or she "really" is and his or her confusion about how, historically, he or she came to be this person. And for the therapist, it is not necessary to work so hard to "figure out" what is going on, what has gone on in the past, and what things "mean." In the course of knowing *each other* through their relationship, both people come to know *themselves* more and more intimately, and this is why the thing we call *treatment evolves.* As an "interpersonally personal" therapeutic milieu, it replaces an analytic *stance*, and regardless of which particular stance it replaces, what is diminished is the intrinsic problem created by the analyst/therapist's *belief* that eventually, albeit slowly, his or her patient will somehow "take in" what the analyst/therapist is offering because the patient will come to *see* that it will lead to a "healthier" reality. The word see is what is most important here because if its meaning is not to be taken simply as a synonym for understanding, it will be valuable if I speak at this point about the difference between "seeing" and "perceiving," and why the mind–brain–body process of perception *underlies* everything in the psychoanalytic relationship that allows it to become *psychotherapy.*

Perception

Let me begin by underlining what you *already* know: (1) As a psychoanalyst I hold that the patient–analyst relationship *is itself* the source of therapeutic action. (2) I hold that what *takes place* in the relationship must be "perceived" in order for what is "talked *about*" to exist in a therapeutic context. That said, I'm going to now address what perception *is*, and while so doing will clarify *why* "simply" by enabling the relationship to be inescapably *personal*, it supports the ability to make *what takes place* in the relationship *therapeutic*.

So, what is perception, and how is it different from seeing? Perception begins at the brain level as *sensory* input, but sensory input is not perception. It is when sensory input to the brain becomes *personal* experience to the mind that the "self" becomes involved. *Perceptual experience exists because of what the person's subjectivity makes out of* sensory experience. Registration on the senses does not provide meaning. But when the neurological impact at the brain level is *experientially* shaped by interaction with the *individuality* of a given person's subjective experience, what Jerome Bruner (1990) calls "an *act* of meaning" takes place. Perception, in other words, underlies the creation of an "*act* of meaning" because *personal* meaning comes into existence when, in any given individual, the brain's sensory neurology engages with his or her mind's subjectivity as it *interacts* with the otherness of what is "out there."

Perception and Verbal Language in Relation to "Acts of Meaning"

As analysts/therapists, when we participate through our own aliveness in increasing a patient's capacity to symbolize experience perceptually, those areas of selfhood that have existed only as internal experience without self-agency become relationally *personal* because the meaning is being *shaped* interactively. Through each person communicating his or her own subjectivity to an "other," an "*act* of meaning" takes place. Bruner puts this point right out there: "The child's acquisition of language requires far more assistance from and interaction with caregivers than Chomsky (and many others) had suspected. Language is acquired not in the role of spectator but through use. Being "exposed" to a flow of language is not nearly so important as *using it in the midst of 'doing'*" (1990, p. 70, emphasis added). Bruner then goes on to address, *indirectly*, the special status of working therapeutically with *attachment-related* interaction, including its seeming inability to access, *experientially*, the trauma associated with it: "It is only *after* some language has been acquired in the formal sense, that one can acquire <u>further</u> language as a "bystander." Its initial mastery can come only from *participation* in language as an instrument of communication" (p. 73, original emphasis). Bruner writes that the initial mastery of language "can come only from participation in language as an instrument of communication." In this developmental phase, however, verbal language as an instrument of communication is either barely present or nonexistent. So, although in an overarching way I agree with Bruner, it must be kept in mind that during the early attachment phase of development, there is a special complexity that is, *for better or worse*, life altering: Even though this phase *lacks* "participation in language as an instrument of communication," it must nevertheless be able to underwrite the core sense of selfhood that is coming into being through *procedural* interaction patterns. When it fails, the outcome is tragic. But the fact that it can even succeed as well as it does makes my mind float between admiration and awe just in *describing* its task.

In analysis or therapy, each patient thereby brings with him or her the residue of his or her negotiation between individuality and otherness in early development—a negotiation that, to one degree or another, was affectively fraught. This requires that the patient and analyst/therapist engage with each other in a way that does not, for a prolonged period of time, dissociatively *sidestep* the fraught areas of experience from being played out in their relationship—and this includes what both Levenson (see above) and I acknowledge as the "messy" parts of the relationship. But for the relationship to be therapeutic, what is enacted as repetitive must include what is *not* repetitive—its *authenticity*—which, from my perspective, is initially most shaped by an analyst/therapist's ability and willingness to be open to a *mutually personal* process of relational self-reflection that includes the analyst/therapist's *perception* of his or her own participation. As Levenson famously put it in his critique of psychoanalysis as fundamentally asking the wrong question, analysts/therapists should be asking, "What's going on around here?" rather than the more usual psychoanalytic inquiry into "What does it mean?" (1989, p. 538).

Over time, through an increasingly broad range of *each* person's self-states, the *relationship* becomes a source of self–other *aliveness*. It endows a patient with ever-increasing capacity of his or her own to hold *in a single state of consciousness* the safe participation of "other" self-states—

both his or hers and the analyst/therapist's—a capacity that formerly had held alternative versions of his or her own self-state *truth*, and were thereby incompatible, adversarial, or a source of *fear*. How can *perception* make this possible?

Let's Get Personal

I've now gotten one step closer to a main point that is rarely discussed in *detail* because it leads to something that makes an analyst/therapist uncomfortable for various reasons, especially in its challenge to the convenient fiction that the patient/therapist relationship is something we can "allow" or "not allow" to be *personal*. The analytic relationship, like any relationship, is *inherently* personal, and all we can do is either *use* that fact in as creative a way as possible or believe that we are able to make it less so by a "stance" that we tell ourselves defines the relationship as something we call professional. By *accepting* its personal nature, psychoanalysis as psychotherapy becomes a process of healing and growth that is *openly* mediated in a perceptual context. Because the personal nature of this process evolves perceptually for *both* partners, it evolves *individually* for each. So now to the *harder* question, about which I will have something to say a bit later: *How* does perception, by making the context personal, enable the patient–analyst relationship to *utilize what takes place in it* as a negotiation between subjectivities that is so deeply therapeutic?

Perception and Self-Narrative

I ask you to pay particular attention to the next sentence: *The patient–therapist relationship becomes an activity that shapes an ongoing and evolving dialectic between seeing and being seen rather than an ideational process in which one person is being seen "into" by another.* Every clinician finds out the hard way that when you try to see *into* someone, all you get is one or another of the person's "self-narratives." Our collection of self-narratives is what we all use to experience ourselves as *staying the same*. It is what gives all of us something solid to hold onto while our self-states are shifting, so that "change" isn't equivalent to loss of personal existence. In this sense, self-narratives in a context that *disregards* the absence of *perecption* are just *words* that have different "user value" for each particular self-state. But the main user value for *all* states is to conceal the core mistrust in human relatedness through *relying* on "just words" to assure they are always in *"safe* hands"—the only safe ones being *their own*.

In areas of the personality where trauma has left its mark, many self-states define not simply *points of view* of their own, but *narrative truths* of their own, which, as I've described earlier, are non-negotiable and protected by a dissociative mental *structure*. The function of this structure is to assure that certain of the person's self-states remain *unbridgeable islands*, allowing each to perform its function, without conflict, by using only its own *truth*. Within this structure, what is "me" to one state will *automatically* be "not-me" to another. Part of our work as therapists—*at times* our sole focus during the initial part of treatment—is participating in the restoration of fluidity between the dissociated self-state gaps—what I call the capacity for "standing in the spaces" (Bromberg, 1998c, 1998d). During the early phases of this process, "safety" is not an authentic relational experience, nor are "hope" and "trust". The more therapists try to demonstrate their trustworthiness, the more they fail. The patient's self-state narratives thus become a central part of the *paradoxical dual role of dissociation* that Allan Schore (2003b) has described, in this case serving as a *counterforce* to growth because personal narrative cannot be "edited" by accurate *verbal input*.

This situation is personally frustrating to most analysts/therapists, and in my opinion is thereby one good reason that, most simply put, the analytic/therapeutic relationship must be *allowed* to provide an experience that is *perceptually* (not just conceptually) different from the patient's pre-established self-narratives. Furthermore, the perceptual context, while it is bridging the gaps *within* a patient's fixed set of self-state narratives about who he or she "really" is, will also be addressing the patient's dissociated *mistrust of the* analyst/therapist. How? Because of the *challenge* that is presented to the patient's lifeless and inauthentic form of "safety" as they increasingly participate *together* in an alive relationship that is *perceived* to be safe, even though not perfectly (Bromberg, 2006a, pp. 4, 189–192).

It is in this way that authentic psychotherapy breaks down the old narrative frame (the patient's "truths") by evoking *perceptual* experience that doesn't quite fit it—which means that the analyst/therapist must be open to being seen *personally*, and this includes the patient's *perceptual awareness* of the analyst/therapist's efforts to wear a "professional mask" when he or she feels in need of one.

Seeing and Being Seen

I cannot overemphasize the importance of the analyst/therapist's openness to being *perceived*. I have been making this point for over 20 years (even though in the early days I used the word see instead of perceive). It started with a 1994 paper titled "Speak! That I May See You" (Bromberg, 1998b)—a line that has been attributed to Socrates. When my final draft of that paper was almost completed and I was about to close the file, I knew I wasn't *completely* happy with the title, but I liked it enough to keep it, and I wasn't about to mess around with Socrates. So I *negotiated* with him. I added a last line to the text, asking Socrates if I could be allowed to *wish* that he had said, "Speak! That I May See *Both of Us*," and Socrates generously agreed—as long as I didn't change the title.

Aside from my enjoyment in revisiting the zaniness, I am underscoring my strong and long-standing conviction that when *perception* organizes our way of relating, our patients are *therapeutically freed* (though not necessarily "free") to actively "do" unto us what we are "doing" unto them. When patients are freed to recognize and actively engage their analysts/therapists *as a center of their own subjectivity* (see Benjamin, 1988, 1990, 1995, 1998), rather than dissociatively hearing their words without *physically embodying a perception* of the person who speaks them, psychoanalysis becomes a process in which affective access to new self-meaning is not "resisted." It is negotiated *among self-states* because affective meaning must feel authentic to each state in its own terms. *Cognitive* meaning will find its natural place *later*—and equally through the relationship. All this is to say that personal meaning is not birthed by the "right words," but by a two-way perceptual context that slowly includes the *cognitive* meaning provided by the personally negotiated affective physicality of its experiential meaning (see Ogden, Minton, & Pain, 2006; Ogden, 2015)

The Trauma of Nonrecognition

The Developmental Phase of Early Attachment

The early attachment phase intrinsically *lacks* participation in language as an instrument of communication. During this period, the mother and child are bonded in a special cocoon of oneness that is developmentally normal. The word symbiosis is not accurate because there is always a physically organized experience of separateness no matter how early—but *psychologically*, the mental quality of the child's experience of reality overlaps with what Peter Fonagy and his colleagues (e.g., Target & Fonagy, 1996), in their work on the developmental evolution of reality, call the *psychic equivalence* mode. Experientially, the child's reality is "I am that which you know me to be, and I am *not that* which you do not know me to be." The *normality* of this phase is that the child has no self-experience that is not organized through being *the child of this mother*. It is a phase of reality that is *especially* ripe for trauma because nonrecognition is communicated as procedurally as the rest of attachment experience.

The special affective state of "oneness" between mother and child that is the hallmark of this phase must be nourished. That in itself is, at least for a while, most frequently a source of enough pleasure for both mother and child to mitigate against serious nonrecognition trauma, but this same phase is also *required* to make room for a transition that allows the oneness of attachment reality to now include *self–other negotiation* as an instrument of communication. It is the latter through which the *representational* expression of self-existence can evolve without losing the pleasure of oneness that, if things go reasonably well, *continues* to be a treasure of its own.

But things do *not* always go reasonably well and when they don't, the developmental transition that enables a child to communicate his or her *subjective existence* as a self can be a nightmare—at times even leading to the phenomenon known as selective mutism. However, the *bigger* tragedy is that the initial relationship that is supposed to provide the basis for a safe and robust adult experience of individuality and self-agency *as well as* assuring continuity in the unique pleasure of oneness, frequently fails to *deliver*, and its failure impairs further self-development, the source of which has always been *confoundingly* inaccessible to analysts/therapists.

The child *continues* to need relational help in making the transition, but if the attachment period has been too infused with the *trauma of nonrecognition*, relational help is most often too little or too late. In later stages of development, the *internal* struggle to negotiate "me and not-me" has already been abandoned as hopeless, but *sometimes*, even against the odds, the act of living may lead to a relationship that feels alive to the challenge—and once in a while that relationship is with a therapist who stumbles his or her way around in new and "unbidden" ways.

Because the early attachment relationship is, at different points, required to facilitate developmentally diverse things, some of which the child will experience as *affectively* in opposition, it is not difficult to understand why, in a relationship that *cannot* be negotiated through language, it *inevitably* will be difficult later in life for a *therapist* to identify a phase-specific relational source. As complicated and affectively dysregulating as it often may be, the therapist's task is to allow the relationship to heal the impaired areas of self in which the expression of individuality and self-agency has been injured, while simultaneously nurturing the *continuing pleasure of oneness* so it is able to evolve into the self–other wholeness I have called "the nearness of you" (Bromberg, 2011a)—a phenomenon I will shortly discuss in greater detail.

Not Simply "Neglect"

Despite the connotation of the word neglect that the term *nonrecognition* may impart, it is *trauma* in every respect, and arguably the most *devastating* aspect of every other form of relational trauma, including those that are assaultive.

Trauma is not intense anxiety. Anxiety is something you *have*. Trauma has *you*. Trauma is a flooding of dysregulated affective experience that, if it cannot be relationally processed, destabilizes a person's *perceptual* experience of his or her own existence and creates an escalating dread of depersonalization that must be stopped at any cost. *The brain then takes over.* To avoid the escalation of what is an indescribable threat to survival, the normally *fluid* dissociative gaps between self-states are hypnoidally rigidified, making self-reflection and in turn intrapsychic conflict *impossible*, not simply difficult—possibly in the total personality, but *inevitably* in certain areas of the mind.

Trauma may imitate neglect, but it is a dissociatively co-created form of "socialization." Why do I place the word *socialization* in quotation marks? Because the best way to turn one's child into what you *need* him or her to be is not by telling the child what he or she *should do* but by showing the child *who he or she is*. In the early attachment phase, reality does not achieve meaning through whatever *words* may be said by the parent. In the face of a mother's dissociative nonrecognition of her child's self-states that hold aspects of the child's subjective experience that are *incompatible* with what she is able to recognize in *herself* as this child's mother, the child's experience of *reality* is destabilized. The "oneness" in their pattern of relating that allows the child to feel known by the mother as *her* child is traumatically ruptured. It is an *affectively traumatic* destabilization of reality, and as such, is not subject to thinking or relational mental representation.

For some children, the experience escalates into what adults may call a tantrum, but whatever it is named, when it happens too frequently, the *brain* will not let it happen again. The dissociatively anticipatory self-state *structure* that I described earlier replaces self-state *fluidity* and becomes the brain's fail-safe survival solution. Even though this anticipatory structure "works," it is similar to living in a haunted house. As therapists, when we allow our patients to remain too long *alone* in that haunted house, something begins to feel "wrong." No matter how hard an analyst/therapist tries, words do not make it better. On his or her own, the analyst/therapist doesn't know what to do. Neither does the patient.

As analysts/therapists, we have reached a place in which our helplessness is not due to something *present* that we can't figure out, but to the *absence* of something we don't necessarily perceive when it is *present*, much less as a *loss* of that "something." It is a loss that is emotionally unsettling enough for the analyst/therapist to dissociate, not only because it involves *both* analyst/therapist and patient, but at least as much because it involves a "not-me" self-state of the analyst/therapist that holds affect toward the patient that the analyst/therapist would much prefer to keep "not-me." The content of the "not-me" affect varies, but for an example of it, go back to my discussion of my *second epigraph* in the initial section titled "Unbidden." The *loss*, however, is what needs the most attention here, because I'm speaking about the *sudden loss* of a special aliveness being tentatively created by the tendrils of an emerging but risky experience of *shared* pleasure that was precipitously and nonconsciously terminated—a lost, shared pleasure that more often than not signals the emergence of what I call "the nearness of you."

The Nearness of You

What do I mean by "the nearness of you?" Even if you *already* know what I mean (Bromberg, 2011a), equally to the point is why I don't simply call it "the capacity to have an intimate relationship?" Some researchers in mother–infant interaction have been extraordinarily illuminating here. Consider what Ed Tronick (2003) has to offer in referring to it as "a dyadic state of consciousness" that, when achieved, leads to what he felicitously calls "feeling larger than oneself:"

> When mutual regulation is particularly successful—that is, when the age-appropriate forms of meaning (e.g., affects, relational intentions, representations) from one individual's state of consciousness are coordinated with the meanings of another's state of consciousness—I have hypothesized that a *dyadic* state of consciousness emerges. Though it shares characteristics with intersubjective states, a dyadic state of consciousness is not merely an intersubjective experience. A dyadic state of consciousness has dynamic effects. It increases the coherence of the infant's state of consciousness and expands the infant's (and the partner's) state of consciousness. Thus, dyadic states of consciousness are critical, perhaps even necessary for development.
>
> An experiential effect of the achievement of a dyadic state of consciousness is that it leads to feeling larger than oneself. Thus, infants' experience of the world and states of consciousness is determined not only by their own self-organizing processes, but also by dyadic regulatory processes that affect their state of consciousness. (p. 475)

It is no easy job for the patient–analyst relationship to restore a patient's trust and joy, and especially trust and joy in the attachment-based wholeness of self that I call "the nearness of you" (Bromberg, 2011a). The *capacity* for it is part of our endowment, but it is not a gift that becomes usable just by our being born. We are born. We are raised. We develop. During the process of development, we are exposed to the impact of early relational trauma. When the *shadow* of early trauma of nonrecognition reduces the capacity to safely trust *oneness*, then future ability is compromised to negotiate the relational transition to self–other wholeness. The success of the transition requires that it carries with it the pleasure that originated in the oneness of early attachment. Without it, each developmental effort to surrender to the experience of "the nearness of you" is aborted by the vigilance of a self-state whose job is to prevent the repetition of past trauma. For some patients, what I have just described is all-encompassing, but for everyone, at least in certain areas of self, it exists in a form that, though "hidden," is always whispering its name.

At the time I wrote the final chapter of *The Shadow of the Tsunami*—the chapter I titled "The Nearness of You"—I was uncertain about the conceptual meaning of the name I gave it, even though I knew I was speaking about something *experientially* alive. I did the best I could by writing about the inherent relationship between the process of early attachment and the development of what attachment theorists consider to be a *core self*, but I wasn't able to write in detail about what I *meant* by the word core because I was uncertain. I let it stay uncertain and allowed it to seem as if I meant it simply as the beginning of selfhood in *whatever* way "beginning" might be conceived.

Happily, I am now able to take this a step further. My view is that "the nearness of you" *is* the core self of early attachment—the core capacity of an affectively organized self to surrender safely, as an adult, to the exhilaration of *dyadic oneness*. When self–otherness has been well enough negotiated relationally to assure that individuality will not be compromised, there is no difference between wholeness and the robust self-coherence that facilitates "*standing in the spaces*" between self-states. In other words, I am saying that the attachment-derived core self *is in fact* the affective state of *oneness* that, little by little, evolves from Tronick's "larger than oneself" experience into a *wholeness* that endures through life—as long as early attachment experience was not ruptured and left unrepaired.

When a patient's anticipatory hypervigilance created by a dissociative mental structure seems to coexist with *attachment instability*, the source of *both*, I have found, is most often located in the trauma of nonrecognition during the early attachment phase of development. This may in fact be *especially* strong evidence that the early joy of oneness became so unsafe that it could not evolve. The subsequent development of wholeness could not take place, leading throughout life to an unreflective, repetitive behavioral pattern: tentative efforts *to give birth to* a shared experience of "the nearness of you," followed by an inevitable need to *abort* it. Because the link between self and other was traumatically ruptured early on, and the felt risk of revisiting it triggers the brain's "survival structure," the patient is unable to feel the *affective* existence of otherness without it becoming automatically a source of potential harm. The brain, supported by certain self-states, attempts to make sure that "other" remains alien to selfhood rather than part of it.

It finally seems time for me to answer the self-inflicted question with which I ended the Section *Let's Get Personal*: I've presented a viewpoint that psychoanalysis as psychotherapy takes place *in the relationship* through an interpersonally/personal process that evolves *perceptually* for both partners, dyadically and individually. Can I now provide some minimally conceptual overview of therapeutic action that accounts for *how* the relationship accomplishes its task *pragmatically*? My answer is *yes and no*. First the *yes*: The structural dissociative protection that is automatically *dictated* at the brain level is *voluntarily surrendered*, little by little, while in the outside world primacy of self-survival at any cost diminishes. The surrender is not automatic. It is earned as the relationship evolves. It is *earned* through the *interpersonally personal* quality of the relationship; it is earned through the *inherently interpersonal* neurobiology of brain structure and function; and it is earned through the body's somatic "mind of its own" being the essential stronghold of selfhood. These *together* allow the miracle of state-sharing to permit self–other wholeness to be achieved. It is a miracle that takes place *in* the relationship, and as a miracle, it doesn't explain how it works.

What takes place pragmatically and explicitly that makes the analyst/therapist a good therapist? What does he or she *do* that enables the patient to grow and heal in a relationship with him or her that is perceptual? I don't know. I believe I will never know. And I'm glad to believe I may be right. If I *wasn't* glad, I would use fewer words like unbidden, nearness, wholeness, and personal, and I would not want to do that because I believe in the meaning of those words. But I also know that sometimes my nonlinear soul takes time off and I catch myself sounding as if I believe there must be empirical answers, as in the notion of enabling patients to *do unto* their analysts/therapists what their analysts/therapists *do unto* them. But don't let this "confession" fool you. This paragraph is the "no" part of the "yes and no." But now comes something that may help you forgive me.

Claudia and Me

State-sharing between *author and reader* is a reality (Bromberg, 2006b), but sometimes it can use a little help. So in hope of making it a little easier to *experience* what I mean by "it takes place *in and between* both partners or it takes place in neither," what follows is the "here-and-now" experience I mentioned earlier. The vignette, excerpted from *The Shadow of the Tsunami* (Bromberg, 2011b, pp. 110–120), was chosen because I believe it captures *both* the uncertainty and the personal aliveness I'm talking about.

Self-states do not exist because of *trauma*. They are what the self *is*, and if they didn't exist, we would wish they did. It is the *normal affective vitality* of our self-states as they dissociatively shift while communicating with each another and with the self-states of another person that is the essential energy source fueling our pleasure as we participate in everyday life. In the patient–analyst relationship it is the essential energy source that *embodies* state-sharing with the physical "chops" that makes the relationship affectively robust enough to be the context in which *psychotherapy* is co-created. Let me introduce the patient I call "Claudia."

Claudia was in her late 30s when she began her analytic work with me. She had been sexually molested at age 5 by her psychologically impaired older brother, but unlike what is more typically observed in the aftermath of such experience, Claudia still retained a clear visual *memory* of it—not "snapshots" or flashbacks. As we began to work together, it became quickly clear that in Claudia's childhood the invalidation of her selfhood had a scope much larger than sexual abuse per se—*so* much larger that her wariness about looking into her past for a single "obvious" cause of her current problems made rational sense, even though it also served a protective function against *my* otherness that was "dissociatively rational."

My perspective on Claudia's childhood was more or less the following: Her normal developmental need for an interested mother who wished to help and support her in coping with the *routine* challenges of growing up had been responded to as invalid. In effect, she was *shown* again and again by her mother that her desire for such attention was a sign of selfishness because, unlike her handicapped older brother, *Claudia* was not "defective." Only if there was a serious crisis that she was unable to handle could she put forth a claim for help, but this could not happen without great shame. As "crises," they were rendered relationally "nonexistent" ahead of time. As a burdened but proudly "nondefective" child, she grew up with the cumulative trauma of expecting that each "next thing" to come along—always something she was determined to handle alone—would be too much for her, but it was this very determination to carry the burden without complaining to her mother that had become the key ingredient in the procedural attachment pattern that shaped her *core sense of self.* Claudia lived, most visibly, in a self-state of *"good little soldier,"* kept in line by an internal voice denouncing the "not-me" part of her that yearned to communicate her inner despair. From the time she was 5 years old she escaped from this inner torment by using her capacity to dissociate.

Claudia eventually married, had a child, and functioned fairly well at a job that entailed considerable responsibility, but, as you might expect, she was always putting out brush fires and felt constantly on the edge of everything falling to pieces. Despite her own early developmental trauma of nonrecognition, Claudia was a pretty good parent in most ways, but for years had been terrified that if she relaxed her maternal vigilance for even a moment, she would be placing her daughter, Alice, in great danger (including, of course, from some other parts of Claudia herself). Alice, who was getting older, was increasingly demanding more freedom, and this was not easy for Claudia. The issue of her hypervigilance in "protecting" Alice was something that Claudia and Alice *were* dealing with together with some interpersonal success, but when Claudia talked to me about their relationship, this progress was never acknowledged. I was not yet responsive to the degree that the adversarial collision between Claudia's dissociated self-states was being *enacted* in our relationship, and for a long time I experienced her as more embedded than she actually was in the single truth of "I must protect my child or disaster will strike." I therefore felt her as more *dependent* on my input to help her sort things out than she was. I was so busy trying *not* to relate to her as her mother did—as the "nondefective child" who didn't need help—that I failed to recognize that we were enacting a version of the way one part of her related to Alice: making sure that I protected *my* child lest disaster should strike, while ignoring another part that was "holding out" on me about her increased growth. But the part of Claudia I was ignoring, as it turned out, was doing something more complex than simply "holding out" on me. Here is where the fun starts:

Claudia had *indeed* grown profoundly, and a central part of her growth was in discovering the *joy* of using her *own mind* as a "private space." I sort of knew about her joy, but the joy in using her own mind as *private space* was the development about which I consciously knew nothing because it was the development that she, at least for the time being, wanted to keep just for herself. In other words, keeping it from *me* wasn't inherently an act of "withholding." In that regard, and notwithstanding my dissociative obliviousness to the enactment, I was at least *uncertainly* aware of a shift that seemed to be taking place in her mental functioning: Periodically, the concreteness of her thinking seemed to diminish, allowing the shadowy presence of something almost like humor to briefly appear. But because this came and went without any *shared* trajectory, the power of our ongoing enactment was strong enough to keep me from looking at it as something to take seriously, and as you will observe in what follows here, I am seeing Claudia through a glass darkly, not only with regard to her capacity for mothering but also with regard to her capacity for sophisticated thinking—and I am being set straight on both counts.

The Session

This particular session was preceded by a voicemail message from Claudia that she had left for me earlier in the day. In it she stated only that since she had not been able to get me on the phone and she would be seeing me for a session in a few hours anyway, she would wait till then to tell me the reason for the call and that it wasn't important for me to call her back.

I did not retrieve the message until just 2 hours before she was due to arrive for her appointment, and although I wasn't "certain" that there was *something* in it beyond her apparent emotional indifference, I was left with an impersonal but nonetheless nagging sense that she had *wanted* me to call her back.

Notice that I here use the word wanted. If I were to be *more* open, I would also admit that I really felt she "needed" me to return her call—a difference so important that I am underlining the nature of the disso-ciative process in *me* that led to my failure to *affectively* "know what I knew." Why did I not want to feel her *need*? One reason was that I didn't WANT to return her call. I was busy and didn't feel like interrupting what I was doing. But there was more to it than that: I also didn't want to admit to myself that a part of me felt uncomfortably like her mother. It was too disjunctive with my self-state that was dedicated to making sure to "protect my child" lest disaster should strike. So, because I told myself that she was being "mature" and that I should heed the *explicit* content of her message, and ignore the *implicit* message conveyed by her affective ambiguity, I felt almost no *conflict* about *not* returning her call. Like most examples of unilateral clinical judgment, my decision was based on a "truth" that was at least partially self-serving, and it is this aspect that I, of course, dissociated.

When Claudia arrived for her session, she began by casually men-tioning that she had left me a voicemail message earlier in the day. In a calm voice she then stated that she had had a "strange and disturb-ing experience" the night before, which was why she had called me. Then, without elaborating on her feelings about the phone call itself, she began to tell me about the "unimportant" reason she had called. She said that she was feeling overwhelmed by everything caving in on her all at once—work, marriage, and motherhood—and that it was all more than her mind could handle.

This time, however, Claudia did not completely give herself over to her old dissociative solution. Even though her brain initially responded dissociatively to the potential for attachment rupture, her mind seemed able to deal with a level of cognitive complexity that transcended her brain's need for automatic protection at any cost. Claudia's use of her cognition was now robust enough to master *the difference between being scared and being scarred*. Indeed, Claudia was frightened and affectively dysregulated, but unlike what would have been characteristic of her in the past, when she "awoke" she telephoned me. Furthermore, the message she left wasn't as much dissociatively *ambiguous* as it was an attempted solution to resolve an internal *conflict* between two self-states that were present simultaneously rather than alternately. One could say that her dissociative response was more against potential dysregulation rather than destabilization of *self-continuity*. I think this is accurate, but what was dissociatively taking place in me is as informative as what I saw taking place in her, and to get to it we are about to look at what was happening *between* us.

Claudia could hold the experience of *conflict*! Sounds hopeful, *RIGHT?* Yeah, it *was*, but *my* part in the ongoing enactment was to enlist my hopefulness as a means of securing my own dissociation. I told myself how wonderful it was that regardless of experiencing psychological overload and in spite of her dissociative symptom, Claudia's ability to hold a state of conflict would enable her to come to her session "fully" present—or so I chose to believe. My preferred definition of fully present was at that moment shaped by my relief that she came ready to "work on her problems" and didn't seem to be bothered that I had not called her back.

It was when she began talking about how much worse her relationship with Alice was becoming, and how awful she felt about having to talk to Alice's therapist about her bad mothering, that the following exchange took place—an exchange that left me breathless.

PB: You may need to give Alice more room to breathe. Your worry that something bad will happen to her if you leave her by herself for even a minute still makes you feel that you would be neglecting her.
CLAUDIA: (primed for confrontation) Are you saying that I'm an overprotective mother?
PB: (nondefensively, because that was in fact what I *was* saying) I suppose I am."
CLAUDIA: (emphatically) Well, you got it wrong! I'm not an overprotective mother to my child. I'm just a normal grandmother.
PB: (bewildered) Grandmother? What do you mean by grandmother?
CLAUDIA: Grandmothers were mothers once already. So with their grandchild it's the **second** time around—being a mother. They know what to look for before it happens because they've been there before.
PB: (*totally* bewildered) What does that have to do with you? You are not a grandmother.
CLAUDIA: *Neglect* is what it has to do with me. I had to mother myself when I was a child, so this is my second time around. I know what to look for before it happens, so I'm just a normal grandmother.

Claudia was clearly enjoying her ability to play with my innocence. But beyond that, she was also enjoying her *own mind*. She was in what before would have been dangerous territory, but her attachment was not threatened—certainly not enough for her brain to trigger automatic dissociation. A new capacity for ironic wit suddenly showed itself through an interpersonal directness that I had not recognized *existed*—a directness that was both an unmistakable challenge to my narrow image of her, and also a clear source of pleasure to Claudia. She could see I was bewildered by this change in her, but she knew me well enough to know that I was also enjoying this delightfully clever person, even if I wasn't certain "who she was." *She* experienced our bond still very much in place, and as it then developed, it was on the threshold of becoming even stronger.

It was *then* that she said it: "I needed you to call me back. You should have known that, and you should have called—even though I said it wasn't necessary."

I could feel my head spinning. Everything that came to mind I discarded, because I could feel my defensiveness and I wanted to hide it from myself as well as from her. Was what she said true? How could it be? How was I supposed to know what she "really" wanted? Almost as if I had asked that question aloud, Claudia continued: "Sure—you're telling yourself you were in a no-win situation, but maybe what I am blaming you most for is that you didn't think about what I was feeling when I left that weird message."

To use my own language, Claudia had given *me* a "safe surprise." She was implicitly inviting me to join her in creating a shared space in which we might explore together what she might indeed have been feeling when she left the phone message—an invitation that, as it turned out, would lead to open exploration not only of *Claudia's* feelings, but to what I might myself have been feeling that made me put the issue of what she "really" wanted out of my mind.

It was not easy. Claudia wasn't being mean, but neither was she keeping anything unsaid. Because she had helped me become aware of how personally distant I had been from her, I was hesitant to look for any more things to say to her that, even if some might be true in the abstract, would feel experientially *inauthentic and empty* to Claudia as they now felt to me.

What to do! It was clear that my cupboard was bare. There was nothing left in it that would "work" any better. The problem was *ME*, not my ideas. So I stopped searching. Strangely, it didn't feel so bad to give up. And even more strangely, it was at that moment that I could feel an option that I had not felt earlier: I could share my experience of what was going on in my mind. I could share it *just because I wanted her to know it*, not because it was supposed to lead somewhere. And so I did; I shared my "formulation," and I also shared my feelings *about* my formulation—my private awareness that I kept *repeating* my formulation because I needed some credible concept that I could offer her so I didn't have to face how hard it was to find a way of just *being* with her. I told her that even though my formulation still seems plausible to me, I have no reason to believe that understanding its logic would be in any way useful to her. She listened attentively, obviously thinking about what I just said, and then tried restating the formulation on her own, after which she declared, quite thoughtfully, that she agreed it *isn't* useful but "it's at least useful that *both* of us now know it isn't useful."

The humor in this moment didn't escape me. I had given up searching because I had run out of ideas, and the result was that we ended up agreeing that my ideas weren't useful anyway. Though it wasn't exactly a gold-medal performance, there was something about what we just did that brought us together experientially in a way that hadn't been possible until that moment. I was no longer feeling disconnected from her despite the fact that the only thing we agreed on was the lameness of my ideas. I was feeling not only close to her, but along with the closeness, I could feel a sense of freedom that was, dare I say it, *JOYFUL.*

One of the things that became clearer as we compared our respective experiences of what was being enacted in our relationship was the powerfully new meaning contained in her "grandmother" story—a meaning that was there to see when she was ready to put words to it, and was willing to invite me to the party. She had constructed a delightfully impish metaphor in which the complex interrelationship among daughter, mother, and grandmother was not only witty but also a form of self-representation. At this *latter* level, Claudia was proudly sharing that, unlike the manner in which her self-states manifested themselves in the phone message, she was experiencing a relatedness among them that felt more natural than the times they became, and might yet again become, "not-me" to one another. Mother, daughter, and grandmother felt more than just separate entities. They felt not only interrelated, but the *fluidity* of their relatedness was now safer. In playing with met-aphor while playing with me, Claudia was simultaneously telling me and showing me that she felt a greater sense of wholeness. And she was having fun doing it. She didn't mind that her pleasure, which was being expressed *just because she was feeling it*, was dysregulating *my* state of mind.

By the time the session ended, the phone message no longer seemed weird, and Claudia didn't feel alien to me. The "Claudia" I had been experiencing as having hijacked our relationship was no longer an alien "other." The boundary between selfhood and otherness had become newly permeable for both of us.

Over time she got in touch with the self-state in her for whom it *didn't* make sense for me to call back, and she then recognized she had not been able to make that explicit because she was protecting another part of her that felt very differently. This was why the message that she left, although it was supposed to be "sort of" a compromise, was actually on the *boundary* between conflict and dissociation. Because there was not *enough* self-reflective negotiation with the part that did *need* to speak with me immediately, the message lacked the hallmark of ambivalence that comes with *sharing* internal conflict with someone else. The needs of each part were, at that moment, still not negotiable enough to be held as *openly shareable* conflict in a phone message, so even though the presence of each self-state could be *felt* in the message, *the synthesizing of conflict resolution with the processing of dissociative enactment* awaited the rela-tional context of the session to take place. And it was *through what took place* in this session that dissociation was most allowed to *not only* demon-strate what Schore (2003b) writes about as its *paradoxical dual role*, but also demonstrate that, as with *any* enactment, there are always "not-me" self-states of the analyst/therapist that are likewise enacting *their* dissoci-ated presence. So it was with an analyst/therapist named Bromberg who was then fortunate enough to meet a twosome named *PB and Claudia*.

We stopped trying to figure out the psychoanalytic *truth*. We freed ourselves from our dissociative cocoon when Claudia could feel what she needed from me, and I could feel my own need. And it was not about whether I should have returned her call. It was about each of us *needing* something from each other—something that transcended concrete behavior. Claudia needed me to experience an *urgency* to which she could not yet claim the right—an urgency that her need for me to return her call would be felt by me and thus have relational *legitimacy*—regardless of whether or not I did return her call and regardless of whether I "wanted" to do so. The issue with which we were struggling was in "feeling into" one another (state-sharing) *while* feeling co-equal legitimacy in having minds of our own—each mind holding and expressing its own reality without experiencing as "alien" the reality of the other.

Let it be clear, however, that the co-created relational space that we came to share was not, nor could it ever be, identical for each partner because individual self-state truths continue to contribute to self-experience. What mattered was that the self-state subjectivities of neither person were *alien* to the self-state subjectivities of the other.

I hope I have been able to convey the strength of my conviction that in psychotherapy, the freeing of *joy* in being "all of one's selves" is an accomplishment of its own. Claudia's private joy was a needed aspect of what enabled her to share it with me, but for her to undertake such a public journey of her private self, Claudia and I had to discover *together* the unspoken parts of her phone message as they existed in the subjectivities of one another. What we discovered was that the message only *indirectly* had to do with her brother's abuse and her mother's indifference. Although as time passed, *both* of those experiences became more and more emotionally vivid and consciously discussible, the "message" that mattered most was not to her mother but to me.

Why so? Because accessing early trauma is, at its heart, *personally* relational: It does not free patients from what was *done* to them in the past, but from what they have had to do to themselves and to others in order to *live* with what was done to them in the past. This is why I argue that the therapeutic context for Claudia was in her relationship with *me*, and only indirectly with her mother or brother, and that the affective and cognitive access to her *childhood* trauma of nonrecognition *became* a useful addition, but not a *prerequisite*, for what took place.

Ultimately, the most salient *message* was what Claudia became more and more able to communicate to me in a variety of ways: "You have the right to not always give me what I need. I have the right to have all parts of me *recognized*. I now claim that right without feeling flooded with dread."

Because Claudia was attuned to my right-brain self-state processes while I had access only to my dissociated left-hemisphere verbal channel, what she was affectively communicating about her experience of me was making me increasingly uncomfortable because I could not experience my own "strange" feelings and thoughts as part of what was taking place between us.

I had been experiencing myself as the all-accepting "doctor" and was connected to Claudia by my earnestness to deliver the "right" formulation. The problem wasn't that I believed my formulation was a good one, but that I needed to experience myself as *only* "the good doctor" in order to remain dissociated from my *own* "not-me" self-states that held the *negativity* in my experience of Claudia—a person I was there to "help."

In *Claudia's* piece of the *enactment*, she was *procedurally* communicating *her* "not-me" negativity, making me increasingly uncomfortable because it became harder and harder for me to dissociate my discomfort—which was being generated by my reciprocal negativity toward *her*, even though the source of my discomfort remained dissociated. Yes, we were in what I call a dissociative cocoon, but what makes this vignette especially interesting, especially with regard to Allan Schore's work on state-sharing, is that Claudia's evolution of self–otherness had *already* made room for enough healing and growth to use the cocoon not only more *flexibly*, but in a joyous and robust way of which I did not know she had become capable. She herself was in charge of it, and *my pleasure in her pleasure* may have been the most powerful part of what led to the "nearness of you." Our relationship continued to develop in newly evolving ways, but I especially like sharing this vignette in this chapter because it allows me to revisit the experience of how state-sharing *comes about*: not as a burst of extraordinary mutuality that has always been there and eventually is "uncovered," but through being earned *together* in a process of healing and growth that belongs to both of us.

The words with which I ended "The Nearness of You" (Bromberg, 2011a) as the final chapter of *The Shadow of the Tsunami* will serve, in an equal way, as a personally warm goodbye to my readers here:

> The link between the legendary 1937 song, "The Nearness of You," and what some now call implicit relational knowing needs few words to explain it. And even though I love Allan Schore's concept of conversations between limbic systems, I prefer the wording of Hoagy Carmichel and Ned Washington. When they wrote the "The Nearness of You" they already knew that "It's not your sweet conversation / That brings this sensation, oh no/ It's just the nearness of you." (p. 186)

Notes

1. Winnicott writes that as a "patient begins to become a whole person and begins to lose her rigidly organized dissociations, she becomes aware [because] she has a place from which to become aware—of the vital importance that fantasying has always had for her" (1971, p. 27). He then goes on to offer what I feel is one of his most brilliant insights. He states that at the same time this is happening, "*the fantasying is changing into imagination . . . [and that] the big differences belong to the presence or the absence of a dissociated state.* In the fantasying, what happens, happens immediately, except that it does not happen at all" (p. 27, emphasis added). In other words, the person that is being *experienced* while fantasying is dissociated from the "me" that is having the fantasy, and is essentially "someone else." It is to this "someone else" that, just as Winnicott says, what is happening is happening immediately, except that it is not happening at all. It is "not happening at all" because the self that is having the fantasy at that moment cannot *imagine* it as "me."

2. To reduce the possibility that I may be misunderstood as if I were speaking about the cited authors of the epigraphs, I wish to clarify that such is not the case and that any perceived similarity is unintended. The words in the *second* epigraph, a direct quotation from *Jennie Gerhardt*, are spoken in the novel on behalf of the title character whose wisdom and loving generosity are being misinterpreted as naive innocence. *Could* Dreiser personally have identified with Jennie? Possibly. The *first* epigraph is attributed to a celebrity. As such, its sensibility as well as its language are inseparable from public image, making it not simply possible, as with my marginal knowledge of Dreiser, but almost *unavoidable* that it would have a degree of influence on my imagination. However, for me to draw upon this issue in *either* epigraph would take the chapter too far from its purpose, an outcome which is indeed avoidable.

3. My most explicit foray into the topic of the *uncanny* (Bromberg, 2011a) was in the context of a phenomenon I call "the nearness of you," to which I return in greater detail later in this chapter. Right now, I want just to mention an article to which I had given special attention: "*Beyond Intersubjectivity: The Transpersonal Dimension of the Psychoanalytic Encounter*" (Tennes, 2007). In it, the author links the therapist's internal experience of uncertainty to "a model of selfhood that resists the need for certainty," and proposes, as do I, that "self and other, subject and object, both are and are not separate" (p. 514). Most centrally, Tennes argues that "as our clinical technique takes us further into intersubjective territory, we are encountering realities for which we have neither language nor context" and that "we discover that they deconstruct in profound and perhaps destabilizing ways, our notions of self and other" (p. 508). Citing research by the biologist Rupert Sheldrake (1999, 2003), Tennes states that Shedrake developed "a theory of the 'extended mind,' which he links to already existing field theories in physics, mathematics, and biology. Our minds, he proposes, are not confined inside of our heads, but stretch out beyond them through morphic fields" (2007, p. 508n).

References

Benjamin, J. (1988). *The bonds of love*. New York, NY: Pantheon.

Benjamin, J. (1990). An outline of intersubjectivity. *Psychoanalytic Psychology*, 7(Suppl.), 33–46.

Benjamin, J. (1995). *Like subjects, love objects: Essays on recognition and sexual difference*. New Haven, CT: Yale University Press.

Benjamin, J. (1998). *The shadow of the other*. New York, NY: Routledge.

Bromberg, P. M. (1998a). The difficult patient or the difficult dyad?: Some basic issues. In *Standing in the spaces: Essays on clinical process, trauma and dissociation* (pp. 119-125). Hillsdale, NJ: Analytic Press. (Original work published 1992)

Bromberg, P. M. (1998b). "Speak! That I may see you": Some reflections on dissociation, reality, and psychoanalytic listening. In *Standing in the spaces: Essays on clinical process, trauma and dissociation* (pp. 241–266). Hillsdale, NJ: Analytic Press. (Original work published 1994)

Bromberg, P. M. (1998c). *Standing in the spaces: Essays on clinical process, trauma and dissociation*. Hillsdale, NJ: Analytic Press.

Bromberg, P. M. (1998d). Standing in the spaces: The multiplicity of self and the psychoanalytic relationship. In *Standing in the spaces: Essays on clinical process, trauma and dissociation* (pp. 267–290). Hillsdale, NJ: Analytic Press. (Original work published 1996)

Bromberg, P. M. (1998e). Staying the same while changing: Reflections on clinical judgment. In *Standing in the spaces: Essays on clinical process, trauma and dissociation* (pp. 291–307). Hillsdale, NJ: Analytic Press.

Bromberg, P. M. (2006a). *Awakening the dreamer: Clinical journeys*. Mahwah, NJ: Analytic Press.

Bromberg, P. M. (2006b). Playing with boundaries. In *Awakening the dreamer: Clinical journeys* (pp. 51–64). Mahwah, NJ: Analytic Press. (Original work published 1999)

Bromberg, P. M. (2011a). "The nearness of you": A personal book-end. In *The shadow of the tsunami and the growth of the relational mind* (pp. 167–186). New York, NY: Routledge. (Original work published 2010)

Bromberg, P. M. (2011b). *The shadow of the tsunami and the growth of the relational mind*. New York, NY: Routledge.

Bruner, J. (1990). *Acts of meaning*. Cambridge, MA: Harvard University Press.

Levenson, E. A. (1974). Changing concepts of intimacy. *Contemporary Psychoanalysis*, 10, 359–369.

Levenson, E. A. (1989). Whatever happened to the cat? *Contemporary Psychoanalysis*, 25, 537–553.

Ogden, P. (2015). *Sensorimotor psychotherapy: Interventions for trauma and attachment*. New York, NY: Norton.

Ogden, P., Minton, K., & Pain, C. (2006). *Trauma and the body: A sensorimotor approach to psychotherapy*. New York, NY: Norton.

Ogden, P., Pain, C., Minton, K., & Fisher, J. (2005). Including the body in mainstream psychotherapy for traumatized individuals. *Psychologist-Psychoanalyst*, XXV, 19–24.

Schore, A. N. (1994). *Affect regulation and the origin of the self.* Hillsdale, NJ: Erlbaum.

Schore, A. N. (2003a). *Affect dysregulation and disorders of the self.* New York, NY: Norton.

Schore, A. N. (2003b). *Affect regulation and the repair of the self.* New York, NY: Norton.

Schore, A. N. (2011). Foreword. In P. M. Bromberg, *The shadow of the tsunami and the growth of the relational mind* (pp. ix–xxxvi). New York, NY: Routledge.

Schore, A. N. (2012). *The science of the art of psychotherapy.* New York, NY: Norton.

Sheldrake, R. (1999). *Dogs who know when their owners are coming home.* New York, NY: Three Rivers Press.

Sheldrake, R. (2003). *The sense of being stared at and other aspects of the extended mind.* New York, NY: Random House.

Target, M., & Fonagy, P. (1996). Playing with reality: II. The development of psychic reality from a theoretical perspective. *International Journal of Psycho-Analysis, 77,* 459–479.

Tennes, M. (2007). Beyond intersubjectivity: The transpersonal dimension of the psychoanalytic encounter. *Contemporary Psychoanalysis, 43,* 505–525.

Tronick, E. Z. (2003). "Of course all relationships are unique": How co-created processes generate unique mother-infant and patient-therapist relationships and change other relationships. *Psychoanalytic Inquiry, 23,* 473–491.

Winnicott, D. W. (1971). Dreaming, fantasying, and living: A case-history describing a primary dissociation. In *Playing and reality* (pp. 26–37). New York, NY: Basic Books.

2

How People Change

Louis Cozolino and Vanessa Davis

The curious paradox is that when I accept myself just as I am, then I can change.
—Carl Rogers

SOMEONE ONCE ASKED me if I knew the difference between a rat and a human being.* I was curious, so I played along; here is what he told me. If you take a hungry rat and put it on a platform surrounded by five tunnels with cheese hidden down the third tunnel, the rat, smelling the cheese, will explore the tunnels until it finds the cheese. Rats have excellent spatial memory, so if you put the same rat in the same place the next day, it will immediately go down the third tunnel. If, in the meantime, you've moved the cheese to the fifth tunnel, the rat will still go down the third tunnel expecting to find the cheese where it was before. So what's the difference between a rat and a human being?

---

* Throughout this chapter, "I" refers to Louis Cozolino.

Rats are realists and soon come to accept that the cheese is gone and move on to explore the other tunnels. Humans, on the other hand, will go down the third tunnel forever because they come to *believe* that's where the cheese *should* be. Within a few generations, humans will develop rituals, philosophies, and religions focused on the third tunnel, invent gods to rule over it, and create demons to inhabit the other four. The rat's simpler brain provides it with no reason to persevere in the face of failure, whereas humans are experts at persevering in the face of frustration. When our brains cause unnecessary suffering, we need our minds to come to our rescue.

Our brains are organs of adaptation and survival, designed to do things as fast as possible with the least amount of information. So once they get things right, like never expressing negative emotions during childhood, brains may become shaped to never express negative emotions again. Such a person might also adopt pacifist philosophies, get into relationships with violent people, and feel like a success because he or she didn't express negative emotions. Brains excel in coming to unconscious conclusions and shaping our conscious experience to reinforce the beliefs we already hold.

Brains are inherently conservative and want to keep doing what's worked in the past: Don't take risks, do what your parents want you to do to, fit in, and contribute to the common good. For the lucky souls whose brains are well matched to their circumstances, life works pretty well. For the rest of us, being stuck between our programming, the expectations of our tribe, and our own needs for emotional health and actualization can make us physically and mentally ill.

When our life isn't working and we are anxious, depressed, or engaging in self-destructive behaviors, we go to therapy seeking change. Often, we are unaware of what is causing our suffering and continue to employ the same unsuccessful strategies in our lives with continued negative results. As therapists, most of us have noticed that our smartest clients can be the most difficult to help change because they are often well rewarded for doing things their way. Successful accountants with obsessive–compulsive disorder (OCD), paranoid policemen, and delusional fortunetellers will shower you with examples of how what you are calling a problem has made them successful.

In contrast to our brains, our minds emerged much farther down the evolutionary path. We still don't understand the origins of the mind, but it probably had something to do with groups of brains coming together to form the superorganisms we call tribes. As attention and memory became stabilized by group process, our interactions grew into a culture, which became the template for mind and the eventual formation of individual identity. At this current point in evolution, our best guess is that the human brain is a social organ and the mind is a product of many interacting brains.

A Social Organ of Adaptation

We are afraid to care too much, for fear that the other person doesn't care at all.
                                        —Eleanor Roosevelt

Human brains are social organs of adaptation—meaning that their growth and organization are shaped and reshaped in the process of ongoing experience. At the same time, our ability to adapt to new situations is constrained by habit and prior aversive and traumatic learning. The dynamic tension between habit and the need for adaptation lies at the heart of psychotherapy. This is why our clients consciously enlist our help in changing suboptimal functioning: Their brains automatically work against our efforts. Although a client's resistance may be seen as an impediment to change, it is actually the central focus of change in psychotherapy. Being a therapist means always skating the delicate edge between stability, flexibility, rigidity, and change.

Despite our natural resistance to it, change is a normal part of life. Sometimes we are forced to change, and sometimes we want to change because old patterns of behavior have become too painful or no longer fit who we've become. That's when we go on a quest to discover something new. Some of us go to the desert, others find a guru, and still others go to therapy; all are learning environments engineered to create change. A brief glance at history reveals that people have been changing long before therapy arrived on the scene. The classic example is the heroic journey from adolescence to adulthood whereby the hero is able to break away from the constraints of his or her childhood in order to discover new ways of being. These kinds of life changes have historically been called redemption, transformation, or salvation.

People change when new experiences disrupt old stimulus–response patterns (habits). Because we depend on the repetitive execution of habits to feel safe and in control, disrupting these patterns makes us anxious. This is where the emotional support of a therapist is most important. The reflexive response to change is either to return to old patterns or grasp onto some new habit or belief system to escape the anxiety of uncertainty. If we can tolerate the anxiety of uncertainty and stay on our journey, change is inevitable. This is why radically different forms of therapy can be successful. We can leverage many aspects of experience in our quest, and the more neural networks we are able to tap in to, the more leverage we will have in service of changing our brains. Because our brains consist of complex and interwoven neural networks, there are many possible avenues of change.

Habits and Flexibility

When I let go of who I am, I become what I might be.
                                                                —Lao Tsu

Robots and humans share the fact that our actions are based on past programming. The actions of robots are organized in algorithms embedded in lines of code; a robot's coding is a long list of "if this, then that" statements that allow it to react to all of the contingencies that the programmer had the foresight to anticipate. This is how Siri is able to know if we should wear a sweater or if the Cubs are playing at home this weekend.

In contrast to a robot's computer code, human habits are maintained by memories stored in ensembles of neural networks. When triggered by internal or external cues, the associated memories activate our behaviors, thoughts, and emotions. The unconscious activation of old programming keeps us doing the "same old same old," which is why every psychology student is told that the best predictor of future behavior is past behavior.

Psychotherapists generally believe in three levers of change: feelings, behaviors, and thoughts. Most traditional forms of psychotherapy use either one or some combination of the three to promote change. For behaviorists, changes in behavior are believed to lead to changes in emotions and thoughts. This is why B. F. Skinner believed that modifying reinforcers within the environment would lead to changes in how we think and feel. For psychodynamic therapists, the primary lever of change is emotions, which will then lead to changes in thoughts and behaviors. In contrast, cognitive therapists believe that thoughts drive feelings and behaviors; change someone's thoughts and changes in feelings and behaviors will follow. More innovative forms of therapy have also discovered the power of movement, body work, art, and meditation to promote change. The underlying theory that guides each therapeutic school assumes that its particular target of intervention is the primary driver of change. Over the years I've seen people have great success in therapies that would fall into all of these categories.

When presented as dogma, each perspective of psychotherapy is simultaneously right and wrong. Each works, or doesn't, depending on the client and the quality of the therapeutic relationship. For many therapists, seeing this reality is a challenge because most of us choose an orientation to therapy based on our own experiences, needs, and defenses. This unconscious egocentric bias leads most of us to believe that our view of therapeutic change is correct to the exclusion of others. This assumption makes us vulnerable to all kinds of biases in judgment. The tendency toward dogma also places us at risk of interpreting treatment failures as problems in our clients instead of in ourselves.

Although my personal bias is in the direction of psychodynamic forms of therapy, if I look closely at what I actually do, I'm also using behavioral and cognitive interventions. As I create experiments in living with my clients, I challenge them to engage in new behaviors and ways of thinking. I work with them to alter the reward contingencies in their lives and challenge dysfunctional patterns of thinking. I encourage clients to consider meditation, yoga, dance, or any other way they can simultaneously sooth their anxiety and explore all corners of their minds and bodies.

The best cognitive therapists I know invest time in forming solid relationships with their clients and include discussions of emotions and behaviors as part of treatment. Behavioral therapists often educate and emotionally connect with clients and their families as they establish the intellectual and interpersonal contexts for their work. So perhaps most well-trained therapists leverage all three neural avenues to some degree, regardless of their orientation.

What we have learned from neuroscience hasn't supported any one of these perspectives over the other. In fact, understanding the interwoven nature of neural networks has challenged us to engage in a higher level of integrative thinking. All three schools, with the addition of systems therapy and other adjunctive techniques such as eye movement desensitization and reprocessing (EMDR), can be synthesized into more efficacious interventions.

The Power of Connection

Experience is a biochemical intervention.

—Jason Seidel

The implications of having a social brain are widespread, including the fact that many things we think of as being objectively true—knowledge, memory, identity, and reality—are largely social constructions. One of the reasons why things seem more real when we experience them with others is because our experience of reality is primarily social. Children show us this in a very straightforward way as they implore us to "Watch this, watch this!" as they do cartwheels or perform a magic trick.

Our social brains allow us to link to those around us, connect with the group mind, and regulate one another's states of mind. In order to tolerate the anxiety of change, we need to feel safe—which is why the quality of the therapeutic relationship is so vital to the success of any form of therapy. Secure attachment to the therapist also activates key drivers of neuroplasticity, such as decreases in cortisol, which inhibits hippocampal functioning, protein synthesis, and new learning.

In addition to the biological consequences of positive relationships, our minds are also more apt to change when linked to other minds. Having a witness activates mirror neurons and theory-of-mind circuitry, making us more aware of others and ourselves while reinforcing our identity. The importance of our brains linking across the social synapse for therapeutic success is probably why the quality of the client–therapist relationship (as perceived by the client) has the stronger positive correlation with treatment success than any other variable studied.

So how do we maximize the therapeutic relationship as an agent of change? The therapeutic stance suggested by Carl Rogers (1951) over a half century ago is likely the best interpersonal environment for neural plasticity and social–emotional learning. His focus on warmth, acceptance, and unconditional positive regard minimizes the need for defensiveness while maximizing expressiveness, exploration, and risk-taking. His orientation to therapy was not to try and solve specific problems, but to help clients gain the broadest possible awareness of their thoughts and emotions. It is not surprising that these same characteristics have emerged as beneficial for positive child development.

What might be going on in the brain and body of a client who is receiving warmth, acceptance, and positive regard? We know that social interactions early in life result in the stimulation of both neurotransmitters and neural growth hormones that participate in the active building of the brain. It is likely that oxytocin and dopamine become activated in states of attunement, enhancing a client's ability to benefit from treatment by stimulating neuroplasticity. A strong therapeutic bond also increases metabolic functioning, which drives blood flow, oxygen availability, and glucose consumption supportive of new learning.

A Rogerian interpersonal context would allow a client to experience the widest range of emotions within the dyadic scaffolding of an empathic other. The trust generated in the context of attunement appears to allow our minds to be open to what we might otherwise reflexively reject. This openness would increase receptiveness to interventions such as supportive rephrasing, clarifications, and interpretations to gain access to conscious consideration. Clients can then link minds with their therapists to co-create new narratives that contain blueprints for more adaptive thoughts, feelings, and behaviors.

It is obvious that we can model the outward behaviors of others and imitate their physical actions. What is less obvious is that the mechanisms of our social brains allow us to attune to the mental activities of those around us. Whereas this attunement is inhibited with those we fear, trust makes it more likely that we will spontaneously imitate the actions, thoughts, and feelings of those we like. A therapist who isn't liked will be unable to leverage the powerful forces of imitation and emotional resonance to drive positive change.

Those who are nurtured best survive best during childhood and more easily benefit from therapy later in life. Unfortunately, the social isolation created by many psychological defenses can separate us from the positive emotional connectedness that drives healing. One of the goals of therapy is to generate trust and connection so that our clients can rejoin the group mind and benefit from its natural healing properties.

Healing Trauma

Never be afraid to sit a while and think.
—Lorraine Hansberry

Fear and terror change our brains in ways that disrupt the continuity of experience and can lead us to disconnect from the group mind. I have had clients from Baghdad, Beirut, and London, separated by culture, language, and generations, who shared the experience of being in buildings as they were destroyed by bombs. These victims of war describe similar experiences: hearing the whistling growing louder, then the explosion, the violent movements of the floor and walls, followed by long periods of silence and struggling to breathe through the clouds of dust. The aftermath involves digging their way out, climbing over the bodies of relatives and neighbors, and then enduring prolonged shock that can last for decades.

One client, fleeing on foot from Eastern Europe to escape the Holocaust, was crossing a field with his older brother. A Nazi plane spotted them and dropped a bomb that landed within feet of where they had taken cover. They stared at the unexploded bomb for what seemed like an eternity before they continued to run. A young woman I worked with was driven to the desert by her sadistic husband and forced to dig her own grave as he sat and sharpened a butcher knife. These are all experiences that terrify us to the point where we can lose our words and disconnect from reality. Meanwhile, the trauma can get locked within us and can become the soundtrack of the rest of our lives.

The value of someone who is willing to go with us to the ground zero of our pain, a witness to our horror, should never be underestimated. Communicating our story to another encourages us to articulate a traumatic experience that may only be represented in our brains as a fragmented collection of images, bodily sensations, and emotions. Once we have a conscious and articulated story, we gain the possibility of integrating the many aspects of what has happened to us in order to find a way to heal. Seeing the reactions of the other to our experiences helps us to grasp their meaning, and having to make them comprehensible to another helps make them comprehensible to us. In addition, telling the story to others provides us with a new memory of the story that now includes a witness, making it a public experience, and making it available to editorial changes. All aspects of this co-creation of our experience support the idea that both reality and memory are social constructs.

Keep in mind that the ability to heal psychic pain through storytelling has been woven into our brains over eons of cultural evolution. When young therapists begin to hear their clients' stories, they usually feel that they have to do something with the information in order to earn their keep. Over time, we come to appreciate the fact that simply bearing witness is an important part of our job. Sometimes the best thing to do, especially at first, is to do nothing. As we weigh in with some of our thoughts and feelings, our clients gradually weave them into stories.

Turning Your Mind Into an Ally

The body benefits from movement, and the mind benefits from stillness.
—Sakyong Mipham

Being in control of your mind first requires remembering that you have a mind, which is not as easy as it sounds. Whereas our bowels and bladders remind us of their existence, our minds are silent and prefer to go unnoticed. There is no reflex to orient us to the mind's existence, no pressure exerted or guilt employed if we ignore it. Remembering we have a mind involves effort and discipline. This is why many people go through life having never noticed they have one, let alone knowing they can use it to their advantage.

If and when we do remember that we have a mind, what do we do with it? One of the first things we may notice about our minds is that they keep generating thoughts all on their own. There may be a momentary interruption in the flow at first glance, but soon enough, your mind will go back to creating an incessant stream of words, thoughts, and images. What you don't want to do is get washed downstream. What you do want to do is to cultivate the ability to observe these thoughts as they flow by without identifying with them or reacting to them. The goal is to learn to let them go by, to be replaced by the next, and the next, and the next. This river of thoughts will go on without effort or intention until you come to realize that the thoughts are not you; you're the one watching.

By gaining distance from this stream of thoughts and feelings, you are in a position to make some choices that you couldn't make before. You can evaluate how accurate and useful they are, and whether or not you choose to believe them. You will soon come to realize that although the brain evolved to help us deal with potential danger, the speed, intensity, and negative bias of all the thoughts it generates have gone too far. In many ways, the cortex has grown too smart for our own well-being. The good news is that although brains evolve over eons, we can change our minds in an instant. It may take decades for that instant to happen, but when it happens, our minds are capable of discovering new ways of being.

Junk Food Junkie

A change in bad habits leads to a change in life.
—Jenny Craig

Years ago, I was telling my therapist that I wanted to get into better shape, but despite all my efforts, I always seemed to fall short. "If only I could eat better," I told her. In good therapeutic form, she replied, "Tell me more." "I exercise every day and eat lots of healthy food. On most days, I eat well all day until the evening, when I become a junk food junkie." I suppose you could call it binge eating, but because I was in such good shape and not overweight, I never labeled it that way. But it was clear that the number and especially the kind of calories I was eating most evenings were not good.

The more I spoke of my evening binges, the more I became aware of how automatic and unconscious the behavior was and how out of control I felt. As the session ended, she suggested that I think about it more, which of course, I promptly forgot until a few days later. One morning, as I lay in bed in that middle state between sleeping and waking, a memory that felt like a daydream began to play in my mind.

I was a young boy, perhaps 7 or 8, walking into the kitchen where my grandmother was cleaning up after dinner. I was telling her that I was sad about something or other. Instead of saying anything, she turned to the right, opened the refrigerator, reached into the freezer, and pulled out a half-gallon box of spumoni ice cream. As she turned back in my direction, she pulled off the paper zippers, grabbed a spoon, and pushed it into the ice cream. I put out my arms, and she placed the box of ice cream in my hands. I turned around in silence and walked into the living room, where I laid down on the sofa, placed the box of ice cream on my chest, and ate until I could eat no more.

An important thing to know about my family is that the direct expression of negative feelings was rare, and discussions about emotions were nonexistent. There was a special injunction against sadness, something I only realized later in life. There had been enough tragedy, loss, and heartbreak already, and I, as the first child of a new generation, was to be saved from sadness. This meant that expressing sadness needed to be staved off at all costs. Everyone used food to distance themselves from emotions, and I learned this lesson well. The downside was that it left all of us without a way to understand or language to communicate the painful aspects of our inner worlds.

So the next question is, how do we use our minds to disrupt the negative patterns stored in our brains? We need to find a tool the mind can use to interrupt the automatic stimulus–response chains in the brain. One that I've found valuable, called HALT, comes from Alcoholics Anonymous. When you feel like having a drink or engaging in any compulsive behavior, say the word HALT and ask yourself whether you are Hungry, Angry, Lonely, or Tired. The idea is that if you are going for a drink, there is probably some emotional trigger. Of course, there are other emotions that you should consider—but they wouldn't spell HALT, which is quite useful.

HALT not only reminds you to interrupt the impulse to drink (or in my case, eat), but also to remember that you have a mind, to be self-reflective, and to engage in a caring relationship with yourself. You are doing what my grandmother was unable to do by asking, "I can see something is wrong; lets talk—tell me what you are experiencing." The added awareness momentarily interrupts the stimulus–response chain and provides the opportunity to reflect, reconsider, and take a healthy detour from your usual route. This is where a well-established and mature relationship with your inner world really comes in handy.

Using the HALT technique is one way to *use your mind to change your brain*. Asking yourself what you are feeling instead of engaging in reflexive behavior allows your mind to reconnect with and learn to retrain the habits of your primitive brain. In a sense, you are giving yourself what you needed as a child—to be seen, to feel felt, and to be helped to grasp and articulate your experience. This corrective internal reparenting—what we strive for in therapy—will eventually create new neural circuitry that allows you to replace symptoms with functional adaptations. In my case, it meant taking better care of myself, investing more in relationships, and being more willing to directly confront emotional pain.

Constructive Introspection

> *Loneliness is the poverty of the self; solitude is the richness of self.*
>
> —May Sarton, *Mrs. Stevens*
> *Hears the Mermaids Singing*, 1965

During the early years of life, we experience ourselves as embedded within the group mind of our families, unaware that we are separate from those around us. For some, especially those in more collectivist cultures, this frame of mind may last a lifetime. For others, there is a dawning awareness of our separateness. What we do with this discovery depends on the quality of our relationships, our personalities, and our life experiences. For some, the awareness of separateness drives us to fear, terror, and despair. For others, solitude and self-reflection become a cherished retreat from the demands and chaos of the outer world.

Learning to look inward to explore the landscape of our internal worlds isn't something with which we are born. It requires time, discipline, and more than a little courage. Fortunately, traditions of meditation and prayer from around the world give us a place to begin. Upon turning inward, we soon discover that our minds are erratic and unsteady instruments. We become aware that our minds shift among different perspectives, emotional states, and modes of language. In fact, there are at least three kinds of inner language that arise during different states of mind: a reflexive social language, an internal narrator, and a language of self-reflection.

Like the river of thought, *reflexive social language* (RSL) is a stream of words that appears to exist to grease the social wheels. It consists of verbal reflexes, clichés, and acceptable reactions in social situations that establish a web of pleasantries with those around us. The best example is the obligatory "How are you?" "Fine, how are you?" "Fine." Most of us also experience this level of language whenever we automatically say something positive to avoid conflict, or when we tell people we are "doing great" regardless of what's troubling us. The clichés of RSL are automatic reflexes, not expressions of our true thoughts or feelings. As our abilities for self-reflection expand, we begin to see that we are able to simultaneously engage in reflexive talk while witnessing ourselves doing it.

When we look within, we also discover an *internal narrator* that is quite different from what we express to others. While RSL connects us to others and has a positive bias, the narrator is a private language we experience as a single voice or inner conversation. The narrator is primarily negative in tone and driven by self-doubt, anticipatory anxiety, fear, and shame. "Did I lock the back door?" "Do I look fat in these pants?" and "I'm so stupid! I should just end it all" are common statements of this inner voice. The inner narrator also turns against others in the form of critical and hostile thoughts. RSL and the internal narrator are reflexive mechanisms that serve to maintain preexisting attitudes, behaviors, and feelings. Whereas RSL is an expression of how we have been taught to interact with other people, our inner narrator reflects our sense of our own lovability, value, and our place in the social world.

Although much of our time is spent alternating between RSL and the internal narrator, we are capable of attainting a state of mind that allows us to be self-reflective and to think about our thinking. This third level, self-reflective language, emerges when we attain a more objective view of our experience. As the language of self-awareness expands through practice and experience, we learn that we are capable of choosing whether or not to follow the mandates of the programming that drives RSL and the internal narrator. Realizing that these reflexive forms of language are not "us," but primitive mechanisms of memory and social control, is a vital first step in being able to use our minds in the service of change.

Shaun's Voices

Who in the world am I? Ah, that's the great puzzle.
                                                    —Lewis Carroll

Well into our therapeutic relationship, "Shaun" sat across from me look-ing exasperated and hopeless. "Why am I still haunted by these voices? My life is great, I've made it, so why can't I just enjoy it? When the voices aren't criticizing me, they are second-guessing everything I do."

I knew Shaun well and these voices weren't a sign of psychosis. "I know, they suck, don't they!" I replied.

"You hear them too?" he asked.

I responded, "Absolutely, never remember a time without them."

"Well, where do they come from and where do I go for an exor-cism?" he asked.

I smiled and said, "I have a theory," I said. "The human brain has a long and complex evolutionary history and works in mysterious ways. It also doesn't come with an owner's manual, so we are still in the process of figuring it out. I've come to believe that these voices are a kind of archeological artifact. What I mean is that they may have once served a survival purpose at some stage of our evolution but have now become a nuisance. Each of us has two brains, one on the left and one on the right. Long ago, primates had brains that were largely the same on both sides, but as brains became larger and more complicated, each hemisphere began to specialize in different skills and abilities. The right hemisphere is in control of very high and very low levels of emotion (terror and shame) and is likely a model for what both hemispheres were once like. It also has an early developmental spurt in the first 18 months of life and connects with caretakers for the purposes of attachment, emotional regulation, and acculturation into our family and tribe.

"The left hemisphere was the experiment that created modern humans. It veered off from this path, in order to specialize in later-evolving abilities such as language, rational thought, social interactions, and self-awareness. Both hemispheres have language; the left hemisphere has the language we use to think through problems and to communicate with others. The right has a language that is usually fearful and negative in tone and programmed very early in our lives. It is the worrier, the critic, and the one designed to keep you in line."

"Well, that does suck!" Shaun said, "but why are they so negative?"

"Well, we know that the right hemisphere is biased toward negativity, and people with more activation in the right than the left prefrontal cortex tend to be depressed. This negative bias was probably shaped because worrying about what others in the tribe were thinking about you most likely correlated with sustained connection and survival. The right hemisphere is concerned with survival, the way both of our hemispheres once were. My best guess is that the voices in our heads are the right-hemisphere remnants of voices of parents and tribal leaders that supported group coordination, cooperation, and cohesion—what Freud called the superego—an inner supervisor of the self that echoes early conditioning.

"Remember that the purpose of the brain is to enhance survival through the prediction and control of future outcomes. In a social context, the right hemisphere leverages our fear of being shamed to keep us in line and obedient to the alphas: Am I acceptable to others? Am I going to get fired? And so on. Concerns about being accepted by the group appear to have been woven into our genes, brains, and minds. Some of us have especially harsh and critical inner voices that never let up. This may be because we had critical parents, have a bias toward depression, or lack self-confidence and feel ashamed of who we are for other reasons.

"Because these voices seem to come from deep inside of us, we don't experience them as memories but rather as part of ourselves—a very painful and unfortunate misunderstanding of how our brains work. A central aspect of becoming the CEO of our lives is to see the voices as primitive memory programming and learn how to interpret, manage, and mitigate their negative effects. I'm not sure they ever go away. This may be because we may still need them in some instances where their input is actually helpful. But we all need to discern which of these voices are counterproductive and learn to tell the destructive ones to get lost. This is one way that understanding how your brain evolved and developed can help to turn your mind into an ally."

I'm sure that Shaun had heard the message of not paying attention to these thoughts many times before. But reasoning with the voices doesn't seem to work—they are deeper, more primitive, and stronger than conscious ideas. Whether or not the explanation I presented to him is correct, this way of thinking about his inner voices captured his imagination. This scientific narrative created a way for him to objectify his enemy—these shaming and critical right-hemisphere voices—and develop a range of strategies to fight them. I'm not telling Shaun that he is being irrational. I am saying that the voices in his head are about his parents and tribe and need to be separated from his sense of self. He now has an enemy to tackle, not just with his mind, but with his body and soul.

Reframing Shame

Nothing you have done is wrong, and nothing you can do can make up for it.

—Gershen Kaufman

Over the last half-century, shame has emerged as the most prevalent and powerful emotion shaping our clients' personal narratives. Jung's shadow, Freud's neurosis, and Beck's depression can all be traced to the origins of shame: Abandonment, exploitation, criticism, and a myriad of other early experiences make us doubt our value and legitimacy as a person. In recent decades, a range of disciplines have revealed the importance of core shame and explored its neurobiological, cognitive, and behavioral dimensions. Shame has come out of the closet and into the spotlight as a topic of TED talks, best sellers, and new therapies.

Where the few who engage in heinous crimes appear to have little or no shame, many who have done nothing wrong are crushed by it.

This incongruity makes us question the evolutionary origins and survival value of shame. One would think that any human phenomenon so prevalent and so powerful must have some survival value to counterbalance all of the pain it causes. Although we experience shame as a private and deeply personal emotion, its survival value may be the result of natural selection at the group level. Let me explain.

As we evolved into social animals, larger and larger groups of individuals needed to cooperate, coordinate their behavior, and follow a leader. But how is this accomplished by a group of prehumans without culture, language, or rational thought? How about making most everyone feel anxious and avoidant of the "spotlight" so they pay close attention to the thoughts, feelings, and behaviors of an alpha? The value of shame may be to make us focus on what others are thinking about us in order to maintain cohesive and well-organized groups. By making us uncertain about ourselves, shame leads us to look to others to make sure we are acceptable and doing the right thing. This explanation could account not only for how groups are able to organize behind a leader but also for the power of celebrity, cult leaders, and dictators. The fact that we feel badly about ourselves as a result of shame may be an accidental byproduct of this method of social organization.

If you were going to design a mechanism of social control that would keep betas in line behind alphas, you couldn't do better than to instill a sense of shame in betas. Those who are psychologically organized around shame are always worried about what others think of them, try to be perfect in the eyes of others, and only feel safe and confident when they are following someone else's orders. What Freud called superego and I call the inner narrator—the voices in our heads that remind us of our shortcomings—reinforces the same type of societal hierarchies that we witness in all mammals.

Understanding and reframing shame is important for change because it is such a powerful agent of the status quo. We can spend years in therapy trying to discover the origins of our shame: what we have done wrong and what wrongs have been done to us. Sometimes we can find the smoking gun, and sometimes we can't—either way, it doesn't really make a difference. We have to root out the manifestations of shame in our day-to-day lives and slowly and systematically alter them, one by one. The manifestations of shame—perfectionism, low self-esteem, powerlessness, and overvaluing the opinions of others—

need to be addressed and combated with energy, assertiveness, and courage. Those of us programmed as betas have to learn that core shame is a primitive form of social organization and not take it personally. Core shame is not about us as individuals; it is a negative side effect of being a social mammal.

An excellent first step to managing shame is to let go of perfectionism and understand that ignorance is a high state of consciousness. When the oracle at Delphi told Socrates that he was the wisest of men, he assumed that the oracle was having a bad day because Socrates was certain of his own ignorance. Later, while watching the folly of those convinced of their knowledge, Socrates realized that the oracle saw his awareness of his own ignorance as wisdom. This same insight is a core teaching of Buddhism in its focus on seeing past the illusions generated by the mind.

People with core shame spend a great deal of energy avoiding risks that might result in failure, and not taking risks ensures that change won't happen. Like many other human struggles, *what we resist, persists,* and our fear control us from the shadows. For change to happen, those with core shame have to convert mistakes and imperfection from evidence of their lack of value as a person into opportunities for new learning. It is always amazing to me how many students have to tell me what they know because they are too frightened to learn something new from me. This is especially poignant given the price of tuition.

Buddhism contains many valuable life lessons, and one of the most important is the difference between pain and suffering. Pain is woven into nature and is an inevitable part of life. To be alive and to love naturally leads to aging, loss, and death. By contrast, suffering is the anguish we experience from worrying about the future and regretting what has or hasn't happened in the past. Shame is a primary cause of suffering. It is relentless; the inner narrator never runs out of material. Coming to grips with past trauma, taking on the risk of connecting with others, and turning our minds into our allies are the levers of change we all need to master in order to alleviate suffering.

Conclusion

We are simultaneously social and isolated creatures, embedded in our groups and in our minds. Because we are social creatures, we become afraid when we feel isolated, making our shame feel all the more overwhelming. The presence of another, like a therapist, allows us to feel safe enough to activate neural plasticity and change our brains and minds. Feeling safe requires that we become familiar with our inner world, root out and battle our demons, and learn to domesticate our minds and turn them into allies. How do people change? We change by connecting with others while cultivating a deeper relationship with ourselves.

Reference

Rogers, C. R. (1951). *Client-centered therapy, its current practice, implications, and theory.* (The Houghton Mifflin psychological series)

3

A Whole-Person Approach to Dynamic Psychotherapy

Margaret Wilkinson

HOW DO PEOPLE change? This question is one that therapists think about in two ways with every patient. Firstly, we need to consider how each patient became a distressed person in need of help. Secondly, we need to decide how we may bring about effective change in that person, change that means our client will leave therapy with a more robust sense of self and a confident approach to living.

Change That Is Destructive to the Developing Mind

The question of how our clients' personalities have developed preoccupies all of us who seek to work with those who have experienced early relational trauma. It may be trauma that arises from inadequate early caregiving, from abuse, from bullying, from an accident, from necessary but intrusive medical procedures, or from sudden, overwhelming loss experienced at an early age. Change in these individuals may take the form of dissociative processes. Dissociation as a defense becomes most severe in those for whom the experience of trauma is persistent, continues over time, and is caused by someone close to them. Moreover, recent studies have shown that the "drip-drip" process of verbal abuse may be just as damaging and lead to neurobiological change within the individual just as much as physical or sexual abuse does (Teicher et al., 2010).

Research into attachment, especially early attachment, has been crucial in developing our understanding of how we change and develop the capacity to relate to one another in a meaningful way that builds a secure sense of both self and other. Research into neurobiology and epigenetics has given us a fuller understanding of how nature and nurture work together for good or ill in the way the individual changes and develops. Kessler observes that "Brains, and in fact, all nervous systems evolved as predictors, as creators of inner *narratives* of future events, for the purpose of the safe navigation of the environment" (2011, p. 202). The plasticity of the brain enables change by using learning from past experience to determine responses to future events. Crucially, *how* people change will depend on their experience. Inevitably, those whose early experience was distressing will develop defensive patterns in their minds; those minds will adapt to help them survive in what is unconsciously perceived as a hostile environment. Our task is to mobilize the plasticity of the human brain to enable therapeutic change.

The accumulated wisdom of years of in-depth psychotherapeutic work with people who have experienced early trauma shows that sexual, physical, verbal, and emotional abuse or neglect in childhood can have profoundly disruptive effects on the development of the mind, on the capacity for affect regulation, alongside long-term effects on the body's well-being. Schore's seminal work on attachment trauma and affect regulation has enriched our understanding of much that occurs in the clinical encounter—in essence, how people may change and develop a more secure sense of self and a more robust way of relating to others (Schore, 1994, 2003a, 2003b). Some of the research conducted by Lanius and her team at the University of Western Ontario has focused on patients who dissociate some aspects of their early traumatic experience and has confirmed that mind, body, and emotions may all be affected in such patients. It also makes clear that, "In addition to its core affective components, PTSD is associated with poor cognitive functioning across multiple domains, including declarative memory, short-term memory, attention, and executive functioning" (Lanius, Frewen, Tursich, Jetly, & McKinnon, 2015). Therapy that emphasizes "putting into words" and "meaning-making" can do much to address these deficits.

Research in the scanner (Lanius, 2012) reveals that some 70% of patients become overaroused when listening to their own trauma narrative. These are the patients who struggle to control and contain feelings, easily becoming dysregulated. In the consulting room such patients may be easily triggered into states of hyperarousal that affect both psyche and soma and blot out the ability to think. One such patient, whom I call "Holly," and have written about in detail elsewhere, painted a frightening image of what she came to call the "bad black cat mother" holding a baby cat that was covered in blood (Figure 5.2 in Wilkinson, 2010). She explained haltingly, with great difficulty as she struggled to find words, how she did not know whether she was the bad black cat attacking me or whether I was the bad black cat mother attacking her. The image spoke volumes about her early experience of her mother and how that had affected her as a person: how it had affected her core sense of both self and others. Such states of mind may escalate very fast in the consulting room, eliciting fight, flight, or freeze responses when even a fragment of current experience, such as a feeling, a noise, a color, a shape, a touch or a smell, reminds the client of previous trauma.

Cozolino stresses that words are problematic at such times of terror because decreased activation in Broca's area occurs in such states and the patient literally finds it difficult to speak (2006, p. 29). Afterward, patients cannot always recall what happened in the session because the encoding for conscious memory as well as unconscious patterns of expectation may be affected in states of such extreme arousal, as it would have been in childhood. This means that patient and therapist struggle with the task of change within the individual and in the relationship. Understanding the way past experience intrudes into present reality helps to explain the intensity of projections that emanate from these patients at these times and the likelihood of the therapist getting pulled into an enactment. The value of consultation or supervision at such times is clear.

In contrast, other patients become detached, "switched off," deadened, and dissociated from their feelings, unable to express or experience them. Some young people today may dissociate by retreating, as much as possible, into the virtual world, "a parallel world where you can be on the move in the real world, yet always hooked into an alternative time and place" (Greenfield, 2014, p. 1). Some will find other ways to switch off from unbearable experience. One patient, whom I will call "Sophie," painted a picture just before the beginning of her therapy (plate 4 in Wilkinson, 2006) that expressed her feeling of being as if entombed. In the picture the layers of her coffin express the layers of her early trauma. The outer layer consists of pointing, slapping hands and clenched fists and represents her early experience with her mother. In the image her hands are clenched, a mirror image of her experience with her mother. She had become frozen as if protected by a layer of wood, but in that very layer of wood she saw her mother's eyes. She commented, "It was as if I needed a skeleton on the outside," and so she painted just that. Inside the body, which is her entombed self-image, is a young child trying desperately to free herself. Thirty per cent of trauma patients, scanned while listening to their trauma narratives (Lanius, 2012), demonstrated deadening dissociative defenses. These defenses also challenge the therapist in the search to help the patient toward greater well-being, and are often reflected in the therapist's countertransferential response in a session. Similar states of mind may be experienced again by therapist and supervisor as the mirroring process informs their work together. For the therapist, the dissociative quality of the patient may be experienced as a struggle to consciously keep the material and the patient in mind, and in supervision to present the material with clarity. For both, there may be a difficulty in following the material and in making the links that are so shunned by the patient. These difficulties may present as bodily reactions, including numbing, distancing, switching off, and drowsiness; all will represent defenses that keep trauma out of mind and hinder meaningful change within the personality. Such trauma does not always consist of what has been traditionally considered active abuse. If early in life, when relationships with meaningful others are simply absent, or the caregiver is too distant or switched off emotionally, the result may be rage, despair, and finally switched-off, dissociative reactions.

In both groups of patients, trauma may affect hippocampal functioning and explicit memory and may leave patients with a highly sensitized amygdala and a storehouse of painful emotional memories held in the body. Haven concludes: "It is not enough, and is actually misguided, to focus exclusively on the cognitive and emotional meaning of the experience. . . . Past traumatic experiences . . . imprinted in the deeper regions of the brain that are only marginally affected by thinking and emotion . . . are embodied in current physiological states and sensations" (2009, p. 216). We should also be aware that there are specific windows of change and vulnerability in brain development in a young life. The hippocampus (the storehouse for explicit memory—the why, when, where, and how of memory) and the corpus callosum (the major link and route between the left and right hemispheres of the brain) are maximally affected at ages 3–5 and 9–10, respectively, and the gray matter volume of the frontal cortex is maximally affected by abuse at ages 14–16 years old (McCrory, DeBrito, & Viding, 2010). McFarlane stresses the difficulties connected with trying to create coherent narratives, and reminds us that traumatic events disrupt the capacity for word formulation and "impact on the areas of the brain concerned with expressive language" (2010, p. 46). Working with cognitions and meaning-making are thus integral to the therapeutic process in dynamic psychotherapy. However, it is the experience-dependent plasticity of the human brain that enables all change in therapy.

Patients who have experienced early relational trauma often carry the marks of that experience in their bodily states of being. Felitti comments that "traumatic events of the earliest years of infancy are not lost but, like a child's footprints in the wet cement, are often preserved lifelong" (2010, p. xiii). He emphasizes that "time does not heal the wounds that occur in those earliest years; time conceals them. They are not lost; they are embodied" (p. xiii). He warns that if we do not explore how to work with these wounds, we ignore "that which is *actually the somatic inscription of life experience on to the human body and brain*" (p. xiv, emphasis added). The importance of the contribution of radiology to assessing the well-being of vulnerable children has been highlighted by researchers: "To the informed physician, the bones tell a story the child is too young or too frightened to tell" (Kempe, Silverman, Steele, Droegmueller, & Silver, 1978, p. 18). The changes in the bones of a patient, whose therapy I will describe as the chapter progresses, documented only too well the effects of adverse early experience on a developing human being.

As a child, this patient, whom I will call "Ella," experienced pervasive early relational trauma. Sadly, it was not until she was an adult that doctors observed and commented on this patient's multiple early fractures. This patient had never forgotten some of her difficult experiences at the hands of her impulsive, volatile, alcoholic mother and the need never to cry or to show her distress. All too easily her mother would respond to such distress with "If you're going to cry, I'll give you something to cry for"—and the violence would escalate, as the mother pulled the child around by her hair or slapped her around the head, at the same time shouting, "If you're hit on the wrong part of your head, you could die!"

For patients such as Ella, it is not just the mind that is radically affected but also the whole person. Those of us whose training is to work with the mind have to grapple with the now urgent question of how to work within the area of our specialty or competence while also taking into account, as much as possible, the complex and sophisticated understanding of the three main elements of mind, brain, and body that constitute our basic humanity. Therapies that focus only on the mind will continue to promote the now outdated Cartesian split.

Fostering Therapeutic Change

Plasticity of the Brain

It is the plasticity of the brain and the importance of the enriched environment evoked in relational styles of therapy that give me hope that meaningful change can come about in our patients. At first, it was thought that we do not make new neurons later in life and that it was only our already established neuronal connections that were open to change. Now we have become aware just how extraordinarily plastic the human brain is (Begley, 2008). Not only do we make new connections when we are stimulated by change, newness, and difference, we also continue to make new neurons throughout our lives. Those new neurons make greater plasticity possible: "New neurons, because they are structurally plastic, are highly susceptible to changes in the environment and to different life experiences (Gould & Gross, 2002, p. 622).

Underpinning my thinking in the whole of this chapter are these research findings concerning plasticity:

- Genes only shape the broad outline of how a living being develops.
- Inheritance may bias us in certain directions, but many other environmental factors, including traumatic early experience. affect how our genes are expressed.
- New neurons continue to be made throughout life; these immature neurons learn easily.
- New connections and patterns of connectivity develop in response to new experience.
- Enhanced environmental stimuli enable change, and (we may infer), the emotionally attuned therapist may provide such an enriched environment.

It was originally assumed that the central nervous system (CNS) became stable soon after birth and remained that way throughout life. Research into plasticity has highlighted the importance of new neurons and new neuronal patterns of connectivity, as just mentioned. Gage and Muotri (2012) investigated the significance of exercise in neurogenesis and in particular genes. Genes known as transposons— one kind in particular, known as long-interspersed or LINE-1 (L.1) retrotransposons—have sometimes been described as "jumping genes," because they have the capacity to "paste" copies of themselves into other parts of the genome, thereby acting as promoters that can alter the level of gene expression. These alterations change the way in which the affected cell will go on to develop, with good or bad results, promoting healthy development or the onset of disease. Such cells are active in the human brain, enabling the ability to adapt quickly to change but with the possibility of affecting behavior, cognition, and risk of disease (Gage & Muotri, 2012).

This research has led to exciting new insights about the way in which DNA may become altered in the embryonic stage of life (particularly in the embryonic forebrain) and in later life when changes occur in the hippocampus, an area where neurogenesis (the creation of new neurons) occurs. Animal studies have revealed that exercise make retrotransposition twice as likely to occur. Because novelty and challenge are also known to stimulate neurogenesis, the same researchers are now questioning whether L.1 jumping increases because "individual brains and the neuronal networks that make them up are constantly changing" in response to new experience, thus making us each unique manifestations of what it is to be a human. The research of Gould and Gross highlighted the importance of the earliest phases of life for the well-being of the whole individual, stressing the activity of these jumping genes. These researchers suggested that "much of the jumping had to have occurred during the brain's development" (2012, p. 24).

What is the significance of all this scientific research for our work in the consulting room? The plasticity of the brain gives us hope for our patients and their ability to change as they experience the emotional engagement that occurs in therapy. Greenfield (2014) stresses the importance of imagination along with her concern that the dominance of the digital technologies may be changing brains, and in particular, eliminating the ways in which children have developed their imagination in the past. Therapy offers an opportunity to remediate this growing lacuna, to explore and develop imagination, whether through the exploration of the patient's unconscious imagination expressed through dreaming or through the transference. Both reveal the unconscious expectations, based on past experience, that affect the way the patient relates to the therapist and to others. Equally important are the novel metaphors that emerge, the new pictures formed in the mind in response to therapy. Some, like Sophie, are able to produce visual images that reflect their inner world experience; others use words to convey their changing emotional world. Gradually, patient and therapist co-construct a narrative that "may play a vital part in assisting the patient not only in coming to terms with the reality of his or her internal world, but also in the process of mourning what was and what might have been, which then enables a greater capacity to live life as it is now in the real world" (Wilkinson, 2010, p. 133). Plasticity is what makes such change possible.

Attachment

Some time ago I spoke in Los Angeles for a Jungian group at the 25th anniversary celebration of the Hilda Kirsch Children's' Clinic. A dinner was kindly given for me by one of the organizers, Harriet Friedman. She asked whether there was anyone I might especially like to be there. I asked if she would invite Allan and Judy Schore because I so appreciated the generous way Allan had encouraged me to develop my thinking and therefore practice. As the group chatted before dinner that evening, we began to speak about the Jungian practice of using sandplay trays as a way to help patients explore their inner world. For some in the group, Jungian sandplay therapy was a new concept, so a small group of us trooped downstairs to look at our hostess's beautiful sandtray room.

One by one we began to choose an object from the shelves and put it into the tray. There was a tree with shimmering gold leaves, a horse running wild and free, a cottage, and an exotic eastern figure, to name but a few. As time went on it became clear that everyone except Allan had made a choice. Then Allan turned to the shelf and carefully chose a little sculpture of a nursing mother and child, saying quietly "It has to be this." As he put it down in the center of the tray, suddenly all the seemingly disparate elements came into relation with one another. For me, it was a vivid expression of the way in which a focus on the quality of early attachment through the lens of neurobiology makes sense of so much that I encounter in the consulting room and, most importantly, guides the way I understand the transference, the countertransference, and the therapeutic response evoked in me. If I keep what I know about early attachment in mind, it all begins to make sense to me. It is for this reason that early attachment has become by far the most important thread in my clinical work.

Let us just consider for a moment the nursing mother and child that Allan placed in the center of the sandtray as surely as he has emphasized the centrality of the nursing couple in our understanding of our clinical work. In order to change and develop in a robust way, each baby needs to experience a meaningful relationship with its primary caregiver (usually, but not necessarily, the mother) in order to make sense of his or her new world. The way the baby is able to achieve this is through the powerful affective engagement that occurs between mother and baby. From the very beginning the warmth of the mother's body is the first experience an infant has of the warmth of human relationship. Also, Schore reminds us that "the mother's face is the most potent visual stimulus in the baby's world" (2002, p. 18), and as such, it becomes the most powerful affective stimulus for the baby's expectation of what relating to another will mean.

The polyvagal system mediates social engagement (Porges, 2007). If activated in its most primitive form, it immobilizes the person in the face of danger. In its more evolved form, it is able to initiate social engagement when it is safe to do so, and, in association with the hypothalamus–pituitary–adrenal (HPA) axis, to mobilize fight and flight strategies when it is not. Porges (2007) suggests that this social engagement system is "online" from birth. In tandem with attachment researchers, he notes that the young baby attempts to elicit interaction with the caregiver through smiling and vocalization. Avoidance of eye contact may be a significant indicator of a baby's very early developing fears about attachment. In Dr. Amanda Jones's video Help Me Love My Baby (2007), a mother struggles with her difficulty in attaching to her baby. There is a moving scene where the mother is struggling with feeling very down while they are on a train journey to the therapy. The baby is sitting in her babychair, which is placed on the table facing her mother. The mother stares at her baby with a blank, almost unseeing expression. The baby repeatedly turns away from her mother and breaks eye contact rather than encounter her mother's emotional absence, which is writ large for all to see. We may also conjecture that the baby's newly developing salience network comes into play as she instinctively avoids experiencing or developing such negative feelings directly from her mother. The price paid is a setback in the development of a robust and secure attachment that would provide a healthy foundation for the building of later relationships.

Even such simple things as the arrangement of our room may be informed by this research. What do I mean? Well, it is important for such patients that the chairs or chair and couch used in the therapy room permit the natural gaze and gaze-away sequence favored in early infant–mother interactions. Such an arrangement encourages the development of direct gaze, which stimulates cortical pathways and facilitates the development of mentalizing processes without forcing it in a way that might be threatening to the patient who has experienced early relational trauma. It can only be counter-productive to positive change if the subcortical alarm system is activated in patients with posttraumatic stress disorder (PTSD).

Affect Regulation

Affect regulation in the consulting room is the key to positive change for patients such as Ella who had difficult early experience. At first, Ella told me of some of her remembered traumas but in a monotonous, switched-off way that made me want to intervene with "Yes, but how did you feel?" If I had asked this question, it would have been far too much for her because it quickly became apparent that as soon as she began to relax, to let her guard slip and to be more in touch with her feelings, she would all too easily descend into the abyss. True affect regulation had never become established for this patient. Ella had achieved an outward appearance of self-control by an almost total denial of her feelings, a survival strategy learned in response to her mother's way of managing her child. The only alternative to this denial of her feelings was a falling into the abyss, much as she must have done at the times when her defense of denial broke down in the face of hostility from her irascible, alcoholic mother. Any early signs of beginning to fall apart by Ella as a child provoked a further attack from the mother, which then overwhelmed her daughter completely.

One might ask, "How did this patient survive well enough to even begin therapy?" Sroufe, Egeland, Carlson, and Collins draw our attention to the importance of the *cumulative* history of care as "a more powerful predictor of outcome than quality of attachment alone" (2005, p. 112, emphasis added), and they identify other emotionally supportive caregivers in childhood as one of three protective factors against an adverse outcome (as cited by Szajnberg, Goldenberg, & Harari, 2010). Some such as Ella may have been protected from the worst effects of abuse by the presence of a loving other—in her case, an aunt—but it was not sufficient to lead to an adequate sense of inner well-being that could sustain a robust sense of self.

Rereading my first draft of this paper, I noticed that I had not yet given a name to the patient in this narrative. This is perhaps in itself an indication of just how much her sense of identity was damaged. I decided to call her Ella because it was the name her beloved aunt once used in addressing her and which she never forgot. This aunt, who had one son but no daughter, used to look after her at least once a week (sometimes more frequently) in her first 7 years of life. Ella knew that her aunt loved her, and she loved her in return; she was the source of fun, stories, laughter, warmth, and love. For example, her aunt bought her a doll and together they made clothes for it; then there were visits to the beach with her cousin and sleeping soundly in her aunt's house at night at the end of a happy day spent with that family. Her aunt taught Ella how to read and introduced her to the world of books; she made Ella a puppet theatre, and they had fun making up plays together. Ella began to do well at school and even loved being there.

At 8 years old, disaster struck for this child. Her father, also an alcoholic, had worked away from home for much of the time, but now lost his job, and she moved with her parents to a different part of the country where he had managed to secure another job. She found herself many miles away from her aunt, alone in a strange place and school, with alcoholic parents who were at war with one another. She would lie in bed at night and listen to the escalating violence; her father would assault her mother verbally, and her mother would then come upstairs and, instead of protecting her child, would drag her into the fray. In the morning neither parent seemed to remember what had happened, but the repeated experience etched a pattern of expectation concerning relationships deep into the mind of their child.

Somehow Ella managed to experience school as a good place where she could achieve in the relative peace that reigned there. When she moved to secondary school, Ella's dramatic ability was encouraged by an empathic drama teacher to whom she became much attached. She filled her life with acting in school productions and those of a local youth theatre group. This way she could dissociate from her own painful feelings as she concentrated on portraying the life of someone else. This acting work helped her to know in some way that there were other ways of being, keeping alive her hope that change might still be possible for her. She went to stay at her aunt's house for as much of the school holidays as she could.

Ella worked hard academically and saw going away to university as offering the beginning of a new life. Just as she left school, her aunt died unexpectedly of a heart attack, and her parents would not let her travel to the funeral. Still grieving, Ella nevertheless escaped, as she thought, to university but then realized, to her horror, that her warring parents had come away with her as part of her internal world. This realization, coupled with the loss of her aunt, led to acute anxiety attacks and to psychosomatic illness that limited her ability to fulfill her potential; her past was fast catching up with her. Her burning desire was to remain independent of her parents and not to have to go home. Sadly, the relationships she made at university seemed to be ones in which she became the victim as she was driven unconsciously by the compulsion to repeat and reexperience the quality of her earliest relationships. Siegel and Sieff explain: "The attachment relationship . . . is the medium through which the infant creates top-down models about how people will behave towards him. In time, these internal models color our perceptions of everybody we meet" (2014, p. 145). As van der Kolk remarks, "Being traumatized means continuing to organize your life as if the trauma were still going on" (2014, p. 53).

Empathy

I believe empathy is what makes possible appropriate understandings and responses in the therapist in the face of such pain. Ella came into therapy in her late 20s to try to resolve her difficulties around anxiety. At the beginning, empathically I experienced her as in a prison with a high stone wall that kept everyone out and kept her safe inside but very alone. Quite early in therapy she described herself as trapped behind a huge glass wall; she could see others and reach out toward them, but she could not touch them. If she tried to do so, it would always end in disaster.

Just as the baby's earliest affective experiencing depends on the tone and musicality, the rhythm and lilt, of the mother's voice, so too does the patient's meaningful affective experiencing of the therapist depend in part on the therapist's ability to speak in "pastel or primary colors" as required (Williams, 2004). This level of attunement involves working in the "right-brained" empathic way advocated by Schore (2002) but also requires a "left-brained" reflective approach, the mirroring of which enables the development of the reflective capacity within the patient. Greenfield directs our attention to studies in the United Kingdom and the United States that suggest that the younger generation may have greater difficulty with empathy because there may be a correlation between amount of time spent interacting with smartphones, iPads, and computers and a reduction in empathy (2014, pp. 36–37). This finding has particular relevance for the generation described as "digital natives" (Prensky, 2001). All these insights are of crucial significance for our understanding of ways to foster change in our patients. I believe that change in Ella came about partly through her coming to understand the significance of her early experience but much more through the quality of the relationship established between us: that is, her freedom to explore and express her feelings, and the opportunity our time together offered for the emergence of the implicit and the chance to reflect upon it together. Many years ago, while working with young people with emotional difficulties in an educational setting, I learned to work from their strengths rather than their weaknesses. Van der Kolk describes reaching a similar conclusion when, as a young intern, he realized "how little attention was paid to their [his patients'] accomplishments and aspirations" (2014, p. 24).

As clinicians we have come to appreciate the importance of attachment and know that therapy will demand a relational approach rather than an impersonal analytic blank screen. Traditionally, we have emphasized words, interpretations, and meaning-making. Over the years that we worked together, slowly I learned from Ella that wordy interpretations did not help her. Brief verbal interventions were easier for her child-self to grasp and to hold on to. Currently, we have come to a greater appreciation of the affective, relational, embodied aspects of the analytic encounter and the way in which they relate to the early right-brained, embodied experience of the child in relation to the primary caregiver—in particular, to the early interactive experience that is held in implicit memory (i.e., in the memory store of the right hemisphere), unavailable to the conscious mind. Shedler, in his discussion of the efficacy of psychodynamic therapy, indicates that the quality of the relationship established with the therapist—the working alliance or the therapeutic alliance—along with the capacity for gaining of "awareness of previously implicit" experience, are the best predictors of "patient improvement on all outcome measures" (2010, p. 104).

Meaning-Making

I understand meaning-making to be both a cognitive and an affective process. Today as analysts and therapists, we work at the interface of what might be termed the cognitive–affective divide. Schore (2002) has made clear that for those whose earliest patterns are derived from relational trauma, therapy must seek to alter responses by providing a different affective experience through relating with another at the deepest levels. Crucial are the unconscious affective exchanges between analyst/therapist and patient, and patient and analyst/therapist, in the service of remaking the patient's experience of relationship. Although interpretation and verbal response to interpretation are the left hemisphere's very necessary contribution to a therapy, they are never enough in themselves. Nevertheless, the left hemisphere enables meaning-making and facilitates our understanding of symbolic material and of the complexity of self and self-states.

When problems occur in treatment, Tymanski (2011) suggests that we consider whether the therapy has become unhelpfully "lateralized," privileging one side of brain functioning over the other. He comments that "this state could lead to miscommunication, empathic failure, and misinterpretation—the long list of therapeutic missteps that occupy nearly every therapist's daily work." Van der Kolk (2014, p. 128) warns that "visiting the past in therapy should be done while people are, biologically speaking, firmly rooted in the present and feeling as calm, safe and grounded as possible" (p. 70). Allen, Fonagy, and Bateman highlight further dangers that may plague the analyst/therapist, such as the danger of confidently imputing to patients "states of which they are unaware" (2010, p. 251); of dealing with the transference in a way that inadvertently stimulates overly intense affect, which then undermines the therapeutic process; of allowing an intense countertransference experience to lead to a distant and avoidant stance in the therapist, which then recapitulates the core trauma in which "the patient feels abandoned . . . in a state of intense distress" (p. 250). Allen et al. see our main task as "to promote a sense of agency" in patients and to help them "become aware of their unwitting re-creation of past trauma in current relationships" (p. 252).

Neurobiological Substrates of Change:
Key Intrinsic Connectivity Networks

I would like to highlight some of the key intrinsic connectivity networks and their relevance to any consideration of the processes of change in therapy. Looking from the point of view as a lay analyst/therapist, I observe how researchers have become increasingly able to identify systems or networks that affect the mind–brain–body system. Studies of such "intrinsic connectivity networks" (ICNs) in individuals (Seeley et al., 2007, p. 2349) have led to an understanding of the brain as being composed of multiple, distinct, and interacting networks that support complex cognitive and emotional functioning. Thinking of brain functioning in this way provides a systemic framework for understanding how people change in therapy. "Three major networks have been identified as critical to our healthy mental functioning" (Menon & Uddin, 2010; Lanius, Wilkinson, & Woodhead 2013; Lanius et al., 2015), all of which are at work in the therapeutic process of change.

The chief executive control network (CEN) deals with both cognitive and emotional decision-making, integrating effective functioning of right- and left-hemisphere activity. The CEN is vital for cognitive decision-making, for maintaining working memory, and for initiating and sustaining goal-directed behavior. Much of our work with every patient involves the functioning of this network in each partner in the therapeutic alliance, as day-to-day aspects of living as well as more crucial decisions get discussed. Some patients are in a flight from thinking. For them to think is to have to confront the unthinkable: the experience of abuse in their earliest relationship. Yet these patients often bring their concerns about relationships in the present, perhaps a flight from the other, maybe a fear of all intimacy, perhaps a retreat into neuter gender identity or a tendency to be repeatedly drawn into relationships that are abusive. Helping patients to think must be an integral part of any sustained process of change.

The salience network can be thought of as the network for meaning-making of the cognitive, emotional, and bodily aspects of experience.

The insula, its hub, is unique in that it lies at the interface of "the cognitive, homeostatic, and affective systems of the human brain" (Menon & Uddin, 2010, p. 656) and mediates "dynamic interactions between other large-scale brain networks involved in externally-oriented attention and internally-oriented or self-related cognition" (p. 655). In addition, the insula facilitates the processing of the "physiological condition of the body" and the development of "subjective feelings from the body" (Craig, 2010, p. 395). It comes as no surprise that meaning-making is at the heart of the therapeutic endeavor.

Damasio (1994, 2003) understands signals from the autonomic nervous system to be the source of our emotions, and feelings to be the mental representation of those emotions; the insula stands at the interface between mind and body: Research demonstrates a strong association between the right anterior insula and the "perception of one's own bodily states and the experience of emotion" (Menon & Uddin, 2010, p. 658). If the degree of connectivity within this network is damaged, then "how one thinks and feels in daily life" may be compromised (Seeley et al., 2007) and there is the potential for the occurrence of pathological difficulties. Links have been made to autism in the case of underactive functioning of the right insula (Di Martino et al., 2009) and to the anxiety disorders when hyperactivity of the right insula is the problem (Stein, Simmons, Feinstein, & Paulus, 2007). It has also been observed that individuals with a high degree of connectivity within the salience network may show a greater degree of anticipatory anxiety, and that an individual's anxiety trait "is coded, to some degree, in the underlying neural architecture of the salience network" (Seeley et al., 2007, p. 2354).

The meaning-making network is inevitably stimulated by the therapeutic encounter. Awareness of both self and others can occur at levels that are less than conscious. For example, "if the size of the pupils of the observed subject change in a way that is discordant with the changes in pupil size in the subject, both anterior cingulate and anterior insula are activated" in the observer (Allman et al., 2010, p. 497). The therapist may experience momentary awareness of this discordance at the first interview and then become increasingly aware of such moments as a therapy progresses. With an extremely gaze-avoidant patient who demonstrates an avoidant attachment style, it may become very marked early in a therapy.

Another patient, who I will call "Melanie," arrived in my consulting room for the first time and stood looking away and down as she entered. She turned out to have an extremely avoidant attachment style born of difficult early parenting from a mother who had repeated psychotic episodes and a father who was away or involved with another woman rather than there to support his children. In the early years, care for the children was provided by a succession of rather strict nannies, none of whom stayed very long. No wonder my patient could not bear to look into the eyes of yet another caretaker. This woman was extraordinarily courageous; she had undergone an analysis with an analyst who had required her to use the couch and who sat at some distance behind her throughout the whole of the therapy. She knew in her heart of hearts that this avoidant, rather abstinent style of analysis did not reach her deepest difficulties but rather colluded with them. When she was a qualified therapist and had been working for a while, she sought out a different style of therapy for herself. It took several months, but eventually she was able to come into my room and take part of the time to rearrange the pillows on my couch at the far end so that she could lean comfortably against the wall and gaze at me, albeit from a safe distance!

Lanius et al. (2015) suggest that in patients with PTSD, altered connectivity within the salience network may result in a change in threat-sensitivity circuits, which then aggravates the symptoms of hypervigilance and hyperarousal. Steuwe et al.'s (2012) research was illuminating concerning an averted or avoidant gaze. The team noted that "healthy controls react to the exposure of direct gaze with an activation of a cortical route that enhances evaluative 'top-down' processes underlying social interactions. In individuals with PTSD, however, direct gaze leads to sustained activation of a sub-cortical route of eye-contact processing" (p. 1), which is an innate alarm system (involving the superior colliculus and the underlying circuits of the periaqueductal gray). The clinical implications for us in terms of how we experience and use gaze in the consulting room are of considerable interest. PTSD seems to be associated with heightened threat sensitivity. Lanius et al. note that "during a virtual reality paradigm, participants with PTSD showed enhanced coupling of the amygdala and the insula within the SN [salience network] as compared to healthy control subjects, providing evidence for an increased sensitivity of the salience network in individuals with PTSD related to prolonged childhood abuse" (2013, p. 6). Van der Kolk observes that "almost every brain-imaging study of trauma patients finds abnormal activation of the insula," the part of the brain that generates a sense of being embodied (2014, p. 247).

"Holly" had such problems with her experience of anger and rejection in her mother's face that for a long while, she would pile the cushions on the couch between her and me in such a way that all I could see was the top of her head, and she did not have to risk looking at my face. Much later, she was to paint a picture (Figure 5.3 in Wilkinson, 2010) of how she had felt at this time. It revealed a very sad little girl, shut away in a bubble, with the pillows as her shield against the all too painful relational reality of her inner perception of herself that had resulted from her early punitive interactions with her mother, with the face and eyes of a caregiver who could not build a bond with her daughter. This patient had a pronounced startle reaction and commented that although sometimes she could not remember some-one's name, she always knew the color of his or her eyes. The picture also gives a graphic description of her fears about what might be in her analyst/therapist's mind, and shows her desperate need for a secure attachment.

The right anterior insula mediates awareness of both positive and negative feelings: empathic and dishonest responses to others, feelings of admiration and of disgust, and the capacity for emotional discrimi-nation and judgment (Menon & Uddin, 2010). It deals with uncertainty and risk as well as intuition and those "aha" moments, characterized by "immediate effortless awareness" (Allman et al., 2010, p. 497). Such moments form the stuff of experience when the process of therapy has engaged both client and therapist at the deepest level. Craig sur-veyed the now extensive literature and concluded that the "anterior insula engenders human awareness" (2010, p. 395). Its role is crucial in that it enables links between outer and inner awareness and cognitive and affective experiences: all vital aspects of the individual personality engaged in the process of change and development.

The default mode network (DMN) also plays a key role in that it is centrally involved in self-referential processing, in building a robust sense of self that is engendered from within. The insula facilitates a switch over to this network when it is no longer necessary for the CEN to be in active mode, when we might be said to be relaxing. The DMN uses past experiences to plan for the future and utilizes moments when we are not otherwise engaged by the external world to do this. This network comes into play when the brain, seemingly at rest, actually uses massive amounts of energy to process experience at an unconscious level.

Some therapists favor an approach to a session that is to be without memory or desire, to seek to be in a seeming resting state out of which a very creative engagement with the material presented by the patient emerges. Although such a notion can only be speculative, it might be that in this unique resting state the DMN is activated, along with its connections into the hippocampus, which allows the creative connections between past and present to emerge and be thought about in the session. As a therapist I find myself wondering about the relationship between the DMN, the salience network, and those underlying pervasive states of fear, sadness, or anger that may affect our patients who have experienced early relational trauma. One patient said that for her, the baseline position that she always felt deep down was one of fear; another said that sadness was always there and only with great difficulty could she keep it out of mind.

Conclusion

I will end on a personal note. I am reminded of the dream I dreamt when finishing my last book, and which was included in it. I want to look at it again here, as I think it perhaps illustrates what we need to take into consideration as we seek to develop our understanding in order to help our clients to change:

> I was visiting a country house that belonged to very close friends of mine called Sally and Alan. It is a very old and beautiful thatched cottage that has been carefully restored and modernized in a way that is in keeping with its original features. Through the front door the large country kitchen is off to the right, down a few steps. On the left is the dining room, so often a hub of conversation and discussion of ideas. As my dream opened, I was in the kitchen with a large group of rather distinguished guests. All were busy preparing their favorite soup, using tried and trusted recipes. My old friend Alan entered the kitchen carrying a very large pan with some new ingredients in it, which he set on the kitchen range. He carefully began to mix and blend quantities of the other soups into this, tasting as he went along

to ensure that he had just the right mix to produce just the right flavor. When all was ready, we trooped out of the kitchen up a beautiful traditional dark oak staircase to the dining room, which in my dream had moved to the left at the top of the stairs. Some of the guests were still clutching the spoon they had been using to taste their favorite old soup.

The scene changed and I was sitting in the middle of one side of a long oak dining table. All the guests were sitting around the table; Alan was just across from me, and an old inglenook fireplace was just behind him. I thought the room had a rather Jacobean feel to it. Some people had chosen to bring the soup of their own old original recipe in the spoons they had brought up with them from the kitchen, wanting at that moment only to conserve the soup with the old familiar much loved taste. Naturally, with this already in their spoons, they found it difficult to taste the new flavor. A tall, distinguished man, who reminded me of a very well respected American psychoanalyst (actually, Philip Bromberg) who has blended the old established psychoanalytic teaching with the new insights from affective neuroscience, asked for a clean spoon. Alan brought fresh silver soup spoons, and several people round the table took one and more readily began to appreciate the new flavor that had been mixed, blending the best of the old with the new ingredients that Alan had added.

As I woke and thought about the dream, I realized almost instantly that Alan, a much valued friend and the master chef of my dream who had blended the old with the new with such care, stood for Allan Schore, who has made such an outstanding contribution to the consideration of how minds are changed in therapy by blending together for us the best of affective neuroscience, attachment theory, infant research, evolutionary psychology and ethology, just as, in my dream, the new is blended with the old to produce something of outstanding worth. (Wilkinson, 2010, pp. 184–185)

As in my dream, it is the Jacobean atmosphere of scientific enlightenment that we need to cultivate in ourselves as therapists if we want to facilitate effective change in those who choose to work with us. The first scene in the dream invited me down into the kitchen on the right of the door: the realm of implicit memory and of sensory experience, the realm of the right hemisphere we will always find ourselves exploring as we work with our traumatized patients. In our work it is also necessary to move up and to the left, to the information-processing center of the left cerebral cortex, to the realm of conscious awareness, of meaning-making, of decision-making, of chief executive control, just as in the dream we moved to the upstairs dining room. The dream warns us that those who cling only to the old familiar "soup"—the old familiar ways of thinking—will not be sufficiently open to change in their own thinking and ways of working. As therapists, we can enjoy a new flavor in our work through the inclusion of new ingredients, blended with the old and supped from a new spoon, but only if we explore the new advances in understanding attachment, affect regulation, and the amazing plasticity of the human brain. It is this extraordinary plasticity that facilitates change in the individual.

References

Allen, J. G., Fonagy, P., & Bateman, A. (2010). The role of mentalizing in treating attachment trauma. In R. A. Lanius, E. Vermetten, & C. Pain (Eds.), *The impact of early life trauma on health and disease: The hidden epidemic*. New York, NY: Cambridge University Press.

Allman, J. M., Tetreault, N. A., Hakeem, A. Y., Manaye, K. F., Semendeferi, K., Park, P., . . . & Hof, P. R. (2010). The von Economo neurons in frontoinsular and anterior cingulate cortex in great apes and humans. *Brain Structure and Function*, 214(5), 495–517. doi: 10.1007/s00429-010-0254-0.

Begley, S. (2008). *The plastic mind*. London, UK: Constable & Robinson.

Cozolino, L. (2006). *The neuroscience of human relationships: Attachment and the developing brain*. New York: Norton.

Craig, A. D. (2010). Once an island, now the focus of attention. *Brain Structure and Function*, 214(5–6), 396–396. doi: 10.1007/s00429-010-0270-0.

Damasio, A. R. (1994). *Descartes' error: Emotion, reason and the human brain*. New York, NY: Putnam.

Damasio, A. R. (2003) *Looking for Spinoza. Joy, Sorrow and the Feeling Brain*. London, UK: Heinemann.

Di Martino, A., Ross, K., Uddin, L. Q., Skar, A. B., Castellanos, F. X., & Milham, M. P. (2009). Functional brain correlates of social and nonsocial processes in autism spectrum disorders: An activation likelihood estimation meta-analysis. *Biological Psychiatry, 65(1),* 63–74.

Felitti, V. J. (2010). Foreword. In R. A. Lanius, E. Vermetten, & C. Pain (Eds.), *The impact of early life trauma on health and disease: The hidden epidemic*. New York, NY: Cambridge University Press.

Gage, F. H., & Muotri, A. R. (2012). What makes each brain unique. *Scientific American* 306(3), 26–31.

Gould, E., & Gross, C. G. (2002). Neurogenesis in adult mammals: Some progress and problems. *Journal of Neuroscience,* 22(3), 619–623.

Greenfield, S. (2014). *Mind change: How digital technologies are leaving their mark on our brains.* London, UK: Random House/Penguin.

Haven, T. J. (2009). "That part of the body is just gone": Understanding and responding to dissociation and physical health. *Journal of Trauma & Dissociation,* 10(2), 204–218.

Jones, A. (2007). *Help me love my baby: Part 1* [Channel 4 TV documentary, made in conjunction with the Anna Freud Clinic].

Kempe, C. H., Silverman, F. N., Steele, B. F., Droegmueller, W., & Silver, H. K. (1962). The battered child syndrome. *Journal of the American Medical Association, 181, 17–24.*

Kessler, R. J. (2011). Neuropsychoanalysis, consciousness, and creativity. *Neuropsychoanalysis,* 13(2), 202.

Lanius, R. A. (2012). A social and affective neuroscience approach to complex PTSD. In P. Bennett (Ed.), *Facing Multiplicity: Psyche, Nature, Culture. Proceedings of the XVIIIth Congress of the International Association of Analytical Psychology.* Einsiedeln, Switzerland: Daimon Verlag.

Lanius, R. A., Frewen, P. A., Tursich, M., Jetly, R., & McKinnon, M. C. (2015). Restoring large-scale brain networks in PTSD and related disorders: A proposal for neuroscientifically-informed treatment interventions. *European Journal of Psychotraumatology, 6,* 27313.

Lanius, R. A., Wilkinson, M. A. & Woodhead, J. (2013). *Report and clinical reflections on the research carried out by Dr. Lanius and her team at the University of Western Ontario.* Paper presented at the triennial congress of the International Association of Analytical Psychology, Copenhagen, Denmark.

McCrory, E., DeBrito, S. A., & Viding, E. (2010). Research review: The neurobiology and genetics of maltreatment and adversity. *Journal of Child Psychology and Psychiatry,* 51(10), 1079–1095.

McFarlane, A. (2010). Part 1: Synopsis. In R. A. Lanius, E. Vermetten, & C. Pain (Eds.), *The impact of early life trauma on health and disease: The hidden epidemic.* New York, NY: Cambridge University Press.

Menon, V., & Uddin, L. Q. (2010). Saliency, switching, attention and control: A network model of insula function. *Brain Structure and Function,* 214(5–6), 655–667. doi: 10.1007/s00429-010-0262-0.

Porges, S. W. (2007). The polyvagal perspective. *Biological Psychology, 74, 116–143.*

Prensky, M. (2001). Digital Natives, digital immigrants: Part 2. Do they really think differently? On the Horizon, 9(6), 1–6.

Schore, A. N. (1994). *Affect regulation and the origin of the self: The neurobiology of emotional development.* Hillsdale, NJ: Erlbaum.

Schore, A. N. (2002). Dysregulation of the right brain: A fundamental mechanism of traumatic attachment and the psychopathogenesis of posttraumatic stress disorder. *Australian and New Zealand Journal of Psychiatry,* 36(1), 9–30.

Schore, A. N. (2003a). *Affect dysregulation and disorders of the self.* New York, NY: Norton.

Schore, A. N. (2003b). *Affect regulation and the repair of the self.* New York, NY: Norton.

Seeley, W. W., Menon, V., Schatzberg, A. F., Keller, J., Glover, G. H., Kenna, H., . . . & Greicius, M. D. (2007). Dissociable intrinsic connectivity networks for salience processing and executive control. *Journal of Neuroscience,* 27(9), 2349–2356.

Shedler, J. (2010). The efficacy of psychodynamic psychotherapy. *American Psychologist, 65*(2), *98–109.*

Siegel, D. J., & Sieff, D. F. (2015). Beyond the prison of implicit memory: The mindful path to well-being. In D. F. Sieff (Ed.), *Understanding and healing emotional trauma: Conversations with pioneering clinicians and researchers.* New York, NY: Routledge.

Sroufe, L. A., Egeland, B., Carlson, E., & Collins, W. A. (2005). *The development of the person: The Minnesota study of risk and adaptation from birth to childhood.* New York, NY: Guilford Press.

Stein, M. B., Simmons, A. N., Feinstein, J. S., & Paulus, M. P. (2007). Increased amygdala and insula activation during emotion processing in anxiety-prone subjects. *American Journal of Psychiatry, 164*(2), *318–327.*

Steuwe, C., Daniels, J. K., Frewen, P. A., Densmore, M., Pannasch, S., Beblo, T., . . . & Lanius, R. A. (2012). Effect of direct eye contact in PTSD related to interpersonal trauma: An fMRI study of activation of an innate alarm system. *Social, Cognitive, and Affective Neuroscience,* 9(1), 88–97.

Szajnberg, N., Goldenberg. A., & Harari, U. (2010). Early trauma, later outcome: Results from longitudinal studies and clinical observations. In R. A. Lanius, E. Vermetten, & C. Pain (Eds.), *The impact of early life trauma on health and disease: The hidden epidemic.* New York, NY: Cambridge University Press.

Teicher, M. H., Rabi, K., Sheu, Y.-S., Seraphim, S. B. Andersen, S. L., Andersen, C. M., . . . & Tomoda, A. (2010) A neurobiology of childhood trauma and adversity. In R. A. Lanius, E. Vermetten, & C. Pain (Eds.), *The impact of early life trauma on health and disease: The hidden epidemic* (pp. 116–120). Cambridge & New York, NY: Cambridge University Press.

Tymanski, R. (2011). The substrate of transformation in psychotherapy and analysis: Review of changing minds in therapy by Margaret Wilkinson. *Jung Journal: Culture and Psyche, 5*(2), *128–132.*

van der Kolk, B. (2014). *The body keeps the score: Mind, brain and body in the transformation of trauma.* New York: Allen Lane, Penguin.

Wilkinson, M. A. (2006). *Coming into mind: The mind–brain relationship—a clinical perspective.* New York, NY: Routledge.

Wilkinson, M. A. (2010). *Changing minds in therapy: Emotion, attachment, trauma, and neurobiology.* New York: Norton.

Williams, G. P. (2004, October 4). Response to "Bodily states of anxiety: The movement from somatic states to thoughtfulness and relatedness." Paper on B. Proner presented at the scientific meeting of the Society of Analytical Psychology, London.

4

Beyond Words

A Sensorimotor Psychotherapy Perspective*

Pat Ogden

NONVERBAL EXCHANGES ARE the heartbeat of all relationships. Ethologists point out the significance of animal behaviors that communicate an invitation for a particular activity, such as to play, to be sexual, or to fight. Infant researchers highlight the body-based communications between infants and attachment figures that generate affect regulation capacities, procedural memory, and so much more. Similarly, implicit dialogues experienced and enacted alongside the verbal dialogue during the therapy hour are receiving increased attention as an essential element of therapeutic change. Therapeutic action is seen as extending far beyond that of understanding and interpreting patients and their behavior to participating in and attending to what is being enacted beyond the words, visibly reflected in gesture, posture, prosody, facial expressions, eye gaze, and so forth.

* A version of this chapter first appeared in Caretti, Craparo, & Schimmenti (2011)

Body-based affective models take into account the dominance of the nonverbal "implicit self" over the verbal "explicit self" (Schore, 2009, 2010, 2011; Schore & Schore, 2007). The unconscious implicit self can be conceptualized as not only having to do with conflicts and emotional pain but also with positive or adaptive retures. The unconscious itself is now thought to serve "much broader adaptive functions" than "primarily a defensive and repressive function" (Cortina & Liotti, 2007, p. 211).

The implicit self takes shape during the rapid, moment-by-moment nonverbal interactions between infants and parents. In a secure attachment, infants learn to repeat the actions that catalyze the desired response from their attachment figures, and they become increasingly effective at nonverbally signaling, engaging, and responding to others (Brazelton, 1989; Schore, 1994; Siegel, 1999; Stern, 1985, Tronick, 2007). Tronick (2007, 2011) has pointed out that movement and posture clearly denote the meaning infants make of interactions with attachment figures. One of his films shows an infant pulling his mother's hair, eliciting a fleeting expressing of anger from her. The infant responds by lifting his arms in front of his face in a gesture that appears protective, apparently interpreting the mother's angry expression as threatening. The mother's anger is momentary, and she swiftly seeks to repair the rupture in their connection, making every effort to reengage and play with her infant. Eventually he lowers his arms, relaxes his body, and smiles. On the contrary, in insecure attachments, the infant may be left in prolonged dysregulated states with little or no interactive repair, or may be frightened, abused, and/or neglected by attachment figures, leading to disorganized attachment (Lyons-Ruth, Bronfman, & Parsons, 1999). In these cases, affect regulatory mechanisms fail to develop optimally, social engagement and nonverbal signaling and proximity-seeking behaviors are compromised, and the infant's nonverbal cues may be unclear or contradictory.

Although the "somatic narrative" is usually beyond the grasp of the conscious mind, it continuously anticipates the future and powerfully determines behavior. This chapter emphasizes the centrality of implicit processes in human behavior, and the significance of nonverbal behavior in the therapy hour. Body-based embedded mindfulness interventions that directly treat the visible physical indicators of the implicit self within the interpersonal context of the therapeutic dyad are illustrated as a way to alter the somatic narrative and change the implicit self.

Implicit Relational Knowing

Through both positive and negative affect-laden interactions with parents, the child acquires "implicit relational knowing"—that is, "how to do things with others" (Lyons-Ruth, 1998). Devoid of verbal descriptions or conscious understanding, implicit relational knowing powerfully informs us how to "be" in relationship; what vocalizations, expressions, or actions will be welcomed or rejected by others; and what to expect in relationships. Lyons-Ruth points out that although implicit relational knowing is procedural, it is markedly different from what is commonly thought of as procedural knowledge (e.g., driving a car). The procedurally learned actions related to this knowing are accompanied by conscious or unconscious emotions and perceptions that are rooted in the past. They have a quality of being on autopilot—we no longer have to think about what we're doing, as when we drive the car or type these words—or when our posture, facial expressions, and gestures automatically change as we interact with our attachment figures.

Although words are unavailable to describe early or forgotten formative interactions with attachment figures, the somatic narrative tells the story of implicit relational knowing and implicit predictions. When "Suzi's" therapist complimented her on her new outfit, Suzi's spine slumped, her head lowered, her shoulders curled forward, and she scooted backward in her chair. However, Suzi was unaware of these action sequences that reflected the appraisal of her implicit self, and she was mystified as to why she suddenly felt fearful when the moment before she had felt fine. Studies show that people with post-traumatic stress disorder (PTSD) tend to respond to compliments negatively (Frewen, Neufeld, Stevent, & Lanius, 2010), and Suzi's reaction seemed to reflect the shame she felt (but could not speak of and was not aware of) and the trauma she had experienced at the hands of her father as she began to grow into an attractive young woman.

Bromberg states, "When self-continuity seems threatened, the mind [and body] adaptationally extends its reach beyond the moment by turning the future into a version of past danger" (2006, p. 5). Suzi unconsciously associated compliments with abuse, turning future interactions with her therapist into perilous ones characterized by shame for what had happened in the past and fear for what she implicitly forecasted would happen in the future with her therapist. Action sequences like Suzi's convey implicit predictions, expectations, intentions, attitudes, emotions, and meanings to others.

Implicit Knowing of the Self

Our sense of self is determined both by the story we tell ourselves verbally and by the story we tell ourselves nonverbally through our affect regulation capacities and other reflexive automatic behavior such as body posture and movement. A variety of studies demonstrate the impact of posture and other physical actions upon experience and self-perception. Subjects who received good news in slumped posture reported feeling less proud of themselves than subjects who received the same news in an upright posture (Stepper & Strack, 1993). Schnall and Laird (2003) showed that subjects who practiced postures and facial expressions associated with sadness, happiness, or anger were more likely to recall past events that contained a similar emotional valence as that of the one they had rehearsed, even though they were no longer practicing the posture. Similarly, Dijkstra, Kaschak, and Zwaann (2006) demonstrated that when subjects embodied a particular posture, they were likely to recall memories and emotions in which that posture had been operational. Suzi's slumped posture conveyed implicit meaning to her about herself. It seemed to diminish her self-esteem and contribute to, if not induce, feelings of shame, helplessness, and fear associated with the past. The patient's behavior is alive in the present with action sequences associated with the past, even in the context of a "safe" therapeutic alliance. Clearly, the implicit self is threatened by that which would challenge the perceived safety of familiar patterns of both relational knowing and self-knowing. The meanings of past experiences might show themselves in the constriction or collapse of the body as they did with Suzi, the shaking of a dysregulated nervous system, tension in the larynx and tightness in the voice reflecting a loss of social engagement, or in the avoidance of or locking in of eye contact. It is clear from such nonverbal behaviors that the implicit selves of our patients predict that the future will repeat the shame and peril that went before, no matter how strongly their explicit selves refute this position and describe the future as different from the past.

Functions of Nonverbal Behavior

Characteristic gestures, habitual postures, and action sequences reflect and sustain long-standing meanings and predictions. They reveal persistent emotional biases (e.g., a forward-thrusting chest and tension in the upper body may contribute to chronic anger, whereas a sunken chest and downward turning head contribute to sadness or grief) and beliefs (e.g., overall tension, quick, focused movements, and erect posture all support working hard and may indicate a belief such as, "I have to be a high achiever to be loved"). Nonverbal behaviors serve many functions in addition to anticipating the future, including affect regulation, emotional expression and communication, and signaling a readiness for or aversion of particular activities or interactions. These behaviors may be enduring action sequences, such as perpetually hunched shoulders, or fleeting expressions and gestures, such as a momentary narrowing of the eyes.

Nonverbal behaviors regulate the here-and-now exchange between people: The intonation of the voice or a thoughtful look away might indicate that the speaker has more to say; tensing the body and lifting the chin might impart a "stay away" message; whereas lowering the head and bending the body slightly forward might signal compliance or submission. Verbal points can be strengthened or emphasized by physical cues, such as the deep sigh and downturned head of a patient describing depression. Nonverbal behaviors might tone down a verbal message or make it more palatable, such as the disarming smile and forward leaning of a patient when she told me how angry she was at me.

These implicit somatic communications may be designed to elicit a particular response from the therapist. One patient responded by narrowing his eyes, tightening his chest, frowning slightly, and looking away when I asked about a relationship he did not want to discuss, effectively conveying his wish that I would drop the subject. Verbal and nonverbal messages might contradict each other as well, and can seek to hide aspects of internal experience as well as make them known. One patient may say she feels fine as her shoulders roll inward and a furrow appears on her brow, whereas another smiles as he speaks of his grief. We often see the signs of dissociative parts of the self in conflicting simultaneous or sequential nonverbal indicators, as when a patient reached out to shake my hand as he leaned his upper body away from me.

Nonverbal communications can be intentional or unintentional, conscious or unconscious, clear or confusing. These cues may represent a unified implicit self or contradictions among dissociative parts of the self. The unconscious, unintentional, and involuntary cues are of most interest to psychotherapists because they tend to indicate that which is under the surface, beyond the words, visibly revealing elements of behavior that reflect and sustain the implicit self or selves. <u>The dance that ensues within the relationship, including the therapist's unconscious responses (by his *or* her own implicit self) to the expressions of the patient's implicit self, is the essence of therapy.</u>

Bromberg states that the "road to the patient's unconscious is always created nonlinearly by the [therapist's] own unconscious participation in its construction while he is consciously engaged in one way or another with a different part of the patient's self" (2006, p. 43). Alongside the verbal narrative, unconscious encoding and decoding are taking place in a meaningful nonverbal conversation between the implicit selves of therapist and patient. Encoding "involves an ability to emit accurate nonverbal messages about one's needs, feelings, and thoughts," and decoding "involves an ability to detect, accurately perceive, understand and respond appropriately to another person's nonverbal expressions of needs, interactions, feelings, thoughts, social roles" (Schachner, Shaver, & Mikulincer, 2005, p. 148). The ongoing interactive process of encoding and decoding shapes what happens within the relationship without conscious thought or intent. Note that the implicit selves of both patient *and* therapist are engaged in this dance.

Nonverbal Indicators in Treatment

Kurtz states that psychotherapists ought to be on the lookout for nonverbal cues he calls "indicators," which are "a piece of behavior or an element of style or anything that suggests . . . a connection to character, early memories, or particular [unconscious] emotions," especially those that reflect and sustain predictions that are "protective, over-generalized and outmoded" (2010, p. 110). Therefore, not every nonverbal cue is an indicator. For example, reaching for a cup of tea or brushing one's hair out of the eyes is not usually an indicator. Indicators are those nonverbal behaviors that help the therapist (implicitly and explicitly) "draw hypotheses about the client: what kind of implicit beliefs are being expressed and what kind of early life situations might have called for such patterns and beliefs" (p. 127).

Indicators encompass both the affect-laden cues reminiscent of early attachment interactions that shape the movements, postures, gestures, prosody, and facial expressions of the child, as well those that reflect dysregulated arousal and animal defenses elicited in the face of trauma. The therapist intends to bring the *experience* of these indicators into the present moment of the therapy hour. Therapy must "activate those deep subcortical recesses of our subconscious mind where affect resides, trauma has been stored, and preverbal, implicit attachment templates have been laid down" (Lapides, 2010, p. 9). Activating these elements requires right-brain to right-brain affective resonance and interaction rather than analytical, cognitive, or interpretive approaches (cf. Schore, 1994, 2003, 2009, 2012).

Indicators that register consciously for therapist or patient can be explored explicitly, along with the associated affect, even while the content they represent remains unconscious. Grigsby and Stevens suggested that recognizing indicators and disrupting automatic behaviors hold more promise than conversing about what initially happened to shape them: "Talking about old events . . . or discussing ideas and information with a patient . . . may at best be indirect means of perturbing those behaviors in which people routinely engage" (2000, p. 361). It may not be enough to gain insight without changing procedural action sequences. There are essentially two ways that implicit procedural learning can be addressed in therapy: "The first is . . . to observe, rather than interpret, what takes place, and repeatedly call attention to it. This in itself tends to disrupt the automaticity with which procedural learning ordinarily is expressed. The second therapeutic tactic is to engage in activities that directly disrupt what has been procedurally learned" (p. 325).

Listening to the somatic narrative along with the verbal narrative naturally stimulates curiosity and awareness of nonverbal indicators. Therapist and client together interrupt the automaticity of these indicators when they become mindful of them, "not as disease or something to be rid of, but in an effort to help the patient become conscious of how experience is managed and how the capacity for experience can be expanded" (Kurtz, 1990, p. 111). Note that the general notion of mindful attention as being receptive to whatever elements emerge in the mind's eye is different from mindful attention directed specifically toward nonverbal indicators. Instead of allowing patients' attention to drift randomly toward whatever emotions, memories, thoughts, or physical actions might emerge, therapists use "directed mindfulness" to guide the patient's awareness toward particular indicators that provide a jumping-off point for exploration of the implicit self (Ogden, 2007, 2009).

Mindfulness is employed not as a solitary activity, conducted in the confines of one's own mind, but as embedded within the verbal and nonverbal dance between patient and therapist (Ogden, 2014). Therapists first observe clients' nonverbal behaviors and ask them to become aware of selected actions postures, expressions, and other nonverbal indicators as these emerge in the present moment during the therapy hour. As clients become mindful of their nonverbal behaviors, they are asked to describe their internal landscape—emotions, thoughts, images, memories, sensations—verbally as well. Therapists are invited to be a part of clients' internal journeys, vicariously experiencing the varied scenery and sensing the many meanings. Through embedded relational mindfulness, awareness of the present moment is shared, mutual, and regulated interactively.

The sections that follow depict some basic somatic indicators that might be significant in clinical practice and describe the use of embedded relational mindfulness to discover their nuances and how to alter the somatic narrative within the therapeutic relationship. Indicators of the implicit self are noticed, outdated action sequences are interrupted, and new actions are initiated.

It is important for the reader to entertain the idea that specific interventions emerge spontaneously from what transpires experientially and implicitly within the therapeutic dyad. Philip Bromberg states that, most characteristically, he does not "plan" in advance what to do or say in the therapy hour, but rather "finds himself" doing or saying certain things that arise spontaneously from within the relationship (personal communication, December 21, 2010). His words and actions are not premeditated or generic techniques, but rather are emerging responses to what transpires in the here and now between himself and his patient. In the description of my own work that follows here, my interventions similarly "came to me" unbidden, arising from what occurred within the relationship. Although I can and will explain the theoretical rationale behind these interventions, they were neither premeditated nor consciously thought out. Although these interventions are "techniques" in principle, they are not generic. They never happen the same way twice, but come forth naturally and unexpectedly while both therapist and patient are subjectively experiencing each other. In other words, they are communicating their affective and somatic responsiveness to an experience of what is taking place within their relationship that is not processed cognitively but is known implicitly.

It takes intention, experience, and practice for the therapist to "know" which nonverbal cues are indicators and which are not. This "knowing" is not cognitive; rather the therapist finds him- or herself being drawn to a specific nonverbal cue, often without knowing why. Typically, later discoveries in the therapy hour reveal that the cue was a significant indicator of trauma and attachment history that reflects and sustains the implicit self.

The subsequent sections describe selected implicit self-indicators and examples of how to work with them in therapy: prosody, eye contact, facial expression, preparatory movement, arm movement, locomotion, posture, and proximity seeking. Obviously, this list is not by any means exhaustive, and many potentially significant indicators of the implicit self have been omitted: the angle and movement in the pelvis; the tilt of the head and the way it sits on the neck and shoulders; the angle, pronation, or supination of the feet, and how they push off the ground when walking; the tension in the knees and other joints; the way the arms hang from the shoulder girdle; range of motion of parts of the body; breathing patterns; and involuntary trembling and shaking often experienced by people with PTSD, to name a few (cf. Ogden, Minton, & Pain, 2006; Ogden & Fisher, 2015).

Prosody

Prosody pertains to how something is said rather than to the content itself. It includes rhythm, intonation, pitch, inflection, volume, tone of voice, tempo (fast, slow), resonance, intensity, crescendos and decrescendos, and even vocal sounds that are not words, such as "um," and "uh-huh." The pauses, rushes, hesitancies, and vocal punctuations that accentuate or downplay what is being said are all part of prosody, as is affective tone:

sarcastic, soothing, patronizing, energizing, joyful, threatening, and so on. Sentences that have identical sequences of words may have different meanings that are disambiguated through prosody (Nespor, 2010). Discourse depends on prosody; in fact, "aprosodic sequences of words are hard to understand. To say the least, communication would not be effective without prosody" (Nespor, 2010, p. 382).

The way the words are said reveals volumes about implicit realms and forecasts of the future. "I am so angry," said in a weak, defeated tone indicates a very different prediction from the same words each said with vigor and emphasis. Prosody reflects the explicit emotional state of the person in the moment, as well as unconscious emotional states. Anger might be revealed through the voice long before the person realizes he or she is angry; a tightening around the larynx may cause a thinning or constriction of the voice and be an early indicator of fear or anxiety.

Prosody may convey a command, request, plea, submission, dominance, or a question. I once observed a therapy session with Ron Kurtz as therapist. The patient's pitch escalated at the end of every single sentence, as if he were asking a question. As the patient focused on the nonverbal indicator of his vocal pitch rising and even exaggerated it a bit, he almost immediately began to cry. He realized his prosody was asking the question, "Do you understand me?" The memories that emerged pertained to early emotionally charged attachment interactions in which he felt he was not seen for who he was and could not "get through" to his parents. Note that the meaning came from the patient, not the therapist. Meaning becomes discovered and conscious through mindful exploration of an indicator, rather than through the therapist's interpretation. Patients' own translation of the implicit meaning of the indicator is elicited, a translation that emerges from their own *experience* rather than from their own or their therapists' analyses or interpretations.

In another example, my patient's voice sounded childlike and dropped almost to a whisper as she reported that maybe she might be a little angry. "Cathy's" prosody was a potent indicator of a childhood filled with abuse and shutting down. I found myself suggesting that she might explore saying "I'm angry" in a louder voice, which at first felt threatening to her and she became quieter—an old habit she had formed in an attempt to prevent drawing attention to herself. Later in the session, after we explored volume and prosody, she looked into my eyes (called a "right-hemisphere modality," according to Lapides [2010]), which were encouraging and accepting, and said, "I'm angry" in a louder voice. She felt more empowered and began to reclaim a healthy righteous anger that she had abandoned long ago because it only made her father's abuse worse. It is significant that nonverbal behaviors like Cathy's childlike whisper not only affect the other person, but also affect Cathy herself, causing her to feel more and more disempowered and submissive.

In the therapeutic relationship, "right brain-to-right brain prosodic communications . . . act as an essential vehicle of implicit communications. . . . The right hemisphere is important in the processing of the 'music' behind our words" (Schore & Schore, 2007, Matching the patient's prosody in terms of volume, tone, and pace is necessary to join and connect, and from there the therapist might slowly up- or downregulate through the same mechanisms. Ron Kurtz (1990) taught his students to speak in the simplest language possible to access early memories and process strong emotion. Lapides states that she knows to "keep [her] sentences simple as LH [left-hemisphere] processing is impaired at elevated levels of arousal and to rely on RH [right-hemisphere] non-verbal means to connect with [hyperaroused patients]" (2010, p. 9).

It bears repeating that all nonverbal indicators convey messages back and forth in the therapeutic dyad that are processed without conscious consideration. Imagine a male therapist who speaks to his female client in clipped, definitive statements and questions without much affect. She implicitly interprets his prosody as indicative of his authority and superiority, which triggers compliance in her and prosody that sounds like a little girl who needs the protection and approval of her father. Colluding together, the therapist feels protective and does not challenge his patient, but is unaware of this. A collusion such as this can lead to an impasse in the therapy; an enactment typically ensues that challenges the therapist to "wake up" and realize that what is going on in the therapy hour pertains to each party's history and what is taking place between the two of them, instead of continuing to believe that what is going on between them pertains to the patient and her history alone (Bromberg, 2006).

Eye Contact

The eyes can speak louder than words. Prosodic communication can be confirmed or contradicted by such movements as downcast eyes, slow or rapid blinking, a flutter of the eyelashes, a look away and back. Proximity is fine-tuned by eye contact, bringing us closer or creating more distance. Eyes can be intent, as the absorbed gaze of a baby with the mother, or blank and unseeing, like the vacant stare of a person in shock. One patient's eyes locked into mine as if her life depended on our eye contact. Her terrified gaze spoke of the huge risk she was taking in telling the "secret" of her abuse for the first time. Other patients scan the environment for potential threat cues, ever hypervigilant, and are unable to make eye contact for more than a fleeting second.

The eyes, like all nonverbal cues, change moment to moment in response to internal and environmental cues. A sudden tightening or narrowing of the eyes might indicate pain, aversion, disagreement, suspicion, or threat, whereas a widening of the eyes might signal excitement, surprise, or shock. Frequency, intensity, insistence on or aversion to eye contact, length of contact, and style (e.g., glancing, pupil dilation, blinks, wide eyed or shrouded, eyes angled downward or upward) can all be important indicators of the implicit self.

Eye contact can be frightening for trauma survivors, and patients may be "beset by shame and anxiety and terrified by being judged and 'seen' by the therapist" (Courtois, 1999, p. 190). In the consulting room, therapist and patient might experiment with making eye contact, being mindful of what happens internally and what changes relationally when one or the other looks away or closes his or her eyes. Repeated patterns of using the eyes can also be explored. One patient who frequently narrowed his eyes explored doing this voluntarily and mindfully and realized he always felt suspicious of me. He eventually traced this pattern back to emotionally charged memories of his unpredictable mother, which had left him feeling on guard, insecure, and suspicious in relationships. Another client, "Marley," had suffered from chronic abuse throughout her childhood. She consistently avoided eye contact with me, only glancing at my face for a split second before looking away. At one point in therapy, I asked her what happened when our eyes met, and she became uncomfortable and withdrawn. The more she tried to make eye contact, the more silent and withdrawn she became. Eventually I asked her to notice what happened if I closed my eyes. Marley immediately became more verbal and relaxed, and she stated that she felt much safer when I had my eyes closed. The absence of eye contact provided the safety Marley needed to arouse her social engagement system.

Facial Expression

The human face has more highly refined and developed expressions than any other animal, which can make looking at faces extremely reward-ing, demanding, and emotionally stimulating. The face is probably the first area of the body to reflect immediate affect, often showing emotion before we are aware of it. The ventral vagal complex governs the mus-cles of the face and is initially built upon a series of face-to-face interac-tions with an attachment figure that empathically regulates the infant's arousal. The "neural regulation of [facial] muscles that provide important elements of social cueing are available to facilitate the social interac-tion with the caregiver and function collectively as an integrated social engagement system" (Porges, 2005, p. 36). Schore (1994) asserts that at around 8 weeks of age, the face-processing areas of the right hemisphere are activated, and face-to-face interactions remain an essential element of interactive regulation throughout the lifespan.

However, adequate dyadic affect regulation does not mean that the mother's facial expressions consistently reflect attunement. Tron-ick and Cohn (1989) report that between 70 and 80% of face-to-face interactions between attachment figures and their infants can be mis-matched. In the majority of cases, these mismatched moments are repaired quickly and any disorganization in the infant is alleviated (DiCorcia & Tronick, 2011). In an attuned interaction, each party rap-idly and unconsciously adjusts their facial expression (as well as eye contact and prosody) in response to his or her own and the partner's affective expressions, and mismatches are quickly repaired.

Research shows that basic emotions have reliable distinctive facial expressions across cultures (Ekman, 1978). However, though we can often be aware of our expression and what we are communicating to others, fleeting microexpressions can implicitly communicate emotional states without self-reflective consciousness. Thus, facial expressions can reveal both intended and unintended emotions. Microexpressions can be visible for as little as one-fifth of a second and can expose emotions that a person is not yet aware of or is trying to conceal. These expressions register implicitly, and "observers make inferences about intention, personality, and social relationship, and about objects in the environment" (Ekman, 2004, p. 412). This is especially significant in terms of the implicit communication between patient and therapist and may help to explain the frequent extreme sensitivity of the traumatized patient to the nuances of the therapist's emotional states.

The remnants of traumatic experience are disclosed in the expressive indicators of unresolved shock: wide open eyes, raised eyebrows, frozen movement, or hypervigilance and tension around the eyes. Increased dorsal vagal tone of the feigned death defense shows clearly in faces that appear flat, with flaccid muscles that reveal little expression (Porges, 2011). In both shock and feigned death, facial expression can be greatly diminished, reflecting a compromised social engagement system. Additionally, clues to affective biases and the beliefs that go with them are etched into face, visible in chronic wrinkles, lines, and patterns: downturned mouth, lifted upper lip, furrowed brow, raised eyebrows, laugh lines, and so on.

"John" had a habit of frowning, and the parallel lines between his eyes were deeply etched although he was only in his 20s. I found myself drawn to these furrows and noticed that they seemed to deepen as he talked about his problems with his girlfriend. I asked him if he would be interested in exploring the frown. He experimented with exaggerating the frown and then relaxing his forehead, being mindful of the thoughts, emotions, and memories that emerged spontaneously as he did so. He saw an image of himself as a small boy hearing the sound of his father's hand striking against his mother's face as his parents argued. I asked him to notice if there were words that went with the frown, and he tearfully said, "What's going to happen to us?" These were the words of a small, helpless boy terrified at the violence in the next room, fearing that his world was coming to an end. John said that his reaction to his present-day conflict with his girlfriend traced back to these early memories, realizing that his current reaction was overblown since he and his girlfriend had a strong, secure relationship. Eventually, he experimented with discussing his current relationship while inhibiting the frown, and he felt calmer. His frown had implicitly communicated the terror of the past to him, which had little bearing on his current situation. Of interest also is that John reported that his girlfriend had interpreted his frown as criticism of her, which triggered her own defensiveness.

Preparatory Movement

Like fleeting microexpressions of the face, small movements of the body can be significant indicators. Anticipatory movements are evident in the minute physical gestures that are made in preparation for a larger movement. These involuntary movement adjustments occur just prior to a voluntary movement. Preparatory movements are reliable signs that predict actions that are about to happen because they are dependent upon the planned or voluntary movement for the form they take (Bouisset, 1991). The first indicators of animal defensive responses and proximity-seeking actions frequently show up in barely perceptible physical movements that antecede a larger movement. Visible prior to the execution of full gross motor actions, these micromovements take a variety of forms: a tiny crouch before a leap, a slight clenching of a fist before the strike, an opening of a hand before a reach, a slight leaning forward, a slight arm movement toward the therapist. Such movements are reliable preparatory cues of actions sequences that "wanted to happen" but had not been fully executed in the original contexts.

Once the therapist catches a glimpse of such a movement, or the patient reports what appears to be a preparatory cue, the patient can voluntarily execute the action "that wants to happen" slowly and mindfully. As "Martin" recalled the first combat he experienced in Vietnam, his hands were resting quietly on his knees. I noticed his fingers lifting slightly just as he reported the "knowing" he had experienced that someone was aiming a gun at him, although he could not see the enemy. Martin's eyes widened, he appeared frightened, and his arousal began to escalate. Rather than focus on the content, I asked Martin to momentarily put the narrative aside in order to focus his attention exclusively on his hands and be aware of what "wants to happen" somatically. Martin described a feeling that his arms wanted to lift upward. As I encouraged him to "allow" the movement, he said that his arms wanted to move upward in a protective gesture. In staying with this movement, Martin started to notice a slight change. Instead of covering his head with his arms and freezing in a habitual immobilizing defense, he said that he had a physical feeling in his arms of wanting to push away. Note that this feeling emerged from his awareness of his body, not as an idea or thought. I encouraged the slow enactment of this mobilizing defense that was not possible at the time of the trauma, holding a pillow against Martin's hands for him to push against. It was important that Martin temporarily disregard all memory and simply focus on his body in order to find a way to push that felt "right." By executing an empowering defensive action, his arousal was downregulated and his terror subsided. Martin's internal locus of control was strengthened because he was the one in charge of how much pressure I should use in resisting his pushing with the pillow, what position to be in, how long to push, and so on.

Through awareness of these preparatory movements and following what the body wants to do, the possibility of a new response emerges, incipient during the original event, ready to be further developed into an action that is more flexible and empowering. The experience of this new action—what it felt like, the sense of oneself as it is executed—seems to have the effect of expanding the patient's behavioral options in his or her life.

Arm Movements

In addition to preparatory actions, a variety of other positions and movements of the arms and hands can be significant indicators. Arms might be crossed over the chest, resting on the lap, or hanging limp at the side. Hands may be fidgeting, placed palm up or down, clenched or open, and so on. One of the most accessible indicators in this category is the simple act of reaching out, which can be executed in a variety of styles that reflects and sustain unsymbolized meaning: palm up, palm down, full arm extension or with bent elbow held close to the body, relaxed or rigid musculature, shoulders curved in or pulled back. If attachment figures are neglectful, a child may cease reaching out to them and depend more upon autoregulation than interactive regulation. Adaptive in that context, these action sequences implicitly predict that no one will respond to proximity-seeking behavior, resulting in the literal abandonment of an integrated, purposeful action of reaching out.

Often I ask patients to simply reach out with one or both arms as a diagnostic experiment as well as an avenue for working through relational issues. One patient reached out with a stiff arm, palm down, braced shoulders, and a rigid spine, whereas another patient reached out weakly, shoulders rounded, keeping her elbow by her waist rather than fully extending her arm. Yet another, always preoccupied with my availability, reached out eagerly, with intense need, leaning forward, both arms fully extended. All these movements reflected a childhood devoid of adequate regulation and support and the abandonment of an integrated, regulated reaching with the expectation of someone reaching appropriately back.

During the course of therapy, I was drawn to the tension in "Robert's" arms and shoulders and his reports of his girlfriend's complaints that he was emotionally withdrawn. I asked if he would be interested in noticing what happened as he reached out with his arm, as if to reach for another person. He said he immediately felt suspicious of my suggestion but was willing to try it. As he reached out with his left arm, his body reflected his words in its tension, slight leaning back, stiff movement, locked elbow, downward palm. His nonverbal message conveyed his discomfort and lack of expectation of a safe, empathic reception. Robert's affect transitioned from suspicion to defensiveness as he stayed with the gesture, saying angrily there was no point in reaching out: "Why bother?" Over time, together we explored his emotionally painful early memories of a father who could abide no weakness or need in his son. Robert learned to abandon this gesture simply because it evoked disgust and criticism from his father. His course of therapy included learning to reach out in an integrated manner, arm relaxed, fully engaged, with eye contact and intent to make real contact with the other—an action that was explored first with anger, but eventually with great sadness.

In addition to reaching out, exploring a variety of other arm movements can be vehicles for change (cf. Ogden, 2009, Ogden et al., 2006). Grasping or beckoning motions; actions of pushing, hitting, and circular motions that define one's personal boundary; expressive movements of opening the arms widely in gestures of anticipatory embrace or expansion; movements of self-touch, such as hugging oneself—all are significant and the manner in which they are executed reflects the implicit self. Whereas reaching out and grasping and pulling movements can be a challenge for many traumatized clients, holding on and being unable to let go can be equally challenging.

Locomotion

Locomotion, the literal act of walking from one place to another, can have a variety of qualities: plodding, springy, tottering, hurried, slow, deliberate, and so on. The angle of the feet and how they come in contact with the ground; the swing of the arms; the pelvic movement forward and back and side to side while walking; the tension in the feet, knee, and hip joints; and the angle of the body (leaning forward or backward, to one side or the other) can all be significant avenues of exploration of the implicit self (cf. Ogden & Fisher, 2015).

One patient walked stiffly, with very little movement through her pelvis, a pattern that we discovered originated in an attempt to conceal her femininity and sexuality in an abusive environment. In one session, she practiced swinging her hips as she walked, which initially elicited fear and increased hypervigalence, but eventually became pleasurable and fun as she learned to separate the present from the past. Another patient walked with a plodding, heavy gait and noticed that, with each step, her heel struck the ground forcefully, jarring her vertebrae. She hunched her shoulders and looked at the ground as she walked, limiting her vision and her engagement with her environment. This pattern reflected and sustained her feelings of hopelessness that had no content. In therapy, she first became aware of her habitual walking style and experienced the negative repercussions both emotionally (hopelessness) and physically (pain with the jarring effect of each moment of impact). Eventually, after processing the hopelessness that had no content, she began to practice a different, more adaptive way of walking: pushing off from the balls of her feet to get a spring in each step. We compared her plodding gait with a bouncy, "head-up" walk, exchanging her hunched shoulders and rounded spine for an upright, shoulders-down posture that encouraged eye contact and engagement with others.

A child in a traumatogenic environment might experience a futile impulse to escape abuse, but these defensive actions are not executed in situations when escape is impossible. The active, mobilizing "flight" response is abandoned in favor of the more adaptive (in that situation) immobilizing defenses of freeze or feigned death. Patients often report pervasive "trapped" feelings, which "Lisa" experienced through a literal sense of heaviness and immobility in her legs, coupled with a foggy, spacey feeling. I suggested that we stand and walk together to notice that our legs could carry us away from certain objects in the room, and toward others. Lisa soon said she felt more present, and observed that it was good to notice her legs. The experience of mobility was a simple resource that Lisa came back to again and again—it helped her feel less immobile and alleviated her foggy, spacey feeling.

Posture

Postural integrity involves the spine, which serves as an axis around which the limbs and head can move (cf. Ogden & Fisher, 2015). The spine is the physical core of the body; it provides support and stability to the entire physical structure and is grounded securely through the inside of the legs and feet. The first movements of an infant are initiated in the core of the body and radiate out to the periphery, then contract back inward to the movements that strengthen the core (Aposhyan, 2004; Cohen, 1993). Kurtz and Prestera note that the core also has a psychological meaning as the "'place inside" to which we may "go for sustenance" (1976, p. 33).

Posture can be upright and aligned, or slumped, twisted, braced, frozen, collapsed, slouched, and so on. A plumb line through the top of the head, middle of the ear, shoulder, hip joint, knee joint, and ankle can be imagined to assess postural alignment and integrity. When these points are in a straight line, each segment of the body supports the one above, and the body is balanced in gravity. Often this imaginary line is jagged as parts of the body are displaced from optimal alignment. Some bodies are bowed forward, others are bent backward; the head may jut forward, or the pelvis may be retracted. Without a strong and stable core, the spine may flex and droop, an indicator that might literally feel like "I can't hold myself up" and might correspond with feelings of dependency, neediness, or passivity. Tronick's Still Face experiments often demonstrate the loss of postural integrity as infants' spines slump and sag when their mothers fail to respond to them. Many patients exhibit this same pattern.

Janet (1925) pointed out that the therapist must be able to discern the action that the patient is unable to execute, and then demonstrate the missing action. If the therapist's posture is slumped, he or she will not be able to demonstrate an aligned posture or help the patient develop alignment. The recent discovery of mirror neurons brings this point home by illustrating that the observation of another's movement stimulates corresponding neural networks in the observer, thus priming the observer for making the same action (Gallese, Fadiga, Fogassi, & Rizzolatti, 1996).

"Doug's" spine began to slump even more than usual as he spoke of his wife. I found myself more interested in his droopy posture than the content, and asked him to become aware of it. He realized his posture reflected and maintained uncomfortable feelings of inferiority and helplessness, familiar feelings in his marriage. After exploring his early experiences of similar painful feelings in his family of origin, we stood up to experiment with the difference between his habitual posture and posture that was aligned and erect, where his head sits centered over his shoulders, his chest rests over his body's lower half, his pelvis supports his torso, and his legs and feet are under his body. With practice of an upright posture, Doug's thoughts started to become less negative, and his feelings of helplessness transformed into a "can do" (his words) attitude. Note that a change such as Doug experienced can help to transform the implicit self, but for more enduring change it was also necessary to address his painful past that brought about his feelings of inferiority and helplessness and the corresponding saggy posture.

Proximity

Infants and children need the proximity of a supportive other to meet their survival needs and protect them from danger. The psychobiological attachment system organizes proximity-seeking behaviors to secure the nearness of attachment figures. This innate system adjusts to the behavior of the attachment figures. If the attachment figure is unreliable, the proximity-seeking behaviors may become hyperactive. If the attachment figure is neglectful or unavailable, or punishing in the face of need or vulnerability, the proximity-seeking behaviors may become hypoactive.

A variety of factors in addition to attachment history contribute to personal proximity preferences: the situation, the specific individuals involved, gender, age, familiarity, content, and so on. Depending upon these factors, Hall, Harrigan, and Rosenthal state that "too much" or "too little" distance between interactants can be regarded as equally negative (1995, p. 21). The childhood attachment figures of traumatized patients usually responded inadequately to proximity needs by providing either too much or too little distance, or vacillated between these extremes. These patients have particular difficulty navigating proximity and seem to not recognize a felt sense of the appropriate distance between themselves and others.

Therapists can help develop patients' awareness of internal somatic barometers to appropriate proximity (cf. Ogden & Fisher, 2015). One patient, "Jill," told me that close proximity made her feel safe and requested that I move my chair nearer to her. However, when I did so, I noticed her muscles tightening, her breath becoming shallow, her body pulling back in her chair, and her eyes looking away. Jill and I agreed to contrast increased proximity with increased distance, and, to her surprise, she found that her body relaxed more when the distance between us was increased. Jill had initially thought that close proximity was preferable, but her implicit self told another story in its somatic narrative. We continued the experiment until she reported a felt sense of "rightness" in her body in terms of the distance between us, which turned out to be about 8–10 feet apart. Jill described this felt sense as one of relaxation, with deeper breathing, easier eye contact, and an internal feeling of well-being.

Negotiating physical distance is a fruitful task because traumatized individuals invariably need to learn about their proximity needs and preferences to be able to tolerate relationships. Patients who have experienced early relational trauma are rarely able to set appropriate distance between themselves and others. Frequently, I ask patients how close or far they prefer me to sit. Experiments (moving toward and away from my patient, or moving an object such as a pillow closer and farther away) can be conducted to explore automatic responses to proximity, such as bracing, moving backward, holding the breath, or changes in orienting or attention. With patients for whom the above experiments are too provocative, introducing simple exercises such as rolling a therapy ball or gently tossing a pillow toward them while they use their arms to push the object away can strengthen the capacity to execute the defensive action of pushing away that was usually not allowed in early relationships.

One patient first stood immobile, allowing the pillow I gently threw to hit her torso. Slowly, she practiced lifting her arms in a gesture of protection against the pillow hitting her body. (Note that when protective actions have incited the perpetrator to more violence in the past, as they did in her extremely abusive childhood, these actions are abandoned; executing them in the "safe" context of therapy can be terrifying, and patients need encouragement and practice to execute these actions.) This built the foundation upon which other proximity exercises could be introduced, such as her making a beckoning gesture and my slowly walking toward her, until she experienced a felt sense in her body that I was close enough. Then she could tell me to stop with her voice or by lifting her arms, palms open and extended outward in a "stop" gesture. It is important that the sense of suitable proximity is founded on the *experienced somatic sense* of preference, safety, and protection, rather than on analysis or ideas.

Self-States and Enactment

Integrated actions are abandoned or distorted when they are persistently ineffective in producing the desired outcome. If no one is there to reach back, we stop reaching out. If our attachment figures ridiculed us when we were vulnerable, we stop seeking proximity when we feel needy. If standing upright with our heads held high brought more abuse, we will slump and keep our heads down. Exploring alternative actions can bring forward a variety of self-states that are "inhospitable and even adversarial, sequestered from one another as islands of 'truth,' each functioning as an insulated version of reality that protectively defines what is 'me' at a given moment and forcing other self states that are inharmonious with its truth to become 'not-me'" (Bromberg, 2010, p. 21).

When Robert explored reaching out, the self-state that had learned to inhibit that action became frightened and oppositional. Having made up its mind that others were never to be relied upon to respond to his need, this part of him believed reaching out to be hopeless and even threatening. New actions, like new words, "are often initially perceived from an adversarial perspective by at least one part of the self, sometimes with grave misgivings, sometimes with outright antagonism, and sometimes even with rage" (Bromberg, 2006, p. 52). Keep in mind that these actions are not simply physical exercises: They are rich with strong attachment-related emotions that were not regulated by the attachment figures in early childhood and/or with trauma-related emotions of terror and rage that accompany animal defenses. Processing these actions and their affects can ultimately encourage self-states to get to know one another and increase the ease of transitions between states.

It warrants reiterating that the therapist's own nonverbal expressions and the self-states they represent have a strong impact on what takes place within the therapeutic relationship. Therapists tend to invite and interact with the parts of the patient with which they are most comfortable, disconnecting from and ignoring the patient's self-states that they would rather not address (Bromberg, 2006). Physical actions that are familiar, easy for the therapist to execute, and do not challenge or stimulate the "not-me" self-states of the therapist are those that he or she is likely to explore in the patient, ignoring or rejecting actions would make him or her uncomfortable. If the therapist is uneasy with reaching out to others for support, and/or uneasy when others reach out to him or her, the therapist will be unlikely to explore this action with the patient. If he or she attempts to do so, the therapist will probably be unable to demonstrate an emotionally and physically integrated reaching action, so the exploration will have little chance of producing the explicitly desired outcome. But this is not cause for undue concern for the therapist who is interested in learning about his or her own participation in what takes place beyond the words. In fact, the real magic and healing power of clinical practice often emerge from the unformulated, unconscious impact of therapist and patient upon one another, which includes the influence of past childhood histories on both parties.

Therapy can be conceptualized as comprising two mutually created, simultaneous journeys (cf. Ogden, 2014). An explicit, conscious journey pertains to what the therapist believes he or she is doing as a clinician, supported by theory and technique. Therapeutic methods, meant to be learned but then be set aside and not reflected upon explicitly in the therapy hour, guide interventions that emerge spontaneously within the dyad. However, inevitably, the implicit selves of therapist and patient communicate beneath the words and even collide in therapeutic enactments. The implicit journey is elusive and unconscious, and although it may feel vaguely familiar, it usually leads relentlessly to outcomes that were not intended or predicted. For one client, "Ellen," our implicit journey together became clear. Ellen had been forced to submit to extreme abuse during her childhood. A pattern of compliance continued into adulthood, long after that abuse was over. Ellen stated that she had great trouble feeling anger, and that when she did, she often turned it against herself through self-harm. As we explored her anger, Ellen discovered an impulse to push outward, along with the words, "Leave me alone." She immediately felt strong and powerful, and I felt relieved. Ellen stated that she had not had much of a chance to practice any assertive action because assertion would have made the abuse at the hands of her father much worse. I suggested that we practice this action in therapy by giving her the opportunity to push away a pillow as I moved it toward her. Ellen agreed, but she was reluctant. I briefly asked if it was OK with her to practice, but I did not pay attention to the part of Ellen that (still) could not say no. She became compliant, and I, in my effort to "do more," did not notice her compliance. I realized that my "pushing" her was a reflection of my own childhood with a demanding mother who conveyed that "more was better." I failed to notice that Ellen was at the limit of her window of tolerance (Siegel, 1999) and at risk of dissociating. Our two histories collided in an enactment that continued to intensify until finally we realized together that Ellen was complying and becoming dysregulated.

The past is commonly reworked in a more powerful and substantial manner through processing an enactment than if the enactment had not occurred. The presence of both our pasts contributed to the enactment. My part reflected my childhood attempts to please my mother by doing more, and Linda's part reflected her childhood pattern of submitting and complying to the wishes of others. Processing the enactment is possible when the therapist or the client (or both) "'wakes up' and *feels* that something is going on between himself and his patient (a here-and-now experience), rather than continuing to *believe* that the phenomenon is located solely in his patient, who is 'doing the same thing again'" (Bromberg, 2006, p. 34). I "woke up" when Ellen's eyes widened fearfully, and she abruptly sat down, shaking. At that moment, I realized that we had gone too far, and that interactive regulation was needed to bring her arousal back into a window of tolerance. At that moment, I was able to acknowledge the part of Ellen that was terrified and provide the reassurance that "nothing bad was going to happen" from executing that action. If Ellen had not experienced her compliance and my failure to notice her dysregulation, interactive repair could not have occurred, and it is the repair and working through of the enacted experience that provided the most beneficial therapeutic impact.

Bromberg (2006) emphasizes that the environment in which change can take place must be "safe but not too safe" for both therapist and patient. If the emotional and physiological arousal consistently remains in the middle of the window of tolerance (e.g., at levels typical of low fear and anxiety states), patients will not be able to expand their capacities because they are not challenging the window by contacting disturbing traumatic or affect-laden attachment issues in the here and now of the therapy hour. Similarly, therapists are challenged by the residue of their past histories that they thought were already resolved, but that emerge in enactments and empathic failures within the relationship. Thus both parties are at the regulatory boundaries of their own windows of tolerance (Schore, 2009). By working at the "edges" of the regulatory boundaries, the windows of both can be expanded.

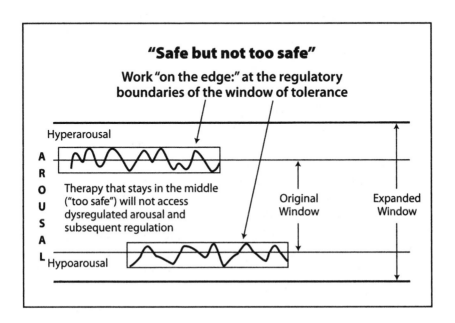

It is the processing of each person's implicit self within the relationship that provides the raw material for new experiences, new actions, and new meanings for both parties. Ellen and I participated together in an unfolding interaction within which we co-created a new experience and challenged early unsymbolized implicit relational knowing for both of us. Eventually, I "woke up" and recognized Ellen's self-state that I had heretofore ignored—the one who was terrified of making an assertive action—by directly acknowledging her fear and reassuring her that this was a different situation from her childhood. This act of recognition challenged Ellen's relational "knowing" that her fear would not be tended to, and that she needed comply to others' wishes rather than assert herself. It also challenged my early relational knowing of never being "enough" and that I had to do more. This intersubjective process cannot be defined, identified, or predicted ahead of time, because it occurs within the context of what transpires within the dyad and thus requires a leap into the unknown not only for the patient, but for the therapist as well.

Conclusion

Visible and tangible nonverbal behaviors tell their own inimitable stories of the past and provide an ongoing source of implicit and explicit exploration in the therapy hour. The therapist listens not only to the verbal narrative, but also to the somatic narrative for the purpose of making the unconscious conscious as well as for "interacting at another level, an experience-near subjective level, one that implicitly processes moment to moment socio-emotional information at levels beneath awareness" (Schore, 2003b, p. 52). Along with the therapist's implicit participation in the nonverbal conversation, explicit exploration of specific nonverbal behaviors provides an avenue to the patient's unconscious. When we experiment with new actions to challenge outdated procedural learning, we challenge habitual implicit processing, including enactments, both explicitly through the use of words and also implicitly at a level at which words are not available and sometimes not needed for therapeutic change to occur. The intimacy and benefit of the therapist–client journey can be heightened by thoughtful attention to what is being spoken beneath the words, through the body.

References

Aposhyan, S. (2004). *Bodymind psychotherapy: Principles, techniques, and practical applications.* New York, NY: Norton.

Bainbridge-Cohen, B. (1993). *Sensing, feeling and action.* Northamption, MA: Contact.

Bouisset, S. (1991). Relationship between postural support and intentional movement: Biomechanical approach. *Archives Internationales de Physiologie, de Biochimie et de Biophysique, 99,* A77–A92.

Brazelton, T. (1989). *The earliest relationship.* Reading, MA: Addison–Wesley.

Bromberg, P. M. (2006). *Awakening the dreamer: Clinical journeys.* Mahwah, NJ: Analytic Press.

Bromberg, P. M. (2010). Minding the dissociative gap. *Contemporary Psychoanalysis,* 46(1), 19:31

Cortina, M., & Liotti, G. (2007). New approaches to understanding unconscious processes: Implicit and explicit memory systems. *International Forum of Psychoanalysis,* 16, 204–212.

Courtois, C. (1999). *Recollections of sexual abuse: Treatment principles and guidelines.* New York, NY: Norton.

DiCorcia, J. A., & Tronick, E. Z. (2011). Quotidian resilience: Exploring mechanisms that drive resilience from a perspective of everyday stress and coping. *Neurosci Biobehav Rev,* 35(7), 1593-602.

Dijkstra, K., Kaschak, M. P., & Zwann, R. A. (2006). Body posture facilitates retrieval of autobiographical memories. *Cognition,* 102(1), 139–149.

Ekman, P. (1978). Facial signs: Facts, fantasies, and possibilities. In T. Sebeok (Ed.), *Sight, sound and sense.* Bloomington, IN: Indiana University Press.

Ekman, P. (2004). *Emotions revealed: Recognizing faces and feelings to improve communication and emotional life.* New York, NY: Henry Holt.

Frewen, P. A., Neufeld, R. W., Stevent, T. K., & Lanius, R. A. (2010). Social emotions and emotional valence during imagery in women with PTSD: Affective and neural correlates. *Journal of Psychological Trauma: Theory, Research, Practice, and Policy,* 2(2), 145–157.

Gallese, V., Fadiga, L., Fogassi, L., & Rizzolatti, G. (1996). Action recognition in the premotor cortex. *Brain, 119,* 593–609.

Grigsby, J., & Stevens, D. (2000). *Neurodynamics of personality.* New York, NY: Guilford Press.

Hall, J., Harrigan, J., & Rosenthal, R. (1995). Nonverbal behavior in clinician–patient interaction. *Applied & Preventive Psychology,* 4, 21–37.

Janet, P. (1925). *Principles of psychotherapy.* London, UK: Allen & Unwin.

Krystal, H. (1978). Trauma and affects. *Psychoanalytic Study of the Child, 33,* 81–116.

Kurtz, R. (1990). *Body-centered psychotherapy: The Hakomi method.* Mendocino, CA: LifeRhythm.

Kurtz, R. (2010). Readings. Retrieved December 3, 2010, from http://hakomi.com/wp-content/uploads/2009/12/Readings-January-2010.pdf

Kurtz, R., & Prestera, H. (1976). *The body reveals: An illustrated guide to the psychology of the body.* New York, NY: Holt, Rinehart & Winston.

Lanius, R. A., Williamson, P. C., Boksman, K., Densmore, M., Gupta, M.,...& Neufeld, R.W. (2002). Brain activation during script-driven imagery induced dissociative responses in PTSD: A functional magnetic resonance imaging investigation. *Biological Psychiatry, 52*, 305–311.

Lapides, F. (2010). The implicit realm in couples therapy: Improving right hemisphere affect-regulating capabilities. *Journal of Clinical Social Work*, published online May 20, 2010. Retrieved January 10, 2010, from http://www.francinelapides.com/newdocs4/Implicit_Realm_Couples_Therapy.pdf

LeDoux, J. (2002). *Synaptic self: How our brains become who we are.* New York, NY: Penguin.

Lyons-Ruth, K. (1998). Implicit relational knowing: Its role in development and psychoanalytic treatment. *Infant Mental Health Journal, 19*, 282–289.

Lyons-Ruth, K., Bronfman, E., & Parsons, E. (1999). Atypical attachment in infancy and early childhood among children at developmental risk: IV. Maternal frightened, frightening, or atypical behaviour and disorganized infant attachment patterns. *Monographs of the Society for Research in Child Development, 64*(3), 67–96.

Nespor, M. (2010). Prosody: An interview with Marina Nespor. *ReVEL, 8*(15). Retrieved December 23, 2010, from www.revel.inf.br/eng

Nijenhuis, E., & van der Hart, O. (1999a). Forgetting and reexperiencing trauma: From anesthesia to pain. In J. Goodwin & R. Attias (Eds.), *Splintered reflections: Images of the body in trauma* (pp. 33-66). Basic Books.

Nijenhuis, E., & van der Hart, O. (1999b). Somatoform dissociative phenomena: A Janetian perspective. In J. Goodwin & R. Attias (Eds.), *Splintered reflections: Images of the body in trauma* (pp. 89-128). Basic Books.

Ogden, P. (2007, March). *Beyond words: A clinical map for using mindfulness of the body and the organization of experience in trauma treatment.* Paper presented at Mindfulness and Psychotherapy Conference, Los Angeles, CA, UCLA/Lifespan Learning Institute.

Ogden, P. (2009). Emotion, mindfulness, and movement: Expanding the regulatory boundaries of the window of tolerance. In D. Fosha, D. Siegel, & M. Solomon (Eds.), *The healing power of emotion: Perspectives from affective neuroscience and clinical practice* (pp. 204-231). New York, NY: Norton.

Ogden, P. (2011). Beyond Words: A Sensorimotor Psychotherapy Perspective on Trauma Treatment. In Caretti V., Craparo G., Schimmenti (eds.), *Psychological Trauma. Theory, Clinical and Treatment.* Rome: A

Ogden, P. (2013). "Oltre le parole: la psicoterapia sensomotoria nel trattamento del trauma" (pp. 183-214). In V. Caretti, G. Craparo, A. Schimmenti (a cura di), Memorie traumatiche e mentalizzazione. Teoria, ricerca e clinica. Roma: Astrolabio.strolabio.

Ogden, P. (2013). Technique and beyond: Therapeutic enactments, mindfulness, and the role of the body. In D. J. Siegel & M. Solomon (Eds.), *Healing moments in psychotherapy.* New York, NY: Norton.

Ogden, P. (2014). Embedded relational mindfulness: A sensorimotor psychotherapy perspective on trauma treatment. In V. M. Follette, D. Rozelle, J. W. Hopper, D. I. Rome, & J. Briere (Eds.), *Contemplative methods in trauma treatment:*

Integrating mindfulness and other approaches (pp. 227-242). New York, NY: Guilford Press.

Ogden, P., & Fisher, J. (2015). *Sensorimotor psychotherapy: Interventions for trauma and attachment.* New York, NY: Norton.

Ogden, P., Minton, K., & Pain, C. (2006). *Trauma and the body: A sensorimotor approach to psychotherapy.* New York, NY: Norton.

Porges, S. W. (2005). The role of social engagement in attachment and bonding: A phylogenetic perspective. In C. Carter, L. Aknert, K. Grossman, S. Hirdy, M. Lamb, S. W. Porges, & N. Sachser (Eds.), *From the 92nd Dahlem Workshop Report: Attachment and bonding—a new synthesis.* Cambridge, MA: MIT Press.

Porges, S. W. (2011). *The polyvagal theory: Neurophysiological foundations of emotions, attachment, communication, and self-regulation.* New York, NY: Norton.

Schachner, D., Shaver, P., & Mikulincer, M. (2005). Patterns of nonverbal behavior and sensitivity in the context of attachment relationships. *Journal of Nonverbal Behavior, 29*(3), 141–169.

Schnall, S., & Laird, J. D. (2003). Keep smiling: Enduring effects of facial expressions and postures on emotional experience and memory. *Cognition and Emotion 17*(5), 787–797.

Schore, A. N. (1994). *Affect regulation and the origin of the self: The neurobiology of emotional development.* Hillsdale, NJ: Erlbaum.

Schore, A. N. (2003). *Affect regulation and the repair of the self.* New York, NY: Norton.

Schore, A. N. (2007). Modern attachment theory: The central role of affect regulation in development and treatment. *Clinical Social Work,* 36(1), 9-20.

Schore, A. N. (2009). Right-brain affect regulation: An essential mechanism of development, trauma, dissociation, and psychotherapy. In D. Fosha, D. Siegel, & M. Solomon (Eds.), *The healing power of emotion: Affective neuroscience, development and clinical practice* (pp. 112-144). New York, NY: W.W. Norton.

Schore, A. N. (2010). The right brain implicit self: A central mechanism of the psychotherapy change process. In J. Pertucelli (Ed.), *Knowing, not-knowing, and sort-of-knowing: Psychoanalysis and the experience of uncertainty* (pp. 117-202). Washington, DC: American Psychological Association.

Schore, A. N. (2011). The right brain implicit self lies at the core of psychoanalysis. *Psychoanalytic Dialogues 21,* 1–26.

Schore, A. N. (2012). *The science of the art of psychotherapy.* New York, NY: Norton.

Siegel, D. (1999). *The developing mind.* New York, NY: Guilford Press.

Stepper, S., & Strack, F. (1993). Proprioceptive determinants of emotional and nonemotional feelings. *Personality & Social Psychology, 64*(2), 211–220.

Stern, D. (1985). *The interpersonal world of the infant: A view from psychoanalysis and developmental psychology.* New York, NY: Basic Books.

Tronick, E. Z. (2007). The neurobehavioral and social–emotional development of infants and children. New York, NY: Norton.

Tronick, E. Z., & Cohn, J. F. (1989). Infant–mother face-to-face interaction: Age and gender differences in coordination and the occurrence of miscoordination. *Child Development, 60,* 85–92.

5

Emotion, the Body, and Change

Peter A. Levine

If your everyday practice is to open to
your emotions, to all the people you meet,
to all the situations you encounter,
without closing down, trusting that you
can do that—then that will take you as far
as you can go. And that you'll understand
all the teachings that anyone has ever taught.
—Pema Chödrön (Buddhist teacher)

How Do People Change?

Neuroscientists can accurately tell us where in the brain various emotions reside.* However, they tell us precious little about how we can change (our relationship to) such difficult emotions as sadness, anger, and fear. Nor do they shed much light on how people change problematic behaviors by altering these troubling emotions. For us to

_____
* See Damasio, Antonio. *The Feeling of What Happens*; Le Doux, Joseph. *The Emotional Brain*

make headway in approaching this critical question, we need to better understand the very components and structure of emotions as rooted in bodily process and central nervous system functions.

Qu'est-ce qu'une émotion?

Alfred Binet posed this very provocative question at the dawn of the twentieth century. He opened the debate with a salvo, which eludes a clear solution, even to this day. Simple to ask, though difficult to answer, the question remains: "What is an emotion?" (Binet, 1908). Theories of emotion, abundant and diverse, have had a long, twisted, confounding and often contradictory history. Philosophy, psychology, and evolutionary biology, have each attempted to define, refine or, simply understand emotion (Gendron, 2009). The first scientific study of emotion was published by Darwin in 1872 with his landmark work, *The Expression of the Emotions in Man and Animals.*

"Emotion as a scientific concept," wrote Elizabeth Duffy, the matriarch of modern psychophysiology, "is worse than useless" (Gendron & Barrett, 2009). On the basis of extensive physiological recording available at the time, she felt that there was no way of differentiating one emotional state from another. In other words, distinguishing an emotion, solely on the basis of physiological measurements (such as heart rate, blood pressure, respiration, temperature, skin conductance, etc.), seemed impossible. Thus, emotions, from her vantage point in 1936, were unworthy of scientific study. Yet recently, there has been a rich vein of inquiry and grounding in the emerging field of the "affective neurosciences," demonstrating distinct brain *systems* involved in the *expression* of various emotions (e.g. fear, anger, sadness and joy) (Panksepp, 2004). However, the question of *felt experience (as opposed to emotional expression)* has been all but neglected, in spite of its great clinical importance. Psychology, questing for objective respectability, has attempted to purge subjectivity from its midst. It has, in the process, unwittingly thrown out the proverbial baby (the subjective feeling experience) with the bathwater, by studying primarily the *expression* and brain mechanisms of emotion.

Much of philosophy (particularly Descartes cogito ergo sum, "I think therefore I am") and early psychology were of the logical, "common sense" conviction regarding the sequence by which an emotion was generated. Let's imagine that when something provocative happened to Renee Descartes—perhaps if someone raised their fist and called him a jerk or alternatively patted him on the shoulder and told him, "you're a great guy"—he might have believed that his brain recognized this provocation as being worthy of an emotional response—anger, fear, sadness, or elation. Had the physiology of his times been more advanced, he might have interpreted the next step, in this "top-down" process, as his brain telling his body what to do: increase your heart rate, blood pressure, and breathing; tense your muscles, secrete sweat, and make goose bumps. For Descartes, and for many clinicians, this sequence makes perfectly logical sense and seems to accurately describe how we experience an emotion. However, to paraphrase his contemporary, Blaise Pascal, in an open letter to Descartes, telling the philosopher: Monsieur Descartes, "I cannot forgive you for what you have said," for Pascal, "The Body has its Reason which Reason cannot Reason."

At the turn of the nineteenth century, however, the experimental psychologist William James made an *experiential* inquiry into the study of emotions. Rather than taking a philosophical and speculative approach, James set up various imagined situations, such as being chased by a bear or losing a close friend. Then, through experiential introspection, he would attempt to infer the chain of events by which the experience of an emotion such as fear was generated. In these subjective experiments he would sense into the interior of his body (what is now called interoception), as well as noting his thoughts and inner images. From these subjective explorations, he arrived at a rather unexpected conclusion. Cartesian common sense dictates that when we see a bear, we are frightened and then motivated by fear, we flee. However, in his careful, reflective observations, *James concluded that rather than running because we are afraid, we are afraid because we are running (from the bear)*. In James's words:

My theory is that the bodily changes follow *directly* (from) the perception of the exciting fact, and that our feeling of the same changes as they occur *is* the emotion. 'Common sense' says, we lose our fortune, are sorry and weep; we meet a bear, are frightened and run; we are insulted by a rival, are angry, and strike. The hypothesis, here to be defended, says that this *order of sequence is incorrect*, that the one mental state is not immediately induced by the other, that *the bodily manifestations may first be interposed* between, and the more rational (accurate) statement is that we feel sorry *because* we cry, angry because we strike, afraid because we tremble. (Wozniak, 1999)

This counter intuitive view challenged the Cartesian/cognitive (*top-down*) paradigm where *the conscious mind* first recognizes the source of threat, and then commands the body to respond: to flee, to fight or to fold. James's *bottom-up paradigm*, that we feel fear *because* we are running away from the threat (while only partially correct), does make a crucial point about the illusory nature of emotional perception. We may commonly believe, for example, that when we touch a hot object, we draw our hand away *because* of the pain. However, the reality is that if we were to wait until we experienced pain in order to withdraw our hand, we might damage it beyond repair. Physiology teaches us that there is *first* a reflex withdrawal of the hand, which is only then *followed* by the sensation of pain. The pain might well serve the function of reminding us not to pick up a potentially hot stone from the fire pit a second time, but it has little to do with our hand withdrawing when it is first burned. Similarly, every student of basic chemistry learns, hopefully after the first encounter, that hot test tubes look just like cold ones. However, what we *falsely perceive*, and believe as fact, is that the (experience of) pain causes us to withdraw our hand.

James was able to recognize that the experience of fear (as well as other emotions) was not primarily a cognitive affair; that there was first a muscular (tension) and visceral reaction in his body (including increased heart rate, cold hands, fast respiration, churning stomach). Then, it was *the perception of this body reaction* (joined with the image of the bear), that generated the felt emotion of fear. What James observed (in terms of neurophysiology) was that, when the primitive brain senses the potential danger, it makes this assessment so quickly that there isn't enough time for the person to become consciously aware of it. What happens instead, according to James, is that the brain "canvases" the body to see how it is reacting in the moment. In what was a revelatory revision, James relocated the consciousness of feeling from mind to body. In doing this he demonstrated a rare prescience about what neuroscience would only begin to (re)discover a hundred years later. In his theory of "Somatic Markers," neurologist Antonio Damasio clearly has resurrected James's perceiving sequence (Damasio, 2000). Let us follow this line of inquiry, beginning with our basic sense of agency.

In the mid 1980s, Ben Libet (1985; 1999), a neurosurgeon and neurophysiologist at the University of California Medical School in San Francisco, conducted a revealing series of studies regarding the sequencing of experience. He essentially confirmed James's observational chain with a series of ingenious investigations. Here's a simple little experiment that you can do right now. Hold one of your arms out in front of you with your palm facing upwards. Then, whenever you feel like it (i.e. of your own "free will"), flex your wrist. Do this several times and watch what happens in your mind. You probably felt as though you first consciously decided to move and then, following your intention, you moved it. It feels to you as though *the conscious decision caused the action.* Common sense?

Libet asked experimental subjects to do this same hand exercise, while he systematically measured the timing of three things: 1) The subjects' "conscious" decision to move, which was marked on a special clock, 2) The beginning of (what is called) the readiness potential in the (pre) motor cortex using EEG electrodes on the scalp, and 3) The start of the actual action—using EMG electrodes on the wrist to measure the electrical activity of the wrist muscles just as they began to contract. So which do you think, based on your experience in the preceding hand experiment, came first? Was it the decision to move activity in the motor cortex, or the actual movement? The answer, defying credulity, dramatically contradicted common sense. The brain's activity, as measured from the motor cortex, began about 500 milliseconds (half a second!) *before* the person was aware of "deciding" to act. *The conscious decision came far too late to be the cause of the action.* It was as though consciousness was a mere afterthought; a way of "explaining to ourselves," an action not evoked by conscious intention, but by something like "perceptual responsiveness." As peculiar as this might seem, it fits in with previous experiments that Libet had carried out on exposed brains as part of a neuro-surgical procedure to treat epilepsy. Here, Libet had demonstrated that about half a second of continuous activity of stimulation in the sensory cortex was needed for a person to become aware of a sensory stimulus (Libet, 1981).

In summary, Libet found that what the subject believed was a "conscious" decision to perform a simple action (such as pushing a button) preceded the action. This conscious decision, however, occurred only *after* the "pre-motor" area in the brain first fired with a burst of electrical activity. In other words, people decide to act only after their brain *unconsciously prepares* them to do so. Much earlier, the evolutionary biologist Thomas Huxley (known as "Darwin's Bulldog" for his advocacy of Charles Darwin's theory of evolution) observed that: *"Consciousness has no more influence on our actions than a steam whistle has on the locomotion of a train."*

Daniel Wegner, working at Harvard University, later reinforced Libet's proposition (Wegner & Wheatley, 1999). In one of his studies, an illusion was created by a series of mirrors. Subjects, thinking that they were looking at their own arms, were actually seeing (in the mirror) the movements of an experimenter's arm. When the experimenter's arms moved (according to the instructions of another researcher), the subjects reported that *they* had made and therefore willed the movements (when, in fact, they had not even moved their arms)! Hence, the strong bias in favor of volitional will is once again challenged. "Nothing seems to us to belong so closely to our personality, to be so completely our property as our free will," decried Wilhelm Wundt, considered one of the founders of experimental psychology.

The results of Libet, Wegner, and others, taken together, seriously challenge our common sense understanding of consciousness and our love affair with free will. The annihilation of free will, suggested in Wegner's book (2013), goes against what we believe is the very core of our existence as autonomous human beings. It challenges such cherished beliefs as the capacity for planning, foresight and responsible action. Who, or what, are we without the power of free will? This dispute of free will, revered in Western thought for 3,000 years, is not just another philosopher's opinion, but rather stems from a variety of dispassionate laboratory research. Einstein, in paraphrasing the philosopher Shopenhauer, re-stated the conundrum of free will with his characteristic understated wisdom: "A human can very well do what he wants but cannot will what he wants."

Is this a farewell to Freud's ego and Descartes' cogito ergo sum? Although this credo, "I think therefore I am," was an important start in freeing people from the power and rigidity of Church doctrine, it's in great need of revision (Damasio, 1995). These different researchers suggest something more like: *I prepare to move, I sense, I feel, I perceive, I reflect, I think, I conclude and therefore I am.*

Together, the studies of James, Libet, Wegner and others confirm that before a "voluntary" movement is made, there is an *unconscious*, let us call it for now, *"pre-movement" impulse*. In addition, there are non-conscious sensory systems that trigger equally unconscious movements. We see this demonstrated in a revealing condition called *"blindsight"* (Weiskrantz, 1986). Oliver Sacks, from his many moving and wise vignettes about the tragic, yet compelling consequences of neurological disorders, describes the case of Virgil. Virgil's entire visual cortex was destroyed rendering him completely blind; yet Sacks describes Virgil's wife's inexplicable observations: "Virgil had told her that he was completely blind, yet she observed that he would reach for objects, avoid obstacles and *behave* as though he were seeing" (Sacks, 1996, p. 146). Such is the enigma of this type of implicit ("bottom-up") information processing derived from pre-motor impulses. These experiments of nature challenge the very "common sense" idea of consciousness. How do we reconcile that he avoided these objects but yet, seemed completely unaware of this.

The primary visual cortex, located in the back of the brain (and known dispassionately as area 17) provides us with conscious visual images. In addition, however, there are multiple visual nuclei in the brain stem and thalamus, which eventually ascends to area 17. Input from the retina to these primitive ("non-conscious") subcortical centers somehow registers basic information that normally has the function of directing eye movements to garner more data. And it does this significantly, before a visual image is recorded in the conscious visual cortex in area 17. These primitive centers also render potential threats as well as a flimsy sketch of which we are largely unconscious. Such was the case with Virgil when, seemingly completely unaware, he avoided the obstacles in his path.* Hence, we are once again appreciative of the *prompting to respond to events before we become overtly aware of them*. Fortunately, these seemingly unconscious impulses can, with coaching, become conscious if we learn how to access and follow subtle physical sensations. This "pre-conscious awareness," as we shall see, is a key to changing difficult emotions.

There has been a tendency in psychology to view consciousness as a binary phenomenon: either "conscious" or "unconscious." However, consciousness occurs on a continuum, a multitude of shades from

---

* This is the same type of unconscious brain stem and limbic system information that evokes the readiness for movement (i.e. pre-movement) we saw with Libet's subjects.

white, through many shades of grey, to black. For the more conscious states (white and greys), awareness is like a flashlight, beamed in a particular direction. On the other hand, the less conscious states are more like distant, glowing embers. As we gently blow our breath in that general direction there is a faint glowing pulsation, just perceived against the dark background. It is just the complex, subtle, ever-shifting interoceptive (body) sensations, that are just this gentle breath. This way we can begin an exploration of "core consciousness." This primal consciousness allows difficult emotions to morph and finally to transform. Indeed, recent work in affective neuroscience, (e.g., see Panksepp, 1998) argues that our core sense of self emerges from our basic mammalian motoricity and emotionality, derived from brain structures in the limbic system, brainstem, and thalamus. We know ourselves, in this perspective, through action, sensation, and feeling.

Consider your response to a fleeting shadow, the subtle gesture of another person, a distant sound. Each of these events can evoke in us survival-bound (movement and emotional) responses without our being "consciously" aware that something in our environment has triggered them. Notably, when traumatized, we are particularly sensitized to (and hyper-aroused into frantic action by) these fleeting sensations, of which we are largely unaware. Our senses of seeing, hearing, and smell provide countless stimuli that provoke us to over-react, even though we may be unaware of the presence of these subliminal stimuli and our pre-motor and emotional responses to them. As a result, we may, and often do, *attribute* our actions and emotions to irrelevant or confabulated causes.*

Causality gets misconstrued for traumatized individuals in two ways. The first one involves the unawareness of the pre-movement trigger; the second involves the extent of the response (see Levine, 2015). Imagine the consternation of an individual trapped in the full-blown ferocious re-enactment of a survival-bound response; for instance the Vietnam vet who wakes up strangling his terrified wife, unaware that it was the backfiring of a distant car, or even the light footsteps of their young child in the hallway, that provoked his "freakish" behavior and grossly exaggerated reaction. However, years earlier, when sleeping in

---

* These specious attributions of causation, are like those of the subjects in Wegner's experiments who, falsely, believed that they had willed the movement of the experimenter's arms.

a bamboo thicket, under fire from the Viet Cong, his immediate kill-response was an essential, life preserving action. It may only take a very mild stimulus to abruptly trigger the tightly coiled spring (his survival kill-or-be-killed reaction sequence) into an intense, out-of-control, emotional eruption.

Thankfully, there is a potent way to break such compulsive cycles of reenactment and diffuse a maladaptive action and corrosive emotion. And in the process, to expand consciousness towards greater response-ability, openness, receptivity, and freedom. Becoming aware of the interoceptive sensations associated with the *pre-movement before it graduates into a full-blown movement sequence allows us to break the compulsive cycles of reenactment*. It is, in the vernacular, to extinguish the spark before it ignites the tinder. As Libet showed, there is a delay of only about one-half a second between the time when we prepare for action and the actual time when we execute it. Let's consider a couple of non-clinical examples that help demonstrate the use of pre-movement postural adjustments:

Many times in the past, I walked with my dog in the Colorado Mountains.

Pouncer, a dingo mix, was imbued with a strong instinctual urge to chase deer and other swift creatures of the upland meadows. Try as I might, it was not possible to neutralize this "habit" by reprimanding him. If I tried to call him back or admonished his behavior when he returned, breathless and panting from the chase, it was of no avail. However, if when we encountered a deer up ahead, at the *very moment* his posture changed (just hinting at his readiness to leap forward), I would firmly, but gently say, "Pouncer, heel." He would then calmly continue on our walk, striding enthusiastically by my side. Then there is the story of a brash young samurai sword fighter and a venerated Zen master.

Two Horns of the Dilemma

There is a vital balancing act, between expression and restraint necessary to neutralize corrosive emotional states. This resolution requires that when we experience a strong emotional feeling we need *not* necessarily act upon it, but rather *experience its underlying sensations*. In the following Zen "teaching story," a young, somewhat brash samurai swordsman confronts a venerated Zen master with the following demand: "I want you to tell me the truth about the existence of heaven and hell." The master replies gently, and with delicate curiosity: "How is it that such an ugly and untalented man as you can become a samurai?" Immediately, the wrathful young samurai pulled out his sword, raising it above his head, ready to strike the old man and cut him in half. Without fear, and in complete calm, the Zen master gazed upward and spoke softly: "This, young man, is hell." The samurai paused, sword held above his head. His arms fell like leaves to his side, while his face softened from its angry glare. He quietly reflected. Placing his sword back into its sheath, he bowed to the teacher in reverence. "And this," the master replied again with equal calm, "is heaven."

Here the samurai, sword held high at the peak of feeling full of rage (and at the moment *before* executing the prepared-for action) learned to hold back and *restrain* his rage; instead of mindlessly expressing it. In refraining, with the master's quick guidance, from making his habitual emotional expression of attack (as I did with my dog, Pouncer), he transformed his rage-full "hell" to peaceful "heaven."

One could also speculate on what sub-conscious thoughts (and images) were stirred when the master provoked his ire. Perhaps he was startled, and at first, even agreed with the characterization that he was ugly and untalented. This strong reaction to this insult (we might hypothesize) derived from his parents, teachers, and others who humiliated him as a child. Perhaps he had a compelling sensation of collapse, along with a mental picture of being shamed in front of his school classmates. And then the other micro-fleeting "counter thought"—that no one would dare to call him that again and make him feel small and worthless. This thought and associated picture, coupled with a momentary *physical sensation of startle*, triggered the emotion of rage that lead him down the driven road to perdition. That was, at least, until his "Zen therapist," precisely at the peak of rage, kept him from habitually expressing this "protective" emotion (really a defense against his feelings of smallness and helplessness) and, by connecting him with his physical sensations moments before striking out in rage, allowed him to redirect his energy and take ownership of his *real* power and gain a peaceful surrender.

How Do We Create Change in Our Emotional Responses

In the above examples (the parable of the Zen master and samurai swordsman, as well as the tale of my dog Pouncer), choice occurred at the critical moment *before* executing attack, during the brief pre-motor readiness. With the Zen master's critical intervention, the samurai held back and *felt* the *preparation* to strike (a bodily sensation) with his sword. In this highly charged state, he paused and was able to restrain and transmute his violent rage into intense energy, and then into a state of clarity, gratefulness, presence, and grace. It is the ability to hold back, restrain, and contain (but not suppress) a powerful emotion that allows a person to creatively channel that energy.

Containment buys us time and, with introspective self-awareness, enables us to separate out what we are imagining and thinking from our physical sensations. It is this fraction of a second of restraint, as we just saw, that was the difference between heaven and hell. When we can maintain this "creative neutrality," *we begin to dissolve the emotional compulsion to react as though our life depends on responses that are largely inappropriate in the present. The uncoupling of sensation from image and thought is what diffuses the highly charged (survival-based) emotions and allow the sensations then to transform fluidly into sensation-based gradations of softer "contoured" feelings.* This process is not at all the same as suppressing or repressing emotions. For all of us, and particularly for the traumatized individual, the capacity to transform the "negative" emotions of fear and rage *is* the difference between heaven and hell.

The power and tenacity of emotional compulsions (the *acting out* of rage, fear, shame, and sorrow) are not to be underestimated. Fortunately, there are practical antidotes to this cascade of misery. With body awareness, it is possible to "de-construct" these emotional fixations. In terms of brain function, the medial pre-frontal cortex is the only part of the cerebral cortex that apparently can modify the response of the limbic system, particularly the amygdala, which is responsible for intense survival-based emotions. The medial pre-frontal cortex (particularly the insular and cingulate cortex) *receives direct input from muscles, joints and visceral organs and registers them into consciousness* (Damasio, 2000). Through awareness of these interoceptive sensations, i.e. through the process of tracking bodily-based awareness, we are able to access and modify our emotional responses, and deepen our core sense of self.

At first, directly contacting our bodily sensations can seem unsettling, even frightening. This is mostly because it is unfamiliar—we may have become accustomed to the (secondary) habitual emotions of distress and to our (negative) repetitive thoughts. We have also become used to searching for the source of our discomfort *outside of ourselves*. We may readily attribute them to other people's actions or inactions. We simply are unfamiliar with *experiencing something, as it is,* without the encumbrance of analysis and judgment.

The first step in creating emotional change requires an active refusal to be seduced into (the content of) our negative thoughts. These thoughts seem so real (as to define us) and, in turn, reinforce the negative emotional states. One simple "cognitive" intervention I have found effective is simply to have the client say something like: *"I have the thought that:* I am a bad person, that I don't deserve to feel good," etc. It is merely by inserting the prefix *"I have the thought that"* which allows the person to begin to cultivate an observer stance, engaging the pre-frontal brain areas that have been shut down by the intense emotional states (see Van der Kolk, 2015). At least as important is the capacity to resist being swept away by the potent drive of an emotion or galvanized into immediate action. Rather, we need to choose to *redirect our attention to the underlying physical sensations as they transform.* This restorative sequence is the basis of Somatic Experiencing, the approach that I have developed during the past 45 years for resolving traumatic states (Levine, 1977, 1996, 2010, 2015; Payne, Levine, & Crane 2015; www.traumahealing.org).

Changing How We Feel; the Posture of Experience

One dreary, rainy, January afternoon in 1972, I was immersed in the warm, musty stacks of the Berkeley graduate library, sorting through the enumerable books on theories of emotion. This was well before the advent of computers and Google, so my search strategy was to find a relevant area in the graduate stacks, those vast literary catacombs, and spend the day browsing for relevant material. It seemed to me that there were nearly as many theories of emotions as there were authors. In this search, I rather accidentally stumbled upon an astonishing treasure trove—the visionary work of a woman named Nina

Bull. This innovative work provided me with a deep appreciation of the nature and structure of emotions and their rooting in the body. Her book, *"The Attitude Theory of Emotion,"* (1951, summarized in Levine, 2010) clarified what I was observing with my early body/mind clients. It suggested a clear conceptual framework and a strategy for the process of emotional change.

In the 1940s and 50s, Nina Bull, working at Columbia University, conducted some remarkable research in the experiential, observational, tradition of William James. In her studies, subjects were induced into a light "hypnotic" trance and various emotions were suggested to them while they were in this receptive state. These emotions included disgust, fear, anger, depression, joy, and triumph. Self-reports from the subjects were noted. In addition, a standardized procedure was devised whereby the subjects were observed by experimenters. These researchers were trained to accurately observe and record changes in the subjects' postures. The postural patterns, both self-reported and objectively observed, were remarkably consistent across multiple subjects and researchers.

The pattern of disgust was noted to involve the internal sensations of nausea, as if in preparation to vomit, along with the observed behavior of turning away first with lip and then with head/neck. This pattern, as a whole, was labeled "revulsion" and could vary in intensity from the milder form of dislike to an almost violent urge to turn away and vomit. This latter acute response could be recognized as an effort to eject something toxic, or as a means of preventing being fed something that one doesn't like. This type of reaction is seen when children are abused or forced to do something against their will; something that they cannot "stomach." This could vary from forced bottle feeding to forced fellatio* or, often, something they cannot stomach, metaphorically and psychologically.

Nina Bull then analyzed the *fear* response and found it consisted of a similar compulsion to avoid or escape and was associated with a generalized *tensing up or freezing of the whole body.* It was also noted that subjects

---

* See A&E's original show, *Intervention*, Episode #74 (Season 6, episode 2), about a girl named Nicole, who was forced to perform fellatio by her next-door neighbor (and father's best friend) for several years. Once her family found out, they tried to cover it up, and Nicole was forced to live next door to the man for years after. Later, Nicole developed an overactive gag-reflex, leaving her unable to swallow anything, including her own saliva. She was placed on a feeding tube.

frequently reported the desire to get away, which was opposed by an inability to move. This opposition led to paralysis of the entire body (though somewhat less in the head and neck). However, the turning away in fear was different from that of disgust. Associated with fear was the *additional component of turning towards potential resources of security and safety.*

In studying the emotion of *anger,* Bull also discovered a fundamental split. There was, on the one hand, a primary impulse to strike out and attack, as observed in a tensing of the back, arms, and fists (as if preparing to hit). However, there was also a strong secondary component of tensing the jaw, forearm, and hand. This was self-reported by the subjects, and observed by the experimenters, as a way of controlling and inhibiting the primary impulse to strike (see Somatic Experiencing Trauma Institute, 2014).

These experiments also explored the bodily aspects of sadness and depression. Sadness was associated with a weakness in the legs and an impulse to cry. However, depression was characterized, in the subject's awareness, as a chronically *interrupted* drive. It was as though there was something they wanted but were unable to attain. These states of depression were frequently associated with a sense of "tired heaviness," dizziness, headache and an inability to think clearly. The researchers observed a weakened impulse to cry (as though it were stifled), along with a collapsed posture, conveying defeat, and apparent lethargy. I have consistently observed similar postures in shame. We easily recognize that there is a fundamental difference between negative and positive emotions. When Bull studied the patterns of elation, triumph, and joy, she observed that these positive affects (in contrast to the negative ones of depression, anger, and disgust) did *not* have an inhibitory component; they were experienced as *"pure energy" and "an unconstrained readiness for action."* Subjects feeling joy reported an expanded sensation in their chest which they experienced as "buoyant," and which was associated with free, deep breathing. The observation of postural changes included a lifting of the head and an extension of the spine. These closely meshed behaviors and sensations facilitated a freer breathing and overall lightness.* This aforementioned "readiness for action" was accompanied by energy and the abundant sense of *purpose* and opti-

---

* This is something that was also observed by F.M. Alexander when his lost speech returned.

mism that they would be able to achieve their goals.* Understanding the contradictory basis of the negative emotions, and their structural contrast to the positive ones, is revealing in the quest for emotional health and well-being. Recall that all of the negative emotions studied were comprised of two *conflicting impulses*, one propelling action and the other inhibiting (i.e., *thwarting*) that action. In addition, when a subject was "locked" into the posture of joy, by suggestion, then a contrasting mood (e.g., depression, anger or sadness) *could not be produced unless the (joy) posture was first altered.* The converse was also true; with feeling sadness or depression, it was not possible to feel joy unless that postural set was first changed. These observations are profoundly important in transforming trauma and its corrosive emotions, particularly that of shame.

There is poignancy to this truth, revealed years ago, in a simple exchange between Charlie Brown and Lucy. While walking together, Charlie, slumped and shuffling, was bemoaning his depression. Lucy suggested that he might try standing up straight to which Charlie replied, "but then I wouldn't have a depression to complain about," as he continued on his way resigned, slouched, and downtrodden. And what are we to do if we don't have an ever vigilant Lucy to elucidate the ever perplexing obvious. However, as correct as Lucy was, in a metaphoric sense, mood-changing is not a matter of simply willing or imposing postural change (like the "proud" military stance). Indeed, altering one's psychological disposition through postural change is a much more complex and subtle process. It is a process that is mediated by interoception[†] and imbued with the quality of spontaneous change.

The extensive life's work of psychologist Paul Ekman adds the role of "facial posture" in the generation of emotional states. In experiments similar to Bull's, Ekman trained numbers of subjects to contract only the specific muscles that were observed during the expression of a particular emotion. When subjects were able to accomplish this task (without being told what emotion they were simulating), remarkably they often experienced those feelings, including appropriate autonomic arousal states (Ekman, 2008).

---

* See Triumph and the Will to Persevere, in Levine 2014.

† Interoception is the composite (experienced) afferent sensory information derived from muscles, joints, blood vessels, and viscera.

In a quirky experiment, Fritz Strack and colleagues of the University of Würzburg, Germany had two groups of people judge how funny they found some cartoons (Strack, Martin, & Stepper, 1988). In the first group, the subjects were instructed to hold a pencil between their teeth *without it touching their lips*. This procedure forced them to smile (try it yourself). The second group was asked to hold the pencil with their lips, but this time not using their teeth. This forced a frown.

The results reinforced Ekman's work, revealing that people experience the emotion associated with their expressions. In Strack's experiments, those with even a forced smile felt happier and found the cartoons funnier than those who were forced to frown.

The Nobel Prize for medicine and physiology was awarded to Nikolaas Tinbergen in 1973 for his contribution to the field of ethology, the study of animal behavior in their natural environments.* In his acceptance speech, Tinbergen took the liberty of extending his field of inquiry to the naturalistic observations of human behavior. In the article titled, *"Ethology and Stress Disease,"* he both speculated on the repetitive (bodily) behaviors of autistic children, as well as describing the beneficial effects of a method of postural re-education called "The Alexander Method" (Tingbergen, 1974). Both he and his family, in undergoing Alexander's treatment process, had experienced dramatic improvement in sleep, blood pressure, cheerfulness, alertness, and resilience to stress, simply by altering their postural states as suggested by the work of Nina Bull. Other prominent scientists and educators had also written about the benefit of this treatment. These included John Dewey, Aldous Huxley, and scientists like G. E. Coghill, Raymond Dart, and even the great doyen of physiology, and earlier Nobel Prize recipient, Sir Charles Sherrington. While admiration from such prominent individuals is provocative, it hardly constitutes rigorous scientific proof. It is unlikely, on the other hand, that men of such intellectual rigor had all been duped.

Alexander's therapeutic work (described in his book, *The Use of the Self,* 1932) consisted of very gentle manipulations, first exploratory and then corrective. It was essentially a re-education of one's entire muscular/postural system. Treatment began with the head and neck, and then

---

* His speech was reprinted in 1974 by the prestigious journal, *Science.*

subsequently included other body areas. *There is no such thing as a right position*, he discovered, *but there is such a thing as a right direction.*

F. M. Alexander and Nina Bull had, each in their own way, recognized the intimate role of postural muscular patterns in behavior and affect. Alexander (in the late 1980s), an Australian-born Shakespearian actor had made his discovery quite accidentally. One day, while performing Hamlet, he suddenly lost his voice. For this condition, he sought help from the finest doctors in Australia. Getting no relief, and desperate, he pursued assistance from the most influential physicians in England. Without a cure, and given that acting was his only profession, Alexander returned home in great despair. As the story goes, his voice returned spontaneously, only to elusively vanish again. Alexander took to observing himself in the mirror, hoping that he might notice something that correlated with his erratic vocal capacity. He did. He observed that the return of his voice was related to his posture. After numerous observations he made a startling discovery that there was a distinctly different posture; one associated with voice and another with no-voice. To his surprise, he discovered that the posture associated with the strong and audible voice felt "wrong," while the posture of the weak or absent voice felt "right." Alexander pursued this observational approach for the good part of nine years. He came to the realization that the mute posture felt "good" merely because it was familiar, while the postural stance supporting voice felt "bad", only because it was unfamiliar. Alexander discovered that certain muscular tensions could cause a compression of the head-neck-spine axis, resulting in respiratory problems and consequently the loss of voice. Decreasing these tensions would relieve the pressure and allow the spine to return to its full natural extension. Attending to this disparity allowed Alexander to cure himself of his affliction. Thus, through better mind-body communication, he was able to recover much of his natural ease of movement, leading to an economy of effort as well as improved performance. Realizing that he had the makings of a new career, Alexander gave up acting and began working with fellow actors and vocalists with similar performance problems. He also began working with musicians whose bodies were twisted and in pain from the strained postures they believed were required for playing their instruments. The great violinist, Yehudi Menuhen was one of his students. A number of famous pop stars and actors including Paul McCartney, Sting, and Paul Newman all received treatments from Alexander Method teachers and sung their praises loudly. However, even today, this method remains rather obscure.* This is largely because the muscles involved in postural adjustments are not under deliberate voluntary control, but involve, rather, minute contractions and relaxations of muscles. These derive from interoceptive awareness and are at the dim continuum (threshold) of pre-conscious awareness. Indeed, it is this challenge that had many of Alexander's clients nearly tearing their hair out in frustration. In addition, it seems that Alexander (and many of his students) was not comfortable in dealing with emotions, and so likely inhibited his clients.

Let us now combine Alexander's observations (of posture's effect on function) with Lucy's wise incite into the cause of Charlie Brown's unnecessary, but self-perpetuating, suffering. Together, they illustrate the centrality of body-self-awareness in the change process. Perhaps the most effective way of changing one's functional competency and mood is through altering one's postural set and thence changing pro-prioceptive and kinesthetic feedback to the brain (Blakeslee, 2007). As previously mentioned, the medial prefrontal cortex (which receives much of its input from the interior of the body) appears to be the only area of the neo-cortex that can directly alter the limbic system, and in turn, emotionality. Hence, *the awareness of bodily sensations is critical in changing stress patterns and emotional states.*

Attitude—Reconciling Emotions and Feelings:

Through a related experiential set of experiments and analysis, Nina Bull demonstrated that *emotional feelings occur only when emotional action is restrained.* Or said in another way, *it is the restraint that allows the postural attitude to become conscious for the attitude to become a feeling-awareness.* We are, once again, reminded that it is primarily through the motivated awareness of internal sensations that the corrosive dragons of negative emotional states can be tamed. Recall how, instead of expressing his habitual rage, the samurai's personal hell was arrested, exposed, and brought into awareness by the impeccable timing of the Zen master. It was when the brash samurai learned to, momentarily, hold back, contain and "feel–into" himself, that

---

* Many of Alexander's principles inspired the work of Moshe Feldenkrais and Ida P. Rolf.

he was able to transform his rage into peaceful bliss. Such is the alchemy of emotional transformation through the felt sense.

What I believe that William James missed, and what Nina Bull has deeply grasped, is the *reciprocal relationship between the expression of emotion and the sensate feeling of emotion*. When we are "mindlessly" expressing emotion that is precisely what we are, in fact, doing. Excessive emotional reactivity (or suppression) almost always precludes conscious awareness of the underlying (body-based) feelings. On the other hand, restraint and containment of the expressive impulse allows us to become aware of our underlying postural attitude. It is the holding back (the restraint) of expression that brings a feeling into consciousness. Deep change only occurs where there is containment and (embodied) mindfulness; and mindfulness only occurs where there is a bodily (felt-sense) feeling, i.e. the awareness of the postural attitude so that it can shift and regulate.

Transforming Terror: A Case Example

It is life's only true opponent. Only fear can defeat life...It goes for your weakest spot, which it finds with unerving ease... You feel yourself weakening, wavering...Fear next turns fully to your body, which is already aware that something terribly wrong is going on...Your muscles begin to shiver as if they had malaria and your knees to shake as though they were dancing. Your heart strains too hard, while your sphincter relaxes too much. And so with the rest of your body.

—Yann Martel, *The Life of Pi*

Louise was working on the 80th floor of the north tower of the World Trade Center, the clear blue morning of September 11, 2001. After witnessing the walls in her office moving twenty feet in her direction, Louise mobilized immediately, springing to her feet and readying to flee for her life. With the help of a courageous off-duty detective, she was slowly and methodically led down 80 floors, via stairwells filled with the suffocating, acrid smell of burning jet fuel and debris. After finally reaching the mezzanine an hour and twenty minutes later, the south tower suddenly collapsed. The shock waves lifted Louise into the air, throwing her violently on top of a crushed bloody body.

In the weeks following her miraculous survival, a dense yellow fog enveloped her in a deadening numbness. Louise felt indifferent by day, merely going through the motions of living. Her great passion for classical music, "no longer interested [her]...[she couldn't] stand listening to it." While numb most of the time, at night she was awakened by her own screaming and sobbing. For the first time in her life, this once highly motivated executive could not imagine a future for herself, terror had become the organizing principle of her life.

During our session, I guided Louise to the experience of being led down the staircase where she encountered a locked door on the seventieth floor. Suddenly, trapped, and unable to complete the escape, her body became paralyzed with fear. In working through this experience, which reestablished her thwarted running reflexes, she opened her eyes, looked at me and said: "I thought it was fear that gets you through...but it's not...it's something more powerful, something much bigger than fear...it's something that transcends fear." And what a deep biological truth she reveals here.

The feeling of danger is the awareness of a *defensive attitude*. It is NOT fear! It prepares us to defend ourselves through directed escape. Similarly, when our aggression is not thwarted, but is clearly directed, we don't feel anger but instead experience the *offensive attitude of* protection, combat-ability, and assertiveness (of "healthy aggression," see Levine, 2014). It is only when the normal orientation and defensive resources have failed to resolve a situation that we see fear, terror, or rage, non-directed flight, paralysis, or collapse. Rage and terror-panic are the *secondary* emotional anxiety states that are evoked when the orientation processes, and the preparedness to flee or attack (felt originally as danger), are not executed successfully. This distortion only occurs when primary escape does not resolve the situation, or is thwarted, as was the case when she came to the locked door.

The emotion of fear may follow from the sensate feeling of danger—that is if we cannot flee or otherwise protect ourselves in an effective way. Thus the normal "unfolding" of activity is suddenly substituted by what Claparede and McDougall (grandparents of modern psychology) titled, a "miscarriage of behavior." It is in this way, that emotional reactivity hijacks the adaptive (feeling/sensation based) behaviors of orientation and defense.

Feelings are the basic path by which we make our way in the world. In contrast, (fixated) emotional states derive from frustrated drives and particularly the thwarted ("last-ditch") mobilization of emergency (fight/flight/freeze). With the paucity of saber-tooth tigers, this critical reaction of last resort rarely makes sense in modern life. However, we are compelled to deal with a myriad of very different threats, such as speeding cars and over-eager surgeons, for which we lack much in the way of evolutionarily prepared protocols.

In conclusion: Emotions are our constant companions, either enhancing our lives or detracting from them. How we navigate the maze of emotions is a central factor in the conduct of our lives, for better or for worse. The question is under what conditions are emotions adaptive and conversely, when are they maladaptive? In general, the more that an emotion takes on the quality of "shock" or "eruption," or the more that it is suppressed or repressed, the more prominent is the mal-adaptation. Indeed, often an emotion begins in a useful (organizing) form and then, because we suppress it, turns against us in the form of physical symptoms or in a delayed and exaggerated explosion. Anger, when denied, can build to an explosive level. There is a popular expression that is apt here: "That which we resist, persists." As damaging as emotions can be, repressing them only compounds the problem. However, let it be duly noted that the difference between repression/suppression and restraint/containment is significant though elusive. While cathartic expressions of emotion in therapy sessions can be of value, reliance on "emotional release" stems from a fundamental misunderstanding about the very nature of feelings and emotions. The work of Nina Bull, described earlier, provides us with insight, both into the nature of habitual emotions and why *feelings accessed through body awareness, rather than emotional release, brings us the kind of lasting change that we so desire.*

When we poses the tools necessary to deconstruct (the postural attitude of) an emotion, and thereby defang even the most intense and corrosive emotions, we begin to make peace with them and enlist their positive qualities. It is essential, however, to take this in small chunks and to titrate our exposure to them so that they can be digested and assimilated (Levine, 1996, 2010). The existential theologian, Henri Nouwen, says it this way: "You have to live through your pain gradually and thus deprive it of its power over you. Yes, you must go into the place of your pain, but only when you have gained some new ground (some inner strength). When you enter your pain simply to experience it in its rawness, it can pull you away from where you want to go." It is, I believe, the capacity to shift our postural attitude, through inter-oceptive awareness, that is just such an effective tool in transforming fixated emotional states.

Reflect, once again, on how the samurai warrior delicately, but defin-itively, arrested his compulsion to strike, allowing himself to feel his (former) murderous rage simply as pure energy, and then ultimately as the bliss of feeling alive, as was advocated by the Buddhist teacher, Pema Chödrön, in the opening of this chapter.

References

Alexander, F.M. (1932). *The use of the self.* London, UK: Orion Publishing.

Binet, S. (1908). L'intelligence des imbéciles. *L'année psychologique* 15(1), 1–147.

Blakeslee, M., & Blakeslee, S. (2007). *The body has a mind of its own: How body maps in your brain help you do (almost) everything better.* New York, NY: Random House.

Bull, N. (1951). *Attitude theory of emotion.* New York: Nervous and Mental Dis-ease Monographs.

Damasio, A. (1995). *Descartes error: Emotion, reason, and the human brain.* New York, NY: Harper Perennial.

Damasio, A. (2000). *The feeling of what happens: Body and emotion in the making of consciousness.* New York, NY: Mariner Books.

Ekman, P. (2008). *Emotional awareness: Overcoming the obstacles to psychological bal-ance and compassion.* New York, NY: Times Books.

Gendron, M., & Barrett, L. F. (2009). Reconstructing the past: A century of ideas about emotion in psychology. *Emotion Review, 1*(4), 316–339.

Levine, P. A. (1977). *Accumulated stress reserve capacity and disease.* (PhD thesis, UC Berkeley, Dept of Medical Biophysics) University Microfilm 77-15-760, Ann Arbor, Michigan.

Levine, P. A. (1996). *Waking the tiger-healing trauma.* Berkeley, CA: North Atlan-tic Books.

Levine, P. A. (2010). *In an unspoken voice: How the body releases trauma and restores goodness.* Berkeley, CA: North Atlantic Books.

Levine, P.A. (2015). *Trauma and memory: Brain and body in a search for the living past: A practical guide for understanding and working with traumatic memory.* Berkeley, CA: North Atlantic Books.

Libet, B. (1981). The experimental evidence of subjective referral of a sensory experience backwards in time. *Philosophy of Science.* 48, 182-197.

Libet, B. (1985). Unconscious cerebral initiative and the role of conscious will in voluntary action *The Behavioral and Brain Sciences.* 8, 529-539. (See also the many commentaries in the same issue, 539-566, and BBS 10, 318-321).

Libet, B., Freeman, A., & Sutherland, K. (1999). *The volitional brain: Towards a neuroscience of free will.* Devon, UK: Imprint Academic.

Payne, P., Levine, P. A., & Crane-Godreau, M. (2015). Somatice: using interoception and proprioception as core elements of trauma therapy. *Frontiers in Psychology, Consciousness Research* doi: 10.3389/fpsyg.2015.00093

Panksepp, J. (2004). *Affective neuroscience: The foundations of human and animal emotions.* New York, NY: Oxford University Press.

Sacks, O. (1996). *The man who mistook his wife for a hat.* New York, NY: Vantage Press.

Somatic Experiencing Trauma Institute. (2014, February 28). *Somatic Experiencing® - Ray's Story.* [Video File]. Retrieved from https://www.youtube.com/watch?v=bjeJC86RBgE

Strack, F., Martin, L. L., Stepper, S. (1988). Inhibiting and facilitating conditions of the human smile: A nonobtrusive test of the facial feedback hypothesis. *Journal of Personality and Social Psychology,* 54(5), 768-777. http://dx.doi.org/10.1037/0022-3514.54.5.768

Tingbergen, N. (1974). Ethology and stress diseases. *Science,* 185(4145), 20-27.

Van der Kolk, B. (2015). *The body keeps the score: Brain, mind, and body in the healing of trauma.* New York, NY: Penguin Books.

Wegner, D. M., & Wheatley, T. P. (1999). Apparent mental causation: Sources of the experience of will. *American Psychologist,* 54, 480-492.

Wegner, D. M., (2013). *The illusion of conscious will.* Cambridge, MA: MIT Press.

Weiskrantz, L. (1986). *Blindsight: A case study and implications.* Oxford, UK: Oxford University Press.

Wozniak, R. H. (1999). *Classics in psychology, 1855-1914: Historical essays.* Bristol, UK: Thoemmes Press.

James, W. (1890). *The principles of psychology.* New York, NY: Henry Holt & Co.

6

The Disintegrative Core of Relational Trauma and a Way Toward Unity

Russell Meares

IN THIS CHAPTER I discuss what I believe to be the central pathological effect of relational trauma and how it might be overcome. A gathering body of evidence suggests that a fundamental feature of those who have suffered repeated traumas during their early years is a relative failure of the integration of mental life. This failure is associated with a loss of coordination among brain systems that normally function together. How integration might be restored is a principal problem facing psychotherapists. No accepted therapeutic approach exists. The proposal put forward here, and in previous publications (Meares, 2000, 2005, 2012; Meares, Bendit, et al., 2012), is that unity of mind is fostered by a specific kind of conversation between the patient and therapist: a conversation that has the quality of analogical connectedness. In its adult form, this kind of conversation has the feeling and "inwardness" that are the cardinal features of intimacy. The feeling involves "warmth," whereas a relationship that is distant is "cold" or "cool."

Intimacy is used here in a quasi-technical way, without confessional or sexual connotations. It refers to a reciprocal sharing of emotional states that leads to a sense of connection between the conversational partners, in turn, generating pleasure. This kind of relationship has a characteristic doubleness that is both psychic and relational. Hobson (1971, 1985) called it "aloneness-togetherness."

Disrupted Rhythms of Psychic Life

Allan Schore introduced the term <u>relational trauma</u> in 2001 to refer to what Freud had called, in pondering the bases of intractable nonpsychotic illness, "alterations of a rhythm of development of psychic life" (Freud, 1937, p. 242). Trevarthen (1974) has termed the normal rhythm a "proto-conversation"—that is, a dynamic interplay of expression and response, a continuing iteration between presentation, representation, re-representation, and so on—in which the continuity depends upon fine-tuning and harmony between the expressions of the dyadic partners, in the manner of music (Malloch & Trevarthen, 2009, Trevarthen et al, 2009).

In 1992, in our first outcome study of the treatment of borderline personality disorder, Janine Stevenson and I suggested that at least some cases of this apparently intractable illness have their basis in the disruption of such rhythms when the caregiver makes responses to the infant's expression that "do not connect with the child's immediate reality and so seem to come from outside" (Stevenson & Meares, 1992, p. 358). In short, such responses have an effect like a loud noise. Winnicott called them "impingements" (1965, p. 86).

At that time no adequate evidence existed that could support the hypothesis that relational trauma—that is, the infant's experience of repeated impingements—might lead to so serious a disruption of personality development as borderline personality disorder. Support, however, soon came from a series of publications from Giovanni Liotti (e.g., 1995, 1999, 2000, 2004), which reported on the outcome of disorganized attachment in childhood. The typical caregiver responses that produce disorganized attachment behavior in a child are those that "do not connect with child's immediate reality" (Stevenson & Meares, 1992). These responses have the effect of a shock. The parent or quasi-parental figure making such responses is likely to be frightening, sometimes frightened, and often unpredictable. The disorganized child may appear as if stunned, as if unable to know which way to turn. The child is manifesting behavior that in the adult is an experience of dissociation. Liotti found that disorganized attachment in children may be the precursor of dissociative disorders and borderline personality disorder in later life.

The Therapeutic Field

When we enter into a therapeutic conversation, we find ourselves in a field governed by two main opposing forces: one positive and the other negative. The first force is toward health and well-being; the second is an effect of unconscious traumatic memory, overthrowing the first, the ordinary sense of existing, the state that Winnicott (1965) called "going-on-being," which is the basis of self. The system of unconscious traumatic memory is a record of inflictions occurring repeatedly, perhaps day after day, some severe, like sexual or physical abuse, and some apparently minor, like those of infancy—"little emotions, each one insignificant in itself, which have left no distinct or dangerous memories" (Janet, 1924, p. 275).

The traumatic memory system is likely to be made up of a number of subsystems relating to traumas of different kinds, at various stages in life, and in different forms of relatedness. Important among them are those that involve "attacks upon value" (Meares, 2004b), in which the individual is subjected to continuing devaluation, humiliation, disparagement, and relentless criticism, usually in a familial context. Such a background has also been associated with intractability as conceived in terms of depression (Meares, 2004b; Kaplan & Klinetob, 2000; Murphy et al., 2002; Kendler, Hettema, Butera, Gardner, & Prescott, 2003; Brown, Harris, & Hepworth, 1995; Farmer & McGuffin, 2003).

Although each subsystem can be conceived as discrete and autonomous, multiple subsystems can connect and trigger each other. Every major therapeutic system approaches interpersonal trauma with its own language. Whether addressing transference phenomena, distorted cognitions, or maladaptive schemas of interpersonal transactions, the approaches are all focused on the negative aspect of the therapeutic field. I do not speak here of this important issue, which has been considered elsewhere (e.g., Meares, 2000, 2005; Meares, Bendit, et al., 2012). Instead, this chapter concerns that which has been neglected, the "self" that has been damaged, distorted, and stunted by trauma. In the case of relational trauma, at least, it must be the primary concern of the therapist. Such trauma is not approached by strategies, techniques, interpretations, and so forth, dictated by the agenda of a particular theory. Rather, it is through the establishment of a specific kind of relationship, which is not artificially imposed or manipulated but is allowed to emerge in conversational interplay. The propensity for it is given to all of us through our biological heritage. A consideration of the form of this relationship necessarily begins with what we mean by self.

The Concept of the Self

Self is an elusive concept. It is hard to define since it is often merely a background sense, a feeling of existing going-on-being. Lévi-Strauss put it this way: "I never had and still do not have, the perception of personal identity. I appear to myself as the place where something is going on" (1979, p. 3). This vague idea, this background feeling, became a highly developed concept in the work of William James (1890, 1892), who can be considered the main descriptor of self. In recent years, he has been reinstated as a cultural hero after a period of neglect during the mid-20th century. James's ideas are now used by the foremost proponents of a neural basis of self: Gerald Edelman (1992) and Antonio Damasio (2012, p. 7). James's description allows us to track the waxing and waning of the experience of self during the therapeutic conversation by the use of linguistic analysis. At least 12 salient features of this experience, which I have noted elsewhere, can be derived from his account (see Meares, 2004a; Meares, Bendit, et al., 2012).

This leads to the idea that we can, to an extent that is useful, observe and measure that which cannot be seen. Words—or more particularly, words as they are spoken and as they fit together syntactically—provide a kind of window into the movements of inner life. In this way, self becomes a subject accessible to scientific inquiry, which, in the past, had not been considered possible (Meares, Butt et al, 2005; Meares & Jones, 2009).

Integration and Conversation

The notion of being able to "observe" psychic change is important. Language gives us a way of testing hypotheses concerning integration and disintegration. Proper "observation" of this kind, however, requires us to go beyond James's work. Although his concept of self implicitly contains a sense of the other—he tells us that, at its heart, is the feeling of "warmth and intimacy"—this idea is not developed.

James's description is of a one-person system. Such a view is an abstraction. Self, as a form of consciousness, cannot exist in isolation. It arises from a brain state. But a brain, seen as a system isolated from the world, is also an abstraction. It is always interacting with the environment, of which, when speaking of self, the social environment is the most important part. This interplay determines the brain state that produces a particular state of mind. The interplay, speaking again of self, is conducted by means of conversation. A particular kind of conversation is associated with a specific form of consciousness. The conversation and the state of mind are aspects of single system of function, made of self and other. The form of the relatedness (i.e., the conversation) both reflects and constitutes the form of consciousness. It is important to note here that integration is not judged by the language of the subject alone but primarily by the linguistic structure of the conversational unit created by both partners.

This main idea is the basis of the Conversational Model (Hobson, 1985; Meares, 2004b; Meares, Bendit, et al., 2012) the project for the development of which was launched by Robert Hobson in 1971. Writing from his experiences with intractable illness, which today would be called borderline personality disorder, a condition we now know to be associated with early trauma, he suggested that "much of the work of psychotherapy is concerned with establishing the state of aloneness-togetherness" (Hobson, 1971, p. 97) out of a prior state of disconnection. Aloneness-togetherness is part of the Jamesian duplex self. The duplex self is one of unified duality.

The simultaneity of relationship and state of consciousness provides a way not only of treating disintegration but also of testing the proposed method of treatment. This theory of self predicts that its main features arise, and can be identified, in a relationship that also has the qualities of connectedness.

Jacksonian Theory of Self and Trauma

The notion that trauma produces disintegration of the mind–brain system requires a fleshing out that takes us beyond James in a second way. He implied that integration of mental function and self are almost the same thing. He wrote: "Thoughts, connected as we feel them to be connected are <u>what we mean</u> by personal selves" (James, 1892, pp. 153–154). Connection is the cardinal quality of self. But James does not tell us <u>what</u> is connected. How can it be conceived?

James's famous image of self as a "stream of consciousness" is not enough to answer this question. This phrase describes the background feeling of existing that is most prominent in reverie. This is not the whole of self. For much of the time, our consciousness in directed toward tasks and events. Our attention is focused on the outer world. Our state of mind, in this circumstance, is quite different from that of the "stream." Can this form of consciousness be thought of as not-self? Such an idea makes no sense. In these moments we also feel our existence.

In order to find an answer to the puzzle presented by these phenomena, we turn to the legendary English neurologist, John Hughlings Jackson. James cited Jackson and spoke of him respectfully. Yet, he was apparently unaware of Jackson's important concept of self, published in 1887, 3 years before the Jamesian magnum opus. Although a neurologist, Jackson had an abiding interest in the concept of mind, or self, and how it might help in the understanding of mental illness. He believed himself to be the first person in the medical literature to use the term <u>self</u>. As he saw it, self is identified by the reflective function of introspection, the capacity to be aware of "inner" events. Such a capacity, however, as he said, is not <u>self</u> itself. This is a more complex conception of a consciousness consisting of paradoxical unity and doubling.

Jackson conceived self as comprised of two coordinated kinds of consciousness. "Each is only half itself" (1887a /1958, p. 93). The first of these he called "subject consciousness;" it is the background feeling, present to a greater or lesser degree all the time. Compared with the second kind of consciousness, which he called "object consciousness," it is comparatively unchanging. Object consciousness is engaged by attention to objects, either external or internal. Although the two kinds of consciousness work together in the creation of self, he believed that subject consciousness (which is akin to Winnicott's [1965] "going-on-being") is the more fundamental. "It is us," he said, emphasizing the verb "to be" (1887a/1958, p. 96). Jackson considered that self arises in development, and arose in evolution, not through any new structures or tissue being added to the brain, but through an elaboration of existing structures, notably the prefrontal cortex, which makes possible a higher coordination of brain systems than previously existed. Self emerges in a hierarchical fashion, each notional tier of the hierarchy decreed by stages in evolutionary history. The appearance of self reflects the culmination of an evolutionary passage from lowest to highest levels of coordination of all elements in the brain, from automatic to voluntary function and from simplicity of organization to complexity. Complexity is reflected in the relationship of the organism to the environment. At its simplest, it is a single stimulus, a sound perhaps. At its highest, it is the relationship of intimacy, which arises out of, and is compounded with, earliest forms of relatedness, most importantly, attachment. This late stage of evolution and development is fragile, the least "hard-wired." It is overthrown by trauma, in which the mind–brain system operates at a lower level of coordination, as if at an earlier level of evolution. Self and intimacy are lost. Attachment becomes exaggerated (Meares, 1999, 2000).

Default Mode Network

Jackson's concept of subject consciousness might have once seemed speculative and without physiological basis. Recently, however, a plausible neurophysiology has been established for this background state of "going-on-being" (Winnicott, 1965), called the "default mode network" (Raichle et al., 2001). This system is active when the mind is apparently at rest, when the "stream of consciousness" becomes salient (Raichle et al., 2001). It is organized around cortical midline structures, with two principal nodes, one prefrontal and the other posterior cingulate/cuneus. Its activity is associated with markers of self such as autobiographical memory (Gusnard, Akbudak, Shulman, & Raichle, 2001; Buckner & Carrol, 2007), "mentalizing" (Frith & Frith, 1999, 2003), and tests of false belief (Gallagher & Frith, 2003).

It is a reasonable hypothesis to suppose that the central pathophysiology induced by relational traumas is a disruption of the connectedness of Jackson's (1887b/1958) "subject consciousness." Bluhm and colleagues found diminished connectivity in the default mode network in a group of subjects with traumatic backgrounds similar to those of patients with borderline features (Bluhm et al., 2009).

Failure in the coordination of brain systems in those subjected to cumulative traumas, of which the archetype is borderline personality disorder, is not limited to the default mode network. Systems that usually operate together no longer do so. Initial evidence of this came from a study of subjects with a history of dissociative disorders and a long history of unexplained medical illness, a condition once called *hysteria* but that now is called *borderline*. Typically, the individuals had histories of trauma and in some cases, severe disruptions of the early life through, for example, institutionalization in infancy. These individuals showed a failure of coordination in excitatory and inhibitory activity; in the normal case, one rises while the other falls. This failed coordination was reflected in electrodermal evidence of disturbed coordination between sympathetic and parasympathetic nervous systems, primarily related, the researchers suggested, to disturbance in the parasympathetic, or inhibitory, aspects of autonomic function (Horvath, Friedman, & Meares, 1980). Similar findings have been reported by Linehan (Kuo & Linehan, 2009) and Porges (Austin, Riniolo, & Porges, 2007).

Autonomic activity occurs at an unconscious level. Failure of coordination has also been shown in conscious function, specifically in the simple matter of the response to a novel stimulus. Such a stimulus produces a large component of the event-related potential, that record of the electrical passage, through the brain, reflecting the processing of a stimulus, called the *P3*. P3 occurs at about 300 milliseconds after the presentation of the stimulus. It is a single peak, suggesting a lone generator. However, it is produced by two main generators: one a largely prefrontal network generating the first part of P3, called *P3a*. The second part of P3, *P3b*, is generated by a mainly parietal network.

In normal circumstances, the function of the two generating networks is coordinated, leading to the unified output of a single peak. In borderline patients, the coordination is lost, resulting in a double peak, a biphasic wave. Onset times of P3a and P3b no longer correlate (Meares et al., 2005; Meares, 2012, pp.63-85).

Later evidence, which I and my colleagues are about to publish, suggests that these abnormalities are markers of dissociation.

Integration and the Right Hemisphere

The observations made thus far in this chapter suggest that a prime therapeutic aim, when treating those who have suffered cumulative traumas, is toward integration of mind–brain function. How is so complex a task to be achieved? A hypothesis derives from Jackson's (1887b, 1958) notion of "coordination." Two systems become coordinated when they somehow "fit" one another, as if their shapes resemble each other, or a part of one also becomes a part of the other. I am suggesting that this coordination first occurs in the outer world in a special kind of conversation that has the characteristic form of "analogical connectedness." An analogue is something that resembles another thing.

The earliest appearance of this kind of conversation is the game mothers play with their babies, which Colwyn Trevarthen (1974) has called a "proto-conversation." In this game the mother portrays, in her face and in the contours of her voice, the "shape" of her baby's immediate experience. In other words, she creates analogues of this experience.

Allan Schore has argued that this interplay between mother and child is essentially one between two right hemispheres (2002, 2003, 2009, 2010). Following this idea, the kind of relatedness that fosters integration and the generation of self depends upon a kind of language that is loosely conceived as right-hemispheric.

Ordinary conversation consists of the coordination of two kinds of language, which Vygotsky (1962) identified in a study of young children. He called them "social speech" and "inner speech," the latter observed during symbolic play. They reflect two different thought forms, which, again following Jackson, depend upon the left and right hemispheres, respectively. Left-hemispheric function, Jackson (1874/1958) pointed out, allows us to "proposition." The right hemisphere cannot construct propositions, but it has a potential language that is abbreviated and emotional.

It would seem that the right hemisphere is particularly suited to the establishment of the proto-conversation, the first form of analogical connectedness (Meares, Schore, & Melkonian, 2011, 2012). It has the functions of "shaping," of rhythm, and of the recognition of faces, especially the emotions they represent. The hypothesis now arises that, since the proto-conversation is likely to be ill-developed in those who have suffered relational traumas, the right hemisphere will have been insufficiently activated, leading to a deficiency in its function. The idea can be tested in the following way.

During the investigation of P3 in patients with borderline features, previously mentioned, we studied the amplitude of P3a and P3b. We found that P3a was greatly enlarged in the borderline individuals, a reflection of deficient higher-order inhibition. This finding is consistent with what Jacksonian theory would predict following trauma. It is found in dissociated patients, but not in those suffering another kind of psychic disintegration: schizophrenia. In a study published with Allan Schore (Meares, Shore, & Melkonian, 2011/2012), we showed that this deficiency, the exaggerated P3a in borderline personality disorder, is confined to the right hemisphere. Consistent with this observation, Bluhm and colleagues (2009) found that disconnections of the default mode network in traumatized people was particularly right-sided.

Analogical Connectedness

Finally, we consider the nature of therapeutic responsiveness that facilitates the integration of consciousness necessary to the experience of self. What follows here is a very simplified attempt to summarize the main elements of a complex matter that is approached in various ways, and in more detail, elsewhere (e.g., Hobson, 1985; Meares & Hobson, 1977; Meares, 2000, Meares, Butt et al., 2005, 2016; Meares et al., 2005; Meares & Jones, 2009; Meares, Bendit, et al., 2012).

First of all, the language is natural and familiar. The response is a refinement and amplification of the innate ability possessed by the typical mother who plays with the baby when the infant is in a state that is free of distress. (She does something different during distress.) Nobody instructed her to do so or taught her how to do it. We might say the behavior is "instinctive."

The behavior, however, is not "instinctive" when it comes to therapy, wherein the therapist is the recipient of quite different interpersonal and emotional signaling. Nevertheless, certain therapists can adapt themselves, without much instruction, to the different situations and are able to respond in a manner that follows the principles implicit in a proto-conversation. Such therapists, in our experience, are the most effective. They may be (linguistic studies are required to verify) those "super therapists" who have been shown, in a number of reports, to have the best results whatever kind of manualized therapy they are applying (e.g. Luborsky et al., 1986; Lambert, 1989).

Although a therapist can foster beneficial change by means of natural talent, this propensity must be trained, honed, and enhanced. It involves a kind of responsiveness that is consistently engaged, in interchange after interchange, in a disciplined way. Change is seen to occur as a result of this continuing relational milieu, rather than as an outcome of intermittent contributions to the therapeutic conversations, such as "interpretations."

The therapist experiences the therapeutic exchange in a particular way by means of empathy. Empathic imagination is the basis of the stereotypic therapeutic response, which has a "picturing" function. It is a "form of feeling" (Hobson, 1985) that shows the "shape" and feeling of the patient's immediate reality. This is not a replica but a second "view" of that reality. It may be merely a vocalization or as large as a story. It is usually brief, having the structure of analogy/metaphor. A positive shift in the conversation often follows a "cascade" of such "analogical representations," each one larger than the one before.

Such "pictures," or "analogues," however, have no positive effect unless they achieve a sense of connection with the reality they attempt to depict. Following this achievement is a positive feeling of a subtle kind. "Fit" is not achieved when the depiction comes as if from an observer, outside the patient's subjective space. In order to achieve the feeling that the therapeutic conversation is going on in shared subjective space, a certain kind of language is required.

A language of connection is likely to have two main qualities. First, it "couples" to that which is essential to the patient's expression.

Secondly, it is of a right-hemispheric kind. In the first case, coupling involves a language that resembles that of the patient's in its style, lexicon, and syntax. It is not a copy, however. For example, a patient begins the session with: "Here I am," speaking in a tiny voice. The therapist's response is firm and positively toned: "Here you are." It seems simple, even banal, yet it is skilled and it works. The sense of "fit," and the pleasure that comes with it, is evident in their laughing together after the response. Whether a therapist's remark is "correct" is judged not in terms of a theory but by "what happens next" (Meares, 2001).

"Right-hemispheric language" is of the kind described by Vygotsky (1962). It is "inner speech," referring to the life of the self, an inner world. It is abbreviated, condensed, emotional, and lacks normal syntax. Sentences are often incomplete. Subjects of sentences may be missing, even verbs may be omitted. It is contrasted with "social speech," which is cast in the form of propositions.

The sense of shared subjective space is enhanced by a language that suggests that the conversational partners are sitting side by side, gazing out at a space, like an invisible screen, where their depictions are jointly cast, in a combined attempt to "visualize" a personal reality (Meares, 1983). This third element of the conversation tends to be referred to as "it." Pronouns are likely to be omitted.

Establishment of connection is evident in a conversation in which the partners finish each other's sentences, speak in unison, use the same words, and utter frequent, non-verbal, emotional vocalizations. An example of a session finishing in this way, showing, in linguistic terms, a high level of connection, will be presented in detail in a later publication. During this conversation, markers of self appear: reflection, mentalizing, and autobiographical memory. These markers are consistent with the main principle of Vygotsky (1978): that higher-order functions have their first form in the outer world as a shared activity between two people. Since the principal characteristic of the mental function we are calling self is cohesion, the shared activity that is a necessary precursor to its appearance will also be cohesive. Vygotsky wrote: "Any function in the child's cultural development appears twice, or on two planes. First it appears on the social plane, and then on the psychological plane. First it appears between people as an inter-psychological category, and then within the child as an intra-psychological category" (1978, p. 163). The intrapsychological category includes, at is core, a remembrance of its origin, the "warmth and intimacy" of which William James spoke so often.

References

Austin, M. A., Riniolo, T. C., & Porges, S. W. (2007). Borderline personality disorder and emotion regulation: Insights from the polyvagal theory. *Brain and Cognition, 65*(1), 69–76.

Bluhm, R. L., Williamson, P. C., Osuch, E. A., Frewen, P. A., Stevens, T. K., Boksman, K., & Lanius, R. A. (2009). Alterations in default network connectivity in posttraumatic stress disorder related to early-life trauma. *Journal of Psychiatry & Neuroscience, 34*(3), 187–194.

Brown, G. W., Harris, T. O., & Hepworth, C. (1995). Loss, humiliation, and entrapment among women developing depression: A patient and non-patient comparison. *Psychological Medicine, 25*(1), 7–21.

Buckner, R. L., & Carroll, D. C. (2007). Self-projection and the brain. *Trend in Cognitive Sciences, 11*(2), 49–57.

Damasio, A. R. (2012). *Self comes to mind.* London, UK: Vintage/Random House.

Edelman, G. (1992). *Bright air, brilliant fire: On the matter of the mind.* New York, NY: Basic Books.

Farmer, A. E., & McGuffin, P. (2003). Humiliation, loss, and other types of life events and difficulties: A comparison of depressed subjects, healthy controls, and their siblings. *Psychological Medicine, 33*(7), 1169–1175.

Freud, S. (1937). <u>*Analysis terminable and interminable.*</u> In *The standard edition of the complete psychological works of Sigmund Freud.* <u>Vol. XXIII.</u> *Moses and monotheism: An outline of psychoanalysis and other works* (pp. 209-254; J. Strachey, Ed.). London, UK: Hogarth.

Frith, C. D., & Frith, U. (1999). Interacting minds—a biological basis. *Science, 286*(5445), 1692–1695.

Frith, U., & Frith, C. D. (2003). Development and neurophysiology of mentalizing. *Philosophical Transactions of the Royal Society B: Biological Sciences, 358*(1431), 459–473.

Gallagher, H. L., & Frith, C. D. (2003). Functional imaging of "theory of mind." *Trends in Cognitive Sciences 7*(2), 77–83.

Gusnard, D. A., Akbudak, E., Shulman, G. L., & Raichle, M. E. (2001). Medial prefrontal cortex and self-referential mental activity: Relation to a default mode of brain function. *Proceedings of the National Academy of Sciences of the United States of America, 98*(7), 4259–4264.

Hobson, R. F. (1971). Imagination and amplification in psychotherapy. *Journal of Analytical Psychology, 16*(1), 79–105.

Hobson, R. F. (1985). *Forms of feeling: The heart of psychotherapy.* London, UK: Tavistock.

Horvath, T., Friedman, J., & Meares, R. (1980). Attention in hysteria: A study of Janet's hypothesis by means of habituation and arousal measures. *American Journal of Psychiatry, 137*(2), 217–220.

Jackson, H. J. (1874/1958). On the nature of the duality of the brain. In J. Taylor (Ed.), Selected Writing of Hughlings Jackson (Vol. 1, pp. 129-145). London: Hodder & Stoughton.

Jackson, J. H. (1887a/1958). Evolution and Dissolution of the Nervous System. In J. Taylor (Ed.), *Selected writings of John Hughlings Jackson* (Vol. II, pp. 92–118). New York, NY: Basic Books. (First published in Medical Press & Circular, 1887.)

Jackson, H. J. (1887b). Remarks on Evolution and Dissolution of the Nervous System. In J. Taylor (Ed.), Selected Writings of Hughlings Jackson (Vol. 11, pp. 76-91. First published Journal of Mental Science, 1887. New York: Basic Books, 1958). London: Hodder.

James, W. (1890). Principles of Psychology (Vol. I & II). New York: Holt

James, W. (1892). Text Book of Psychology: Briefer course. London: Macmillan.

Janet, P. (1924). *Principles of psychotherapy*. London, UK: Allen & Unwin.

Kaplan, M. J., & Klinetob, N. A. (2000). Childhood emotional trauma and chronic posttraumatic stress disorder in adult patients with treatment resistant depression. *Journal of Nervous and Mental Disease,* 188, 596–600.

Kendler, K. S., Hettema, J. M., Butera, F., Gardner, C. O., & Prescott, C. A. (2003). Life event dimensions of loss, humiliation, entrapment, and danger in the prediction of onsets of major depression and generalized anxiety. *Archives of General Psychiatry, 60*(8), 789–796.

Kuo, J. R., & Linehan, M. M. (2009). Disentangling emotion processes in borderline personality disorder: Physiological and self-reported assessment of biological vulnerability, baseline intensity, and reactivity to emotionally evocative stimuli. *Journal of Abnormal Psychology, 118*(3), 531–544.

Lambert, M. J. (1989). The individual therapist's contribution to psychotherapy process and outcome. Clinical Psychology Review, 9(4), 469-485.

Lévi-Strauss, L. (1978). Myth and Meaning. New York: Schocken Books.

Liotti, G. (1995). Disorganized/disoriented attachment in the psychotherapy of the dissociative disorders. In S. Goldberg, R. Muir, & J. Kerr (Eds.), *Attachment theory: Social, developmental and clinical perspectives* (pp. 343–363). Hillsdale, NJ: Analytic Press.

Liotti, G. (1999). Disorganized attachment as a model for the understanding of dissociative psychopathology. In J. Solomon & C. George (Eds.), *Disorganized attachment as a model for the understanding of dissociative psychopathology* (pp. 291–317). New York, NY: Guilford Press.

Liotti, G. (2000). Disorganized attachment, models of borderline states, and evolutionary psychotherapy. In P. Gilbert & K. Bailey (Eds.), *Genes of the couch: Essays in evolutionary psychotherapy.* Hove, UK: Psychology Press.

Liotti, G. (2004). Trauma, dissociation, and disorganized attachment: Three strands of a single braid. *Psychotherapy: Theory, Research, Practice, and Training, 41,* 472–486.

Luborsky, L., Crits-Christoph, P., McLellan, A. T., Woody, G., Piper, W., Liberman, B., . . . Pilkonis, P. (1986). Do therapists vary much in their success?

Findings from four outcome studies. American Journal Orthopsychiatry, 56(4), 501-512.

Malloch, S., & Trevarthen, C. (2009). *Communicative musicality: Exploring the basis of human companionship.* In S. Malloch & C. Trevarthen (Eds.). Oxford, UK: Oxford University Press.

Meares, R. (1983). Keats and the "impersonal" therapist: A note on empathy and the therapeutic screen. *Psychiatry, 46*(1), 73–82.

Meares, R. (1999). The contribution of Hughlings Jackson to an understanding of dissociation. *American Journal of Psychiatry, 156*(12), 1850–1855.

Meares, R. (2000). *Intimacy and alienation: Memory, trauma and personal being.* London, UK: Routledge.

Meares, R. (2001). What happens next?: A developmental model of therapeutic spontaneity—commentary on paper by Philip A. Ringstrom. *Psychoanalytic Dialogues, 11,* 755–769.

Meares, R. (2004a). Attacks upon value: A new approach to depression. In R. Meares & P. Nolan (Eds.), *The self in conversation* (Vol. III, pp. 10–22). Sydney, Australia: ANZAP Books.

Meares, R. (2004b). The conversational model: An outline. *American Journal of Psychotherapy, 58*(1), 51–66.

Meares, R. (2005). *The metaphor of play: Origin and breakdown of personal being (Rev. ed,).* London, UK: Routledge.

Meares, R. (2012). *A dissociation model of borderline personality disorder.* New York, NY: Norton.

Meares, R., Schore, A., & Melkonian, D. (2012). Is Borderline Personality a Particularly Right Hemispheric Disorder? A study of P3a using Single Trial Analysis The Science of Psychotherapy (pp. 320-338). New York: Norton.

Meares, R. (2016). *The poet's voice in the making of mind.* London, UK: Routledge.

Meares, R., Bendit, N., Haliburn, J., Korner, A., Mears, D., & Butt, D. (2012). In D. J. Siegel & A. Schore (Eds.), *Borderline personality disorder and the conversational model: A clinician's manual.* New York: Norton.

Meares, R., Butt, D. G., Henderson-Brooks, C., & Samir, H. (2005). A poetics of change. *Psychoanalytic Dialogues, 15*(5), 661–680.

Meares, R., & Hobson, R. F. (1977). The persecutory therapist. *British Journal of Medical Psychology, 50*(4), 349–359.

Meares, R., & Jones, S. (2009). The role of analogical relatedness in personal integration or coherence. *Contemporary Psychoanalysis, 45*(4), 504–519.

Meares, R., Melkonian, D., Gordon, E., & Williams, L. (2005). Distinct pattern of P3a event-related potential in borderline personality disorder. *NeuroReport, 16*(3), 289–293.

Meares, R., Schore, A., & Melkonian, D. (2011). Is borderline personality a particularly right-hemispheric disorder?: A study of P3a using single trial analysis. *Australian and New Zealand Journal of Psychiatry, 45*(2), 131–139.

Meares, R., Schore, A., & Melkonian, D. (2012). Is borderline personality a particularly right hemispheric disorder?: A study of P3a using single trial analysis. In A. Schore, *The science of the art of psychotherapy* (pp. 320–338). New York, NY: Norton.

Meares, R., Stevenson, J., & Comerford, A. (1999). Psychotherapy with borderline patients: I. A comparison between treated and untreated cohorts. *Australian and New Zealand Journal of Psychiatry, 33*(4), 467-472; discussion 478-481.

Murphy, J. M., Nierenberg, A. A., Laird, N. M., Monson, R. R., Sobol, A. M., & Leighton, A. H. (2002). Incidence of major depression predictions from subthreshold categories in the Stirling County Study. *Journal of Affective Disorders, 68*(2), 251–259.

Raichle, M. E., MacLeod, A. M., Snyder, A. Z., Powers, W. J., Gusnard, D. A., & Shulman, G. L. (2001). A default mode of brain function. *Proceedings of the National Academy of Sciences of the United States of America, 98*(2), 676–682.

Schore, A. N. (2001). The effects of early relational trauma on right brain development, affect regulation, and infant mental health. *Infant Mental Health Journal, 22*(1-2), 201-269.

Schore, A. N. (2002). Dysregulation of the right brain: A fundamental mechanism of traumatic attachment and the psychopathogenesis of posttraumatic stress disorder. *Australian and New Zealand Journal of Psychiatry, 36*(1), 9–30.

Schore, A. N. (2003). *Affect dysregulation and disorders of the self.* New York, NY: Norton.

Schore, A. N. (2009). Relational trauma and the developing right brain: An interface of psychoanalytic self psychology and neuroscience. *Annals of the New York Academy of Sciences, 1159*, 189–203.

Schore, A.N. (2010). Relational trauma and the developing right brain: The neurobiology of broken attachment bonds. In T. Baradon (Ed.), *Relational trauma in infancy* (pp. 19–47). London, UK: Routledge.

Stevenson, J., & Meares, R. (1992). An outcome study of psychotherapy for patients with borderline personality disorder. *American Journal of Psychiatry, 149*(3), 358–362.

Trevarthen, C. (1974). Conversations with a two-month old. *New Scientist, 62*(2), 230–235.

Trevarthen, C., Delafield-Butt, J. T., & Schögler, B. (2009). Psychobiology of musical gesture: Innate rhythm, harmony and melody in movements of narration. In A. Gritten & E. King (Eds.), *Music and gesture* (Vol. 2, pp. 381–403). Aldershot, UK: Ashgate.

Vygotsky, L. S. (1962). *Thought and language* (E. Hanfmann & G. Vakar, Trans.; E. Hanfmann & G. Vakar, Eds.). Cambridge, MA: MIT & Wiley.

Vygotsky, L. S. (1978). *Mind in society: The development of higher psychological processes.* Cambridge, MA: Harvard University Press.

Winnicott, D. W. (1965). *The maturational process and the facilitating environment.* New York, NY: International Universities Press.

7

How Children Change Within the Therapeutic Relationship

Interweaving Communications of Curiosity and Empathy

Dan Hughes

RECIPROCAL INTEREST AND care are wonderful things with regard to good conversations as well as to good relationships. The world of each person is both known and felt by the other. It is hard to imagine a good relationship that does not develop and thrive without good conversations. It is hard to image good conversations that we might have with a person over a period of time that do not lead to a good relationship. There is a strong consensus that the therapeutic relationship is at least as important to the outcome as the specific model of therapy employed (Norcross & Wampold, 2011). There is an equally strong consensus that one of the most important components of a therapeutic relationship—empathy—

has a central place in successful treatment outcomes (Elliott, Bohart, Watson, & Greenberg, 2011).

It is next to impossible to separate acts of empathy from acts involved in being with the child in discovering the nature of herself and others in her world (Elliott et al., 2011). Curiosity represents the open and engaged stance of the therapist who, jointly with the child who is coming to trust the process, is in the act of coming to know the child and her experiences of the events of her life. This stance represents the core of the social engagement neurological system that is central in our coming to know ourselves and others (Porges, 2011). The therapist's curiosity activates the child's curiosity about her relationships and her life. The therapist is communicating to the child that it is safe—going along with the mind of the therapist—to wonder about shame and doubts as well as pride and joy. The therapist's curiosity facilitates the child's integration and development of her reflective mind so that she may begin to make sense of her world and begin to explore its challenges and opportunities (Siegel, 2012). Cozolino states that "children need their parents' curiosity about them as an avenue of self-discovery" (2006, p. 322). Children in therapy need the same from their therapists.

This chapter specifically focuses on good conversations, relationships, and how curiosity and empathy facilitate the development of both between a child and therapist. When they develop, the therapy leads to significant change for the child, and, possibly to a lesser extent, for the therapist. But this process may be difficult for the child and hence for the therapist. Being known? Many children would rather not be known when they anticipate that the adult will discover that they are lazy, dumb, selfish, or bad. Being cared for? Many children would rather not evoke an emotional response from an adult when they anticipate it is likely to involve anger, disgust, pity, ridicule, indifference, or dislike. So children in therapy often hesitate to have their experience (and their self) be known and felt by the therapist, and so they avoid reciprocal conversations. They distract, ask repetitive questions, remain silent, disagree, and simply don't listen, again and again.

So what is a therapist to do? Ask repetitive questions? Remain silent? Disagree? Not listen to the child's expressions, which the therapist thinks aren't relevant to solving the problem? The therapist might even lecture, though it would be given in mild, therapeutic terminology: "I know you have the ability to work this out if you would just trust me and let yourself get involved with the process."

If we want a relationship with children, let's acknowledge that we need to be able to have a conversation with them, not lecture them as to what is best for them nor try to fix them. Let's acknowledge that this is going to be hard for them to start with, and hard for us too. Most therapists are great at experiencing empathy for children when they express their sad and vulnerable parts. Most therapists are deeply committed to helping children to feel safe and to grow. But how to get into that conversation with children who just don't know how, or who are too angry or terrified to do so? How can we commit to finding ways to get conversations going?

And we must get conversations going because although we might have some good ideas, we don't know what is best for a child. We must discover what is best together with the child, within the unique features of his world, and we must do so by joining in his experience of his world. We need to join him with our minds and hearts so that he is known and felt. Will he let us join him in his world? He might, if we openly share our experience of his world; our experience that develops and deepens through our not-knowing stance of curiosity and unconditional empathy. If we want to help children to develop coherent narratives that serve to give direction and organization to their lives, we need to become engaged with them in good conversations. These conversations, also known as affective–reflective dialogues, are central in the treatment of children who have experienced abuse and neglect (Hughes, 2011). Curiosity and empathy are core components of these dialogues.

Not-Knowing Curiosity

Often children who are seen for psychological treatment have weak reflective functioning. This deficit is especially noted in maltreated children where chronic terror and shame greatly impede their ability to wonder about the inner life of either themselves or their parents (Toth, Cicchetti, Macfie, Maughan, & Vanmeenen, 2000). They do not have the habit of noticing their thoughts, feelings, and wishes, and they have even less ability to communicate their inner life to another

person. This may be due to their having had parents who were not sufficiently interested in what they thought, felt, or wanted. It may also
be due to their core sense of unspeakable shame as to who they are, so
they are reluctant to turn their gaze toward qualities that they assume
are inadequate, bad, or unlovable. These assumptions limit their curiosity about themselves and cause them to avoid conversations that
focus on their thoughts, feelings, or wishes. Too often, when adults
try to lead them into such conversations, the adults' comments involve
judgmental questions such as, "WHY did you DO that?"; "WHAT
were you THINKING?; "WHAT did you WANT?" Such efforts to
understand often assume negative, inadequate reasons to account for
the child's negative behaviors (and even if they don't, the child is likely
to assume that they do). No, the child is not likely to follow that line of
questioning. (Asking "why" is not, in itself, judgmental. It is, though,
when the tone in which "why" is asked conveys annoyance before the
child has a chance to answer. Asking, "I wonder why you did that?" in
a tone that is relaxed and rhythmic contains no assumptions, and does
not imply that a wrong choice was made.)

For too long, asking questions of children in therapy has been considered intrusive ("He'll tell us when he's ready!") or shaming ("If she
can't answer, she'll feel that she should be able to") or developmentally
inappropriate ("He was too young to remember" or "Children can't
express their emotions with words—they need to use play"). These
assumptions might be valid if the therapist is entering into a conversation with a child that is judgmental and rational with the intention of
teaching the child something rather than getting to know her. But that
is not the conversation that I am describing here.

Children in therapy may not know the answers to our questions
because their reflective functioning may not be well developed. (This
reality was made clear to me by my three children, who could answer
questions at home that children in therapy, who were years older than
them, could not.) Questions in therapy will not evoke shame if there is
no judgment made about the child not knowing.

Words alone are not likely to contain much psychological meaning
for most children. Words presented in a monotone are even less likely
to hold meaning. Words joined with nonverbal expressions involving
voice, face, and bodily movements, conveyed with descriptive terms
and wondering about their meanings, are another thing entirely! And

yes, most children are not likely to tell us about events that happened when they were 2—but they are likely to listen most attentively when we begin a conversation with them about those events in a storytelling manner, so that they become actively engaged with us in co-creating stories of possible meanings of those events. Through this process, we get a gut sense of how those events impact the children today.

Too often, in life if not in therapy, children are told "Use your words" when they do not have the words to use. That three-word injunction could easily become a shaming experience, and the answer is *not* to give them words to parrot. Nor is the answer simply to assume that they do not have the ability to enter into conversations. That assumption is likely to lead to another assumption that the best approach is to influence them either with behavioral reinforcers or through giving them the opportunity to express themselves only with metaphor. It may be that an important therapeutic goal for children would be to empower them by developing their ability to communicate their inner life with trusted adults and peers. The way to attain such a goal is through engaging these children in therapeutic conversations so that they are able to engage trusted others in similar conversations.

Therapeutic curiosity that is more likely to evoke children's curiosity about themselves and lead to a reciprocal conversation about their inner world has the following characteristics:

1. *No assumptions.* No matter how many children have similar histories and similar symptoms, each child is unique and we cannot assume that we know what was the child's experience of abuse, loss, failure, or conflict. When we are curious about a child's story, our curiosity truly reflects a state of "not-knowing." Any guesses are tentative and conveyed only as possibilities, with the child being the only one who knows what her experience might be. If we assume the child has a given experience of an event, we may be restricting the child's curiosity to the limits of our assumptions about children in given situations, and in doing so, fail to provide her with the opportunity to discover what is uniquely hers.

2. *No evaluations.* A child's experience of an event is his best way to make sense of it, given the limitations of his life and relationships. It must never be evaluated as being right or wrong. It simply is. The

moment a parent or therapist suggests that a child should not think, feel, or want something, the child is likely to become defensive, have no interest in discovering another way to experience the event, and be less likely to have further conversations about his inner life. The child's experiences—his inner life of thoughts, feelings, dreams, and intentions—are accepted as they are, truly accepted. Only then will the child begin to openly explore these areas with his therapist and share in the discoveries that he is making.

3. *No conversation-induced shame.* Many children lose curiosity about their inner life because of their assumptions that what they would discover there is wrong, selfish, bad, or deficient in one way or another. Every experience that the child has needs to be met with acceptance and understanding. This attitude reflects the belief that whatever the content was it was, in her mind, the best or only possible response to the overall situation. When this is clear within the conversation, the child's mind will greatly expand into new possibilities, no longer restricted by shame.

4. *Storytelling voice.* When we tell stories, our voices naturally vary in rhythm and intensity as we place emphasis here or there, building suspense and surprise, with our voices attempting to convey an experience of the event being described. Such a storytelling voice also tends to be the best way to engage with another in a personal conversation about the events of each other's lives. The content of the storytelling conversation is more interesting and engaging, and thus reduces distractions and defensiveness. This voice is the opposite of a serious lecture voice, which, for children (and adults), tends to create distancing and discouragement. When we are truly engaged with co-creating the child's story—making sense of it together—we will be using this voice. Our engagement will be evident to the child in the subtle and obvious inflections in our tone and rhythm. We will be lively and gentle, excited and subdued as we move through the events of the child's life and help him to develop a coherent story. Such stories make sense of the child's life and are created together in a way that reduces shame and fear.

5. *Elements of wonder, suspense, and surprise.* We need to help the child increase her interest in her own story. We can do this naturally through our own deeply felt fascination with that child's inner world and through conveying this interest to the child as events are being explored. The child is unique and the therapist is committed

to understanding her. The therapist is conveying a wide-eyed desire to know the child, who she is under her problems, and who she was before the traumatic events entered her life.

Case Examples of Curiosity in Conversation

The therapist's wondering mind gazes both broadly and deeply for the meanings held by the child of the important events of her life. The following example shows what might result when the therapist is able to gently lead a child into wondering about the events of her life and developing an awareness of how she experiences those events. An 11-year-old girl had frequent conflicts with her mother that had been escalating over the past few years. As the child entered into a conversation with the therapist, many themes emerged, with both child and therapist discovering the nature of and reasons for the acute distress that the child felt. These included (grouped according to similar themes):

- "She [Mom] thinks I'm a baby. She doesn't care what I want. I'm not important to her. She loves my little sister more than me. She's disappointed in me."
- "Nothing ever seems to go right for me. I have so many things that I have to do that I never have time for what *I* want to do. I don't even know what I want to do anymore. I wish that things weren't so hard."
- "Sometimes I think that there's something wrong with me. I'm stupid. I'm lazy. I'm a loser. I wish I was more like other kids. I'm afraid that I'll never have any friends. I'll never amount to anything."
- "I never realized that I think that my dad loves my little sister more. I guess that I'm lonelier than I thought. Sometimes I think that I hate my sister, and then I think that I'm just awful for feeling that way. It just occurs to me that the worst part is that I don't think it will ever change."

As the story develops, co-created by child and therapist, and the child's mind is wandering over these various themes, some seem to strike a chord whereas others have less felt meaning. The child is sensing, through this conversation with the therapist, that any aspect of her inner life is safe to explore. Her thoughts, feelings, and wishes are not right or wrong. They do not seem too hard for her to be aware of, and they seem to be helping her to feel that things are starting to "make sense." She feels safe enough in conversation with the therapist to feel vulnerable, rather than to have to hide the experiences that make her feel vulnerable behind anger, distractions, or indifference.

Ideally, after helping the child develop a coherent story that makes sense of her struggles and enables her to experience her sense of vulnerability, the therapist then assists her in communicating this story to her parent or caregiver. But this next step only occurs if the therapist is confident that the parent will respond to the child's newly developing story with a similar attitude of curiosity and empathy that is conveyed by the therapist. When the therapist has this confidence, the parents are present when the therapist is developing a conversation with their child. Most often, the child quickly senses their open and nonjudgmental attitude and their presence does not interfere with the child's willingness to co-create a story with the therapist. The therapist will have had one or more prior sessions with the parent to ensure that he or she is willing and able to accept the child's experiences that reflect the meaning of her behaviors about which the parent is concerned. The parent is assisted in becoming able to respond with curiosity and empathy to her child's experience before beginning to bring reassurance, information, and/or a nonjudgmental problem-solving mind into the conversation.

When parents or other caregivers are not willing or able to have such conversations with the child, the therapist may need to go forward in individual therapy. This format may well be of considerable value to the child even if his parents are not willing or able to assist him with developing his story, which now contains less fear, shame, or loneliness and an increased sense of hope, confidence, and pride. Part of the value of individual therapy in that instance is for the child to develop a story that makes sense of his parents' inability or unwillingness to assist him in this process of discovering new qualities about his self and his world. He may develop a new story where the meaning of the family conflicts no longer contain the belief that he is a bad and selfish kid, but rather that the new meanings reflect his parents' struggles that are indicative of other hardships in their lives, stretch back into their childhoods, or simply reflect the routine challenges and conflicts of family life.

The following case example hopefully demonstrates how a therapist helped a traumatized child to begin the process of developing a new story to make sense of the different type of care that he is receiving in his adoptive home compared to his previous homes. His adoptive parents are actively present to assist him in wondering about the meaning of his place in their family.

Andy, now 8 years old, was adopted at 4, following 2 years of neglect and 2 years in which he lived in five foster homes. He spent many of his days living a story that he organized as well as he could, given the assorted traumas that he experienced. These might primarily be characterized as the trauma of absence. The self that he lived was unremarkable, being special to no one. Periodic efforts to develop significant relationships were met with failure. It dawned on him that he was unlovable, so there was no value in trying. After 4 years of being rejected by their son, his adoptive parents, Arlene and Tom, had difficulty in continuing to try to relate to him. He was not interested in joint activities, cooperating, learning from them, or taking comfort from them.

During the seventh treatment session, Andy's therapist, Susan, conveyed a sense of sadness that Andy did not seem to trust his parents.

SUSAN: Andy, living with your parents seems to be so hard for you. It seems that you don't like most of what they do for you or with you. Sometimes it makes me wonder if you don't like them very much . . . like you wish that you had been adopted by someone else.

ANDY: I do like them! You don't know me at all! I even love them! I don't know why I fight with them all the time. I don't know why.

SUSAN: (*with an intensity that conveyed a sense of urgency to understand*) What could it be then, Andy? What could it be? It seems sometimes when they set aside time to do things with you that you like, even when they work hard to find out what you might like, you ignore them more! Or don't talk with them when they try to find out what's happening.

ANDY: I don't want them to!

SUSAN: What, Andy, you don't want them to what?

ANDY: I don't want them to love me!

(*There was a sudden silence. Susan, Arlene, and Tom looked at Andy, and he looked down.*)

SUSAN: (*very slowly and quietly*) Why, Andy . . . why don't you want them to love you?

ANDY: It's too scary! I'll start to want it . . . and it will just go away.
SUSAN: Why will it, Andy, why will it go away?
ANDY: It always does. There must be something wrong with me.
SUSAN: Tell your parents that, Andy, tell them.
ANDY: You'll change your mind! Someday you'll get tired of loving me and you'll just stop.
ARLENE: (*with tears*) We will never change our mind. We will always love you!
TOM: You are our son, we are your parents, now and always.

For the next several months Andy seemed anxious, trying to be good, trying to please. He seemed to now want his parents' love, but he still thought he had to earn it. If he let out the 'unlovable Andy,' he would only be rejected again, of that he was sure. But there was doubt now . . . and hope. Doubt and hope were allowed in because he had shared something that was so important with his parents about his inner world: his belief that unconditional love could not exist for him and his deepest fear that one day his parents would give up on him. It was a few years before his hope turned to confidence and to a new realization: His parents *did* love him unconditionally. He was lovable.

Andy's experience of self-discovery was a gradual thing, first in his mind, then his heart, and finally settling throughout his body so that he knew it with his heart and soul. During this puzzling, working-it-out time of exploring who he was and what love was while his old and new learnings were coming together in new ways, he was likely to have experienced a great deal of confusion. This period of discovering the new while still living in the shadow of the old is beautifully articulated by the author Marilynne Robinson in her book *Lila*. Following an extremely hard childhood, the protagonist, Lila, marries a man who offers her unconditional love. After several years of marriage, Lila says to her husband: "I guess there's something the matter with me, old man. I can't love you as much as I love you. I can't feel as happy as I am."

Unconditional Empathy

Often, children who are seen for psychological treatment have developed a life of self-reliance, which restricts their range of emotional connections with others. Avoiding conversations about their inner lives, they feel alone and lonely. They avoid emotions of vulnerability—sadness, fears, doubts, and shame—because these feelings are painful, especially when they are felt alone. When they rely on someone, they feel vulnerable, so best not to rely on anyone.

If therapy is to assist these children to begin to rely on someone else, it will have to convince them that it is safe to be sad. This sense of safety will only develop when the children realize that they will not be alone in their vulnerability. The therapist's unconditional empathy helps children feel safe, knowing that if they share their distress with their therapist, they will no longer have to carry it alone. They might be able to experience life without continuous sadness and fear.

Therapeutic empathy that is likely to evoke children's empathy for themselves, leading to compassion and self-acceptance, is likely to have the following characteristics:

1. It is an end in itself, not a means to an end. Empathy is seen as a central component of the child's treatment, not a technique that is done to the child in order to make the later problem solving more effective. It is a way of being with the child that is expressed, not something that you give to him.

2. It involves both observing and participating in the child's world. Empathy involves being fully open to the world of the child and experiencing it along with the child. The therapist is not a detached observer, but rather is experiencing the child—alongside her—through whatever events the child is experiencing.

3. It involves being touched by the child and his world. The child and his world have an impact on the therapist, and this impact, in turn, has a greater impact on the child than if the therapist simply understood the child's world. This is the nature of intersubjectivity, in which being together becomes a joint experience that has an influence on both child and therapist. If the therapist is a detached observer of the child's experience, the child's experience becomes diminished—it is not significant enough to truly affect the therapist.

4. Empathy involves being able to remain emotionally strong and present in the child's pain. The therapist needs to be able to remain emotionally present while the child explores her pain or she will avoid experiencing it further. If it seems to be too much for the therapist to contain, then most likely the child will think it is more frightening or

shameful than she had previously imagined. Empathy involves being able to remain in the child's pain as long as it is being experienced by the child. The therapist is not working to pull the child out of the distress, but rather to stay with him while he is in it, walking with him out of it when he is ready. The therapist needs to be able to assess if the child's experience of his pain is being regulated and remains therapeutic, and then remain with the child in the experience as long as it seems to remain important and integrative to the child. The therapist needs to closely observe the child's nonverbal expressions to determine if the level and nature of the distress are continuing to be therapeutic.

5. Empathy is conveyed primarily nonverbally (bodily) with facial expressions, voice prosody, and movement. While the empathic words convey understanding, the nonverbal expressions enable the child to experience the therapist as also experiencing the event being explored.

6. Empathy is unconditional. The therapist does not experience and communicate empathy for a child only when the therapist thinks that the child's distress could not have been avoided and that it matches the seriousness of the event. When the child is in distress, the therapist experiences empathy, with no strings attached. Later, with nonjudgmental curiosity, the therapist might wonder with the child about the nature of the distress and if it might be changed. With curiosity, the therapist is wondering about the child's experience, and with empathy the therapist is experiencing it with the child. In neither case is the therapist judging it.

Case Examples of Unconditional Empathy

In the following excerpt of a session between a child and her mother, the power of empathy to start the process of creating new meanings is evident. This excerpt also demonstrates how the therapist may instruct the parent in experiencing and communicating empathy for her child, without reducing the impact of the parent's empathy for her child. Of course, the therapist needs to first establish a trusting relationship with the parent to prevent the parent from becoming defensive.

Sarah, 12 years old, was finding middle school to be a challenge—a big challenge. Sarah had done well in her first 6 years of school, both academically and socially—so well, in fact, that that her relatives were comparing her to her mother, Rachel, who had been a high-achieving student, along with being popular and athletic throughout all of her childhood and adolescence. Currently, however, Sarah was not only falling behind in her studies but she also was increasingly reluctant to go to school. Efforts from her parents to talk with her about this problem were met with further withdrawal and anger. She seemed to need to deal with whatever troubles she was having on her own and she was not doing very well.

When Rachel and Sarah met with Jon, a therapist who specialized in family therapy, Sarah was not very verbal or cooperative. Jon had spoken with Rachel and Sarah's dad, Dave, the week before, and had a general sense of Sarah's history and recent troubles. Initially, Jon spoke about Sarah's interest in soccer and her recent acceptance onto the school team. Sarah responded briefly, then seemed to catch herself becoming more open than she intended to be, and she spoke with annoyance.

SARAH: Why don't you just say it—I'm a loser! I'm not doing well, and Mom wants you to fix me!

JON: Oh, Sarah, I'm sorry if you think that you're here for me to fix you. That would not be something you'd want. No one wants to be fixed!

SARAH: Then why am I here? I didn't want to come!

JON: Because you seem to be unhappy and your mom was hoping that I could help you, and her, to figure out what was going on for you. I want to understand you, not fix you.

SARAH: Maybe you do, but she doesn't! She wants me to be perfect! She's never satisfied with how I do!

RACHEL: That's not true, Sarah, there's much that you do that I could not be more pleased about.

JON: I wonder, Rachel, if you would be OK just understanding Sarah's experience and supporting her in whatever feelings she's having, before giving your view of things. That's what I meant last week when I spoke with you about the importance of empathy. She just said something very important, and now she needs us to get what she is feeling, not reassure her. (turning toward Sarah) If you think that your mom wants you to be perfect, that would be hard for you!

SARAH: She does! Sometimes I feel that she wishes she had a different daughter! That she's disappointed in me!

JON: Would you tell your mom that, Sarah. And Rachel, would you just tell your daughter you understand how hard it would be for her if she thought that.

SARAH: You are, Mom! You *are* disappointed in me because I'm not like you! I'm not as good as you were!

RACHEL: Oh, honey. I'm so sorry if you think that! If you think that I'm disappointed in who you are! I'm very sorry if I've done something to make you think that. I'm not disappointed in you at all.

SARAH: What do you think then, Mom? I'm messing up a lot! I can't get anything right and no one thinks I'm any good. And I don't either.

RACHEL: I know it's hard now, honey, I know it's hard. We'll get through this together. We'll make sense of it and we'll work it out. I love you now as much as ever.

SARAH: You do?

RACHEL: Yes, I do. (*Rachel now moved over on the couch and held her crying daughter in her arms, rocked her back and forth. Soothing sounds from her mother matched Sarah's cries.*)

Over the next few weeks, Sarah realized that she could talk about her struggles at school with her mom and that her mom was not disappointed or annoyed with her. Her mom gave her comfort, helping her to get through the hard times, and within 2 months, Sarah had discovered herself at school again. She was less wobbled by the differences and the new challenges and was able to enjoy school and learning once more, struggles and all. She did not have to be perfect, safe in the knowledge that her mother's love for her did not change regardless of whether or not she was successful.

Empathy for the child in pain is central in treatment regardless of the severity of the child's problems or the traumatic experiences that led to the problems. Experiencing the pain with the child reduces the child's experience of the pain. Pain shared is pain reduced by half, or maybe more. Once that occurs, whatever challenges remain tend to be smaller and the way forward clearer.

In the following excerpt, the transforming power of empathy to reduce a child's sense of shame is demonstrated. Shame often is a central contributor to a child's inability to construct a new story of his life.

Carl was 7 years old, adopted at age 3, after severe neglect while living with his parents. He was particularly aggressive toward his adoptive mother, and he would take food whenever he was not being supervised and gorge himself if he could. He lied intensely when any of his challenging behaviors were addressed. His pervasive sense of shame made it very difficult for him to face anything wrong that he had done.

The therapist was able to evoke a strong emotional engagement with Carl in his story first through animation and then gentleness as he explored what he knew to have been the reality of Carl's early years. Carl appeared very sad when he heard the therapist's deeply moving description of how lonely he must have been when he was home alone for hours and how he most likely felt that no one thought of him or cared for him. The therapist then made a connection between the loneliness during his years of neglect and how alone he feels when his adoptive parents scold him for doing something wrong:

THERAPIST: Oh, Carl, how hard that would be when your parents are correcting you for your behavior. Your brain knows that they love you, but, when you do something wrong, your heart probably does not feel it! (*Carl looked very sad and nodded his agreement.*) Tell your mom, Carl. Tell her that what I said was right. (*Carl said that it was right and then he fell into his mom's arms and she held him and rocked him.*)

THERAPIST: (*continuing and a pause*) Now, Carl, I'd like to see if you could feel your mom's love another way. Would you look into her eyes for a few seconds? (*Carl sat in his mom's lap and looked into her eyes. Then he burst into tears and held his mom tightly.*) Oh, Carl, what did you feel when you looked into your mom's eyes. What did you feel?

CARL: My mom loves me no matter what! (*They continued to rock, with Mom's arms around Carl and her tears joining his.*)

This was the beginning of a long journey toward trust and self-worth for Carl, with the strong, accepting presence of his adoptive parents. This conversation enabled Carl to experience the shame that he felt whenever his parents corrected his behavior. He was able to experience how this threat to his relationship awoke his prior sense of being unlovable when he was being neglected. This awareness led him to recognize that although he knew that his parents loved him, he did not feel it when they corrected him. This awareness, emerging from the experience of both curiosity and empathy over his story, enabled him to experience the restorative power of being comforted by his adoptive mother.

The Dynamic Story: Weaving Together Curiosity and Empathy

Children who are seen in therapy are often likely to have a fragmented and disorganized story that lacks coherence because of frightening and shameful emotions associated with many of the events of their developing lives. Their story is not coherent because many of the events that they have encountered are terrifying and shameful. These events remain terrifying and shameful because they lack the restorative meaning that would make them coherent. It is not enough to prevent the events in the child's life that have been traumatic from recurring. It is necessary to revisit those events with curiosity, while regulating the associated emotions with empathy. These are interwoven processes. Curiosity is limited without empathy, and empathy will not lead to new possibilities without curiosity.

However, curiosity and empathy do not exist as techniques, whether separately or interwoven. They are words that reflect our intentions to understand and be with the children we treat. We need to communicate our intentions within conversations that will engage these children so that they invite us into their world. Yes, we must become invited guests who help these children discover who they are once the cover of shame and fear are lifted from the stressful events of their lives.

Our conversations with the children we treat have the components of good stories, filled with suspense and surprise, moments of fear, and struggles to heal and grow. We communicate both our not-knowing curiosity and our unconditional empathy through the rhythms of our voice, the expressions of our face, and the movements of our hands and arms. All of these bodily expressions show vividly that we are experiencing their world with them and, most importantly, that our experience of their world is safe and accepting—completely accepting—without shame and fear. Being with them, our experience of their world will help them to re-experience the events of their past. The presence of our minds and hearts within their world will enable them to re-experience their world in a manner in which they are able to accept, reflect upon, and have compassion for themselves as they discover new ways to understand and resolve the various obstacles of their life.

When we have good conversations with children, we are not simply sharing stories but co-creating them. We are entering the child's world and using our minds and hearts to assist the child in developing her story so that it is safer and more coherent. We are assisting her in developing a story that involves more pride and less shame, more joy and less fear, more confidence and less doubt. We are assisting her to develop a greater sense of acceptance of her story—and herself—while at the same time having the confidence to develop abilities that are needed for new meanings to be discovered.

When we have good conversations with a child, we are providing his inner world with a companion whose curiosity opens the way toward greater reflection and whose empathic presence provides safety for any emotions that result. With curiosity we are co-creating the child's story and with empathy, we are co-regulating any emotion that is emerging.

References

Cozolino, L. (2006). *The neuroscience of human relationships: Attachment and the developing social brain.* New York, NY: Norton.

Elliott, R., Bohart, A. C., Watson, J. C., & Greenberg, L. S. (2011). Empathy. *Psychotherapy, 48,* 43–49.

Hughes, D. (2011). *Attachment-focused family therapy workbook.* New York, NY: Norton.

Norcross, J. C., & Wampold, B. E. (2011). Evidence-based therapy relationships: Research conclusions and clinical practices. *Psychotherapy, 48,* 98–102.

Porges, S.W. (2011). *The polyvagal theory: Neurophysiological foundations of emotions, attachment, communication, and self-regulation.* New York, NY: Norton.

Siegel, D. J. (2012). *The developing mind: How relationships and the brain interact to shape who we are* (2nd ed.). New York, NY: Guilford Press.

Toth, S. L., Cicchetti, D., Macfie, J., Maughan, A., & Vanmeenen, K. (2000). Narrative representations of caregivers and self in maltreated pre-schoolers. *Attachment and Human Development, 2,* 271–305.

8

The Therapeutic Use of Optimal Stress

Precipitating Disruption to Trigger Recovery

Martha Stark

The Use of Optimal Stress to Provoke Healing

What is our understanding of how people change? By the same token, how do we understand the resistance to change that characterizes so many of our patients? In other words, what fuels their inertia and reluctance to relinquish their unwitting and compulsive re-enactments, their infantile and ambivalent attachments, and their relentless but futile pursuits? The answers to these pivotal questions are of not only academic but also clinical interest.

In the psychodynamic literature, a number of explanations have been proffered for why patients would seem to be so resistant to letting go of their dysfunctional defenses, despite the fact that their defensive ways of being and doing have long since outlived their usefulness. Although these self-protective mechanisms might once have been necessary for survival, they have now become more hindrance than help. To set the stage for understanding the therapeutic use of optimal stress to provoke change by overriding these maladaptive defensive structures, I first briefly discuss Freud's (1937, 1990) time-honored concepts of repetition, compulsion, and adhesiveness of the id. I also introduce my concepts of ambivalent attachment to dysfunctional defense and relentless pursuit of the unattainable as explanatory constructs for the almost universal resistance to change that we encounter in patients with longstanding emotional injuries and scars.

Once the stage has been set, I turn to the field of chaos theory to inform our understanding, on a more fundamental level, of both how people change and what must first be overcome if they are to do so. When, as is now being done in some scientific circles, people are depicted as open, complex, adaptive, self-organizing systems with emergent properties that remain fairly constant over time, then the maladaptive patterns of behavior with which people present to treatment can be understood as demonstrating the same well-known resistance to perturbation that characterizes all such complexly ordered systems—be they neural networks, fashion trends, the stock market, natural disasters, traffic jams, or a person's ways of acting, reacting, and interacting, to name a few. Despite apparent underlying randomness, a self-organizing structure will emerge as these chaotic systems evolve over time—a robust orderedness that will indeed be resistant to change.

Healing Cycles of Disruption and Repair

As I myself have evolved over the course of the decades, so too has my understanding of the healing process shifted from one that emphasizes the internal workings of the mind to one that is more holistic and recognizes the complex interdependence of mind and body. Long intriguing to me has been the idea that superimposing an acute physical injury on top of a chronic one is sometimes exactly what the body needs in order to heal.

For example, the practice of wound debridement to accelerate healing speaks directly to this concept of controlled damage. Not only does debridement prevent infection by removing foreign material and damaged tissue from the site of the wound but also it promotes healing by mildly aggravating the area, which will in turn activate the body's innate ability to self-heal in the face of challenge.

Another example of causing physical irritation or injury to provoke recovery is the practice of prolotherapy, a highly effective treatment for chronic weakness and pain in such vulnerable areas as the lower back, shoulder, hip, and knee. This technique involves injecting a mildly irritating solution (a relatively innocuous substance like dextrose, a local anesthetic like lidocaine, and water) into the affected ligament or tendon to induce a mild inflammatory reaction, which will then activate the body's healing cascade, resulting ultimately in overall strengthening of the damaged connective tissue and alleviation of the pain. Prolotherapy is believed by many holistic practitioners to be significantly more effective than cortisone injections because these latter treatments, although sometimes able to provide immediate short-term relief of pain, will—because of their catabolic effect—cause destruction of tissue and exacerbation of pain over the long run.

Just as with the body, where a condition might not heal until it is made acute, so too with the mind. Indeed, I have come to appreciate that the therapeutic provision of optimal stress—against the backdrop of an empathically attuned and authentically engaged therapy relationship—is sometimes the magic ingredient needed to overcome the seemingly intractable resistance to change so frequently encountered in our psychiatric patients (Stark, 2008, 2012, 2014). To demonstrate the use of optimal stress to provoke psychological change, here I introduce a particular kind of psychotherapeutic intervention that I have developed to target the maladaptive but deeply entrenched patterns of behavior that have emerged in the patient over time and are now proving resistant to perturbation; these conflict statements are intentionally designed to precipitate disruption in order to trigger repair.

Strategically formulated to offer just the right combination of challenge (whenever possible) and support (whenever necessary), these anxiety-provoking but ultimately growth-promoting interventions repeatedly call to the patient's attention the inherent conflict that exists within her between the objective reality that she knows with her head and the subjective experience that she feels with her heart. More specifically, these optimally stressful statements alternately address the patient's adaptive capacity to know certain painful truths (which will constitute the anxiety-provoking challenge) and then, with compassion and without judgment, resonate with the patient's defensive need to deny knowing those painful truths (which will provide the anxiety-assuaging support).

By way of example, the therapist might first challenge (by speaking to the patient's adaptive capacity to recognize the price she is paying for refusing to let go of her dysfunctional defenses) and then support (by resonating empathically with the patient's defensive need to cling to them even so), all with an eye to creating incentivizing tension within the patient between, on the one hand, her dawning awareness of just how costly her defenses are and, on the other hand, her new-found understanding of just how invested she has been in holding on to them despite her awareness of how maladaptive they are.

As we shall see, ongoing use of these custom-designed, optimally stressful interventions will trigger recursive cycles of destabilizing disruption (as a defensive reaction to the anxiety-provoking challenge) followed by restabilizing repair (as an adaptive response to the anxiety-assuaging support). The cumulative impact of each such iteration results in ever more evolved levels of complex understanding and nuanced awareness. This will in turn generate more and more cognitive and affective dissonance within the patient as she comes increasingly both to know and to feel how untenable it is for her to be still so invested in her dysfunctional ways of being and doing. It is hoped that, ultimately, the increasing dissonance resulting from her evolving capacity to reflect upon her internal process and her expanding insight into both the cost and the benefit of preserving her (dysfunctional) status quo will galvanize the patient to resolve her internal discomfort and discord. The wisdom of the body (Cannon, 1932) is such that it cannot tolerate disequilibrium for extended periods of time and will therefore be prompted to take action to resolve the tension and restore the order.

Although the therapeutic use of optimal stress is designed to engage both the patient's head (her objective knowledge) and the patient's heart (her subjective experience) and thereby to create opportunity for the development of both cognitive and affective awareness of her internal process, at the end of the day it will be by way of tapping into the patient's evolving adaptive capacity to recognize the fundamental conflict between cost and benefit that she will be forced simply to let go. In other words, with each cycle of disruption (in reaction to challenge) and temporary repair (in response to support), the patient will come increasingly to understand—with both her head and her heart—that she has almost no choice but to relinquish her tenacious attachment to dysfunctional defenses that she now appreciates cause more pain than gain, no choice but to surrender her maladaptive patterns of behavior—despite their erstwhile robustness—in favor of more adaptive ways of acting, reacting, and interacting. What had once been relatively ego-syntonic will now have become ego-dystonic, as dysfunctional defenses are incrementally transformed into more functional adaptations. And, of course, as with all change, this letting go of dysfunctionality will necessarily constitute a loss and, as such, will need to be mourned.

Indirect and Direct Advancement of the Therapeutic Endeavor

Importantly, by challenging the patient to work through the optimal (nontraumatic) stress created in the here and now of the treatment situation through the use of therapeutic interventions that both challenge and support, the therapist will be both indirectly and directly advancing the therapeutic endeavor. By virtue of the patient's transference to the therapist, whereby the here and now is imbued with the primal significance of the there and then, mastery in the here and now of nontraumatic experiences at the hands of the therapist (who, whenever possible, will be provoking disruption to create opportunity for repair) will be tantamount to mastery in the there and then of traumatic experiences sustained at the hands of the infantile objects.

But, in addition to this indirect benefit of working through transferential ruptures (thereby enabling extrication from the bonds of infantile attachments), mastery in the here and now of nontraumatic experiences at the hands of the therapist will directly reinforce the patient's resilience and replenish her internal reserves, such that she will be better equipped to process and integrate the impact of the multitude of environmental stressors with which she will continue to be confronted as she moves forward both in the therapy and, more generally, in her life. In essence, with every successive and successful negotiation of first rupture and then repair, the patient will evolve to ever higher levels of functionality and adaptive capacity, thereby progressively increasing her capacity to cope with stress—certainly an important hallmark of mental (and physical) health.

From Defensive Reaction to Adaptive Response

Behind my "no-pain/no-gain" approach is my firm belief in the underlying resilience that patients will inevitably discover within themselves once they are forced to tap into their inborn ability to self-correct in the face of optimal challenge—an innate capacity that will enable them ultimately to advance from less evolved defensive reactions to more evolved adaptive responses (Cannon, 1932; Sapolsky, 1994; McEwen, 1998, 2002; Bland, 1999). In fact, growing up (the task of the child) and getting better (the task of the patient) can be conceptualized as stories about the gradual transformation of unhealthy, low-level defenses—mobilized as knee-jerk reactions to stressors that cannot be adequately processed and integrated—into healthier, higher-level adaptations, for example (and relevant for both child and patient), (a) from dissociating to becoming more present, (b) from externalizing blame to holding oneself more accountable, (c) from denial to confrontation, (d) from being self-indulgent/self-destructive to being more self-affirming/self-respecting, (e) from the need for immediate gratification to the capacity to tolerate delay, (f) from the need to hold on to the capacity to let go, (g) from the need for external regulation of the self to the capacity for internal self-regulation, (h) from the need for perfection to the capacity to tolerate imperfection, and (i) from cursing the darkness to lighting a candle.

This transitioning from unevolved defense to more evolved adaptation is an evolutionary process that involves mastering—either during one's formative years (in the case of the child) or during one's treatment (in the case of the patient)—the myriad environmental impingements to which one will be constantly exposed over time. This mastery is the result of incremental processing, integration, and internal adjustment. In fact, it could be said that adaptation is a story about making a virtue out of necessity.

In sum, psychodynamic psychotherapy can be viewed as a method of treatment that affords the patient an opportunity—albeit a belated one—

to master experiences that had once been overwhelming (and therefore defended against) but that can now, with support from the therapist and by tapping into the patient's underlying resilience and capacity to cope with stress, be processed and integrated (and thereby adapted to). This graduated transformation of dysfunctional, unhealthy, rigid defenses into more functional, healthier, more flexible adaptations will produce deep and enduring change.

Again, stressful stuff happens. But how well we are ultimately able to manage its impact will make all the difference. In other words, how well we are ultimately able to manage the impact of stress in our lives will either derail our development when all we know how to do is to react defensively or trigger our growth once we have learned to respond adaptively to the myriad disappointments, frustrations, and losses with which life will confront us. As they say, what doesn't kill you only makes you stronger.

Repetition Compulsion

How has it been understood, historically, that people keep playing out, in their lives, the same scenarios over and over again, even when they know, in their heart of hearts, that the outcome will be just as disappointing this time as it was the time before, and the time before that, and the time before that? A well-known quip, usually attributed to Albert Einstein, captures beautifully the essence of these unconscious re-enactments: "Insanity is doing the same thing over and over again and expecting different results." Indeed, perhaps part of being human is that we find ourselves continuing to do that which, at least on some level, we know we ought not to be doing and find ourselves not doing that which, at least on some level, we know we would rather be doing.

I am here reminded of a *Saturday Night Live* skit in which two men are seated around a fire chatting, and one says to the other: "You know how when you stick a poker in the fire and leave it in for a long time, it gets really, really hot? And then you stick it in your eye, and it really, really hurts? I hate it when that happens! I just hate it when that happens." A popular song that speaks to the need so many of us have to recreate that with which we are most familiar and, therefore, seemingly most comfortable is a rock song by the late Warren Zevon (1996) titled "If You Won't Leave Me I'll Find Somebody Who Will."

The fact that we keep re-enacting the same dysfunctional (not only self-destructive but also self-indulgent) scenarios on the stage of our lives has been described in the psychoanalytic literature as the *repetition compulsion.* This concept speaks to the hope that springs eternal in all of us—the hope that perhaps, this next time, there will be a different outcome, a better resolution. What is thought to drive these compulsive and unwitting repetitions that underlie the robust resistance to change manifested by so many of our patients?

On the one hand, the unhealthy piece of the repetition compulsion is thought to speak to the desire to have more of the same, no matter how dysfunctional, because that is all we have ever known. Having something different would make us anxious because it would highlight the fact that things could be, and could therefore have been, different. In truth, it is often just too painful to be forced to think about what might have been. And so we remain stuck, clinging to the safety and security of what is familiar—thereby making the same dysfunctional choices (and falling into the same mistakes) over and over again. On the other hand, the healthy piece of the repetition compulsion has to do with our need to achieve mastery—albeit belatedly—of early traumatogenic experiences that we were not able, for whatever complex mix of reasons, adequately to process and integrate at the time. We are unconsciously searching for some kind of closure, completion, or resolution so that we can extricate ourselves from the infantile ties that bind us to our past and will then be freed up to move on to embrace a future replete with realizable opportunities and realistic hope. No longer slaves to our past, we will become masters of our destiny.

We all have, however, a tremendous investment in maintaining the status quo of our lives—no matter how dysfunctional, misguided, maladaptive, self-sabotaging, self-destructive, or recklessly self-indulgent that might be. And it has long been understood that this investment in maintaining what is familiar gives rise to our inertia and fuels our resistance to change. Along these lines, Patrick Casement (1992) has written compellingly about the need in all of us (some aspects of which are unhealthy and some healthy) to be failed in ways specifically determined by unresolved experiences that we had during our formative years, traumatogenic experiences that, never fully processed and integrated, are instead internally recorded as pathogenic structures—which then become the bedrock for how we position ourselves in our lives going forward. In other words, these defensively derived ways of being and doing become a template for dysfunctionality that we will replay again and again, addictively and unwittingly, on the stage of our lives in a desperate, but for the most part futile, attempt to achieve mastery.

Relentless Hope

A specific instance of the operation of the repetition compulsion is the concept of relentless hope, a term I coined to describe a self-protective defense to which patients cling in order not to feel the pain of their disappointment in their objects—the hope is a defense ultimately against grieving (Stark, 1994a, 1994b, 1999). A patient's refusal to deal with the pain of her disappointment in the object (be it the infantile, a contemporary, or the transference object) will fuel the relentlessness with which she pursues it, both the relentlessness of her hope that she might yet be able to make the object over into what she would want it to be and the relentlessness of the outrage she experiences in those moments of dawning recognition that, despite her best efforts and most fervent desire, she might never be able to make that actually happen.

Even more fundamentally, however, what ignites the relentlessness of the patient's pursuit is the fact that the object is separate from her, outside the sphere of her omnipotence, and unable therefore to be either possessed or controlled (Winnicott, 1960). In truth, it is this very immutability of the object—the fact that the object cannot be forced to change—that provides the propulsive fuel for the patient's relentless pursuit. Even in the face of incontrovertible evidence to the contrary, the object of her desire will be pursued with a vengeance, the intensity of this pursuit a result of her entitled conviction that the object could give it (were the object but willing), should give it (because that is her due), and would give it (were she but able to get it right).

Ironically, such patients are never relentless in their pursuit of good objects—their relentless pursuit is of bad objects. In other words, it is never enough that the patient simply find a new good object to compensate for how bad the old (infantile) object had been. Rather, the compelling need becomes first to create or, more accurately, to recreate the old bad object—the comfort of the familial and therefore familiar (Mitchell, 1988)—and then to pressure, manipulate, prod, force, coerce this old bad object to change. And so it is that the patient pursues the (bad) object of her desire with a vengeance, refusing to accept the reality of what it is and intent upon compelling it to be what it is not.

Clinical Vignette: The Transformation of Heartbreak

Many a psychiatric patient, as a child, has suffered great heartache at the hands of a misguided, even if well-intentioned, parent, be it in the form of psychological trauma and abuse (too much bad) or emotional deprivation and neglect (not enough good). Such a patient may never have had occasion to confront the pain of her grief about the parent's unwitting but devastating betrayal of him. Instead, she has defended herself against the pain of her heartache by pushing it, unprocessed, out of her awareness and clinging instead to the illusion of her parent (or a stand-in for her parent) as good and as ultimately forthcoming if she (the patient) could but get it right.

Under the sway of her repetition compulsion, the patient—as she struggles through her life—will find herself delivering into each new relationship her desperate hope that perhaps this time, were she to be but good enough, want it badly enough, or suffer deeply enough, she might yet be able to transform this new object of her relentless desire into the perfect parent she should have had as a child but never did (Stark, 1999). As long as she continues her relentless pursuits, however, and refuses to come to terms with the reality of the limitations, separateness, and immutability of the people in her world—and the limits of her power to make them change—she will be consigning herself to a lifetime of chronic frustration, heartache, and unremitting feelings of impotent rage and profound despair.

If the patient is ever to relinquish her passionate but self-sabotaging pursuits, then she must someday dare to let herself first remember the outrage and the anguish of just how heartbreaking it really was—both the parental errors of commission (presence of bad) and the parental errors of omission (absence of good)—and then confront the pain of her disillusionment in the parent, grief against which she has spent a lifetime unconsciously defending herself. Only once the patient has been able to master and integrate the dissociated grief will she be able to relinquish her relentless and infantile pursuit of the unattainable. She will have transformed dysfunctional defense (the need to hold on) into more functional adaptation (the capacity to let go) once she has grieved and, in the process, developed a more refined awareness of the limitations inherent in relationship and a more evolved capacity to accept that which she cannot change.

The bad news will be the sadness patients experience as they begin to accept the sobering reality that disappointment is an inevitable and necessary aspect of relationship. The good news, however, will be the wisdom they acquire as they come to appreciate ever more profoundly the subtleties and nuances of relationship and begin to make their peace with the harsh reality of life's many challenges—sadder, yes, but also wiser.

Ambivalent Attachment to Bad Objects

As noted earlier in this chapter, not only is the repetition compulsion implicated as a resistive force that must be overcome if the patient is ever to evolve to a higher level of integration, balance, and harmony and not only does the patient's relentless hope create seemingly intractable inertia but also the adhesiveness of the id must be recognized as a powerful force that reinforces the patient's resistance to letting go of the old and moving on to embrace the new.

To appreciate fully this concept, let us now turn to W. R. D. Fairbairn (1963), who advances our understanding of the patient's resistance to change by deconstructing the patient's attachment to her internal bad objects. As we shall soon see, because these bad objects excite, they are longed for (and therefore libidinally cathected); because these bad objects reject, they are hated (and therefore aggressively cathected). And it is this ambivalence that will fuel the relentlessness with which the patient pursues her objects—not only the relentlessness of her hope that something good might someday be forthcoming and of her entitled sense that this is her due but also the relentlessness of her outrage in the face of its being denied.

Over the years many psychoanalytic scholars have written about internal bad objects (or pathogenic introjects) to which the patient is tenaciously attached, but few have addressed the critical issue of what exactly fuels these intense attachments. So it is indeed to Fairbairn that we must look in order to understand the nature of the patient's attachment to her internal bad objects, an attachment that makes it difficult for her to separate from the infantile object and, therefore, to extricate herself from her compulsive repetitions, repetitions that impel her again and again to recreate the early traumatic failure situation in the hope that perhaps this time it will be different, this time the resolution will be better.

Fairbairn writes about how bad experiences at the hands of the infantile object are internally recorded and structuralized.

First of all, what constitutes a bad experience? Fairbairn postulates that when a child's developmentally appropriate need for contact is frustrated by her mother, the child defensively deals with her frustration by introjecting the bad mother. It is as if the child finds it intolerably painful to be disappointed by her mother; and so the child, to protect herself against the pain of having to know just how bad her mother really is, introjects her mother's badness—in the form of an internal bad object.

As we know, this happens all the time in situations of abuse. The patient will recount episodes of outrageous abuse at the hands of her mother (or her father) and will then say that she feels not angry but guilty. After all, it is often easier to experience oneself as bad (and unlovable) than to experience the parent as bad (and unloving), just as it is often easier to experience oneself as having deserved the abuse than to confront the intolerably painful reality that the parent should never have done what she did.

More generally, a child whose heart has been broken by a parent will defend herself against the pain of her grief by taking on the burden of the parent's badness as her own, thereby enabling the child to preserve the illusion of her parent as good and as ultimately forthcoming if she (the child) could but get it right. In essence, by introjecting the bad parent, the child is able to maintain an attachment to her actual parent and, as a result, will be able to hold on to her hope that perhaps someday, somehow, some way, were she simply to want it badly enough, then she might eventually be able to compel the parent to change.

And so it is that the child remains steadfastly attached to the (now internalized) bad object. Were she to disengage herself from the infantile object, were she to renounce her dependence upon the object, in her eyes such renunciation would be tantamount to forfeiting all hope of ever securing gratification of her unsatisfied longing for connection, acceptance, and love. Although the object is bad, the child can at least hope that the object might someday be good, which is why Fairbairn advances the idea—at once both simple and quite profound—that a relationship with a bad object is infinitely better than no relationship at all.

But what does Fairbairn suggest is the specific nature of the child's attachment to the internal bad object?

As we have just seen, the child who has been failed by her mother takes the burden of the mother's badness upon herself. Introjection is therefore the first line of defense. As noted above, according to Fairbairn, a bad mother is a mother who frustrates her child's age-appropriate longing for contact. But, writes Fairbairn, a seductive mother, who first says *yes* and then says *no*, is a very bad mother.

Fairbairn's interest is in these very bad mothers—these seductive mothers. So when the child has been failed, more specifically, by a mother who is seductive, the child will introject this exciting but ultimately rejecting mother.

Splitting is the second line of defense. Once the bad object is inside, it is split into two parts: the exciting object that offers the enticing promise of relatedness and the rejecting object that eventually fails to deliver. Is the rejecting (depriving) object a good object or a bad object? Yes, it is a bad object. But is the exciting (enticing) object a good object or a bad object? Actually, it too is a bad object!

Splitting of the ego goes hand in hand with splitting of the object. Parenthetically, Fairbairn's ego is a dynamic structure with objects and its own energy. In his theory, the endopsychic situation does not include an id. Rather, the so-called libidinal ego attaches itself energetically to the exciting object and longs for contact, hoping against hope that the object will deliver. By the same token, the antilibidinal ego (which is a repository for all the hatred and destructiveness that have accumulated as a result of frustrated longing) attaches itself energetically to the rejecting object and rages against it.

So what, then, is the actual nature of the patient's intense attachment to the bad object? It is, of course, ambivalent: it is both libidinal and antilibidinal (or aggressive) in nature. As noted earlier, the bad object is both needed (because it excites) and hated (because it rejects).

Repression is the third line of defense, repression of the ego's attachment to the exciting/rejecting object.

According to Fairbairn, then, at the core of the repressed is not an impulse, not a trauma, not a memory; rather, at the core of the repressed is a forbidden relationship—an intensely conflicted relationship with a bad object that is both loved and hated, both desired and detested, both longed for and loathed. Importantly, however, because the attachment is repressed, the patient may be unaware that both sides exist.

What this means clinically is that patients who are relentless in their pursuit of the (once again externalized) bad object must ultimately acknowledge both their longing for the object and their hatred of the object for having failed them, and that until they are able to do this, they will remain stuck in their relentless, infantile, and futile pursuits.

Adhesiveness of the Id

Akin to Fairbairn's intensely ambivalent attachment to bad objects as a source of the patient's resistance is Freud's (1937) adhesiveness of the id (to which he also refers as psychic inertia). Although historically Freud's interest was always more in the id's libidinal cathexes than in its aggressive cathexes, it is probably not too much of a stretch for me to suggest that the adhesiveness of the id is ultimately a story about not only intense yearning but also intense aversion. As such, the adhesiveness of the id is therefore implicated in the patient's resistance to relinquishing not only the earlier-referenced infantile attachment to bad objects but also, more generally, her tenacious attachment to dysfunctional defenses. Indeed, I conceive of the patient's intensely ambivalent attachment to her maladaptive thoughts, feelings, and behaviors as a manifestation of Freud's adhesiveness of the id. To the extent that the patient's dysfunctional defenses help her (and are therefore consonant with her sense of self), she will be libidinally, or positively, cathected to them; to the extent that they hurt her (and are therefore dissonant with her sense of self), she will be aggressively, or negatively, cathected to them. But until the patient comes to understand not only the price she pays for having her defenses but also her investment in having them (one or both aspects of which may be unconscious) and until those defenses become more ego-dystonic than ego-syntonic, then she will be destined to continue playing out, unwittingly and compulsively, her unresolved childhood dramas in the arena of her life.

Only by way of working through iterative cycles of defensive collapse and adaptive reconsolidation at ever more evolved levels of awareness and insight will the patient gradually come to recognize—with head and heart—that the cost of living in the way that she does outweighs the benefit she so derives. It will then be the cognitive and affective dissonance created by her ever-expanding awareness that will ultimately become the fulcrum for therapeutic change and provide the leverage needed for transformation of dysfunctional defense into more functional adaptation.

Clinical Illustrations of Ambivalent Attachment to Dysfunctionality

Whether described as instances of the patient's repetition compulsion, unwitting re-enactment, relentless hope, adhesiveness of the id, or ambivalent attachment to dysfunctionality, the following are examples of self-sabotaging behaviors that patients will be reluctant to surrender until they are optimally challenged to recognize that the cost to them of clinging to their dysfunctionality supersedes the benefit they are deriving from remaining entrenched in their maladaptive ways.

It is not just serendipity that a patient who had an emotionally abusive parent will find herself choosing partners who are emotionally abusive. Clearly, something is being played out by way of this compulsive and unwitting re-enactment on the patient's part—something that is not only painful but also pleasurable, not only frustrating but also satisfying, not only costly but also beneficial. If the patient is ever to relinquish her dysfunctionality, she must become aware of both the price she pays for having the dysfunctionality and the investment she has in holding on to it. Her ever-expanding capacity to reflect upon her internal dynamics will generate ever-increasing dissonance, which will then become the fulcrum for her to let go and move on.

As further examples: A patient may compulsively overindulge in drugs and alcohol in a desperate attempt to deal with her emptiness and in the hope thereby of overcoming her longstanding feelings of deprivation and neglect. Her abuse of alcohol and drugs may temporarily satisfy her by offering the promise of filling up the void inside, but her reckless overindulgence will also defeat her because it will interfere with her ability to live a productive and fulfilling life. Her self-indulgent/self-destructive drug and alcohol addiction will continue until the patient is able to work through the (libidinal and aggressive) adhesiveness of the id to her dysfunctional, self-defeating behavior.

Or a patient may be relentless in her pursuit of an unattainable love object because she has never resolved the conflicted feelings she has about her first partner, namely, her parent. The patient's relentless pursuit of the perfect parent (be it either the actual parent or a parent substitute) serves her because it enables her not to have to confront—and grieve—the reality that the actual parent was far from perfect. But the patient's relentless pursuit also costs her because her heart is being constantly broken as a result of the dysfunctional object choices that she finds herself making again and again. The patient will continue to experience heartbreak until she begins to face the reality that the suffering she is causing herself (by choosing inappropriate love objects) far exceeds the protection she has secured for herself by not dealing with the early parental failure. Only once the pain of her devastating heartbreak becomes greater than the gain of her self-protective refusal to grieve will the patient be able to overcome the adhesiveness of the id and relinquish the dysfunctional attachment to her relentless pursuit.

Or, finally, a patient may be drawn to partners who are critical and controlling because she has not yet worked through the complex mix of feelings that she has about a critical and controlling parent. Her choice of critical and controlling partners serves her by fueling her hope that perhaps someday, somehow, some way, were she but to try hard enough, she might yet be able to find a critical and controlling partner whom she could force to be kind, gentle, and accepting of her. But her dysfunctional object choices also defeat her because they consign her to a lifetime of chronic frustration and feelings of helplessness and defeat. The patient will continue to choose inappropriate and, sadly, all-too-familiar bad objects until she has come to appreciate, deeply, both the lure of the familiar and the price she pays for refusing to let go of her compulsive and unwitting re-enactments.

The Process of Grieving and Evolving to Acceptance

In all the situations above, as part of the working through that the patient must do to be released from the stranglehold of her tenacious attachments and relentless pursuits, the patient must come not only to know with her head that her dysfunctional defenses have become too costly for her to maintain but also to feel with her heart that these self-protective mechanisms are no longer serving her.

All change, even if for the better, involves loss and, as such, must be grieved. As part of that mourning process, the patient will need to deal with disappointment, frustration, and heartbreak experienced in relation to not only her transference object and her contemporary objects but also her infantile objects. And, more generally, she will need to deal with the destabilizing stress and upset of having her time-honored, albeit maladaptive, ways of being and doing challenged and her all-too-familiar and oh-so-comfortable but fundamentally flawed defensive stance in the world called into question. Again, all change involves loss—and a letting go as one grieves—and, at least initially, a tentative repositioning of oneself in one's life.

Only more recently have I come to appreciate that genuine grieving requires of us that we be able, at least for periods of time, to be fully present with the anguish of our grief and the fury we will experience when we are confronted with inescapable and shocking realities about ourselves, our relationships, and our world. We must not absent ourselves from our grief; we must enter into and embrace it, without running away. We cannot effectively grieve when we are dissociated, missing in action, or fleeing the scene. We need to be present, engaged, in the moment, mindful of all that is going on inside us, grounded, focused, and in the here and now. If, instead, we are in denial, unwilling to confront, closed, shut down, numb, retreating, refusing to feel, protesting, or unwilling to accept, then no real grieving can be done.

Genuine grieving—usually accomplished only incrementally and over time—is an ongoing and tortuous process of alternately falling into the depths of devastation and heartbreak and then raging against the world and railing against our fate. But, ultimately, it involves forgiving, relenting, letting go, separating, and moving on. It is what it is; it was what it was—and we must have the wisdom to accept that.

Self-Organizing (Chaotic) Systems Resist Perturbation

Let us shift now from a conceptualization of the patient's resistance to change as a story about the regressive pull of (a) unwitting and compulsive re-enactments of unresolved childhood dramas, (b) relent-less pursuits of that which can never be, and (c) intensely ambivalent attachments that both satisfy and frustrate to a conceptualization of the patient's inertia as speaking, more fundamentally, to the inherent resistance to change manifested by all self-organizing chaotic systems.

In the language of chaos theory (Strogatz, 2001; Kauffman, 1995; Buchanan, 2000), I depict patients here as complex, adaptive, self-organizing chaotic systems. Although at first glance seemingly random (i.e., chaotic), as noted earlier, these systems have an under-lying and robust orderedness that will emerge over time as the sys-tem evolves.

First, some definitions. Systems are *complex*, which speaks to the intricate interdependence of their constituent components; *adaptive*, signifying their capacity to adjust to experience and not just to react; *self-organizing*, referring to the spontaneous emergence of system-wide patterns arising from the interplay of components; and *chaotic*, speaking to the underlying orderedness despite the apparent randomness.

An example of a quintessential self-organizing chaotic system, whereby order emerges from chaos as the system evolves over time, is crystallization: the spontaneous emergence of beautifully patterned crystals from solutions of randomly moving molecules. Other exam-ples of self-organizing systems include the assemblage of rippled dunes from grains of sand and the generation of swirling spiral patterns in hurricanes—the rippled dunes and the swirling spirals are *emergent prop-erties* of self-organizing systems.

Consider the phenomenon whereby female roommates will, over time, begin to menstruate on the same cycle—this synchronization is an emer-gent property of a self-organizing system. Or consider the phenomenon whereby thousands of fireflies gathered in trees at night and flashing on and off randomly will, after a while, begin to flash in unison—their syn-chronization is an emergent property of a self-organizing system and a dramatic illustration of the phase-locking of biorhythms. Consider also the phenomenon whereby a number of grandfather clocks with their pen-dulums initially swinging randomly will eventually entrain, such that all the pendulums will swing in precise synchrony (Bentov, 1988).

Well known about self-organizing (chaotic) systems is that they resist perturbation. No matter how compromised or dysfunctional, self-organizing systems, fueled as they are by their homeostatic tendency to remain constant over time, are inherently resistant to change; they have an inertia that must be overcome if the system is to evolve to another level.

It took many years for me to appreciate something about the therapeutic process that is at once both completely obvious and quite profound, namely, that it will be input from the outside and the patient's capacity to process, integrate, and adapt to this input that will ultimately enable the patient to change. Only more recently, however, in light of my relatively new-found appreciation for the clinical significance of viewing the patient as a self-organizing chaotic system with an intrinsic resistance to perturbation, have I come to understand that the patient will need something more than simple input from the outside to incite change. Indeed, it will actually be stressful input from the outside and the patient's capacity to process, integrate, and adapt to the impact of this stressful input that will provoke change and the emergence of new patterns of behavior.

Consider a patient who is clinging tenaciously to dysfunctional defenses that had once served her but no longer do so. By conceptualizing the patient as a self-organizing chaotic system, it becomes clear that the patient must be sufficiently perturbed (i.e., impacted) by input from the outside (i.e., the therapist's interventions) that there will be impetus (i.e., force needed to bring about change) for the patient to relinquish the attachment to her maladaptive patterns of acting, reacting, and interacting in favor of healthier, more adaptive ways of being and doing.

In essence, the therapist's interventions must have enough stressful impact that they will be able to challenge the homeostatic balance (i.e., the status quo) of the patient's dysfunctional defenses. By the same token, however, the therapist's interventions must also provide enough support that this input, in combination with the patient's innate striving toward health (i.e., her resilience), will create opportunity for the patient to evolve to ever-higher levels of complexity and nuanced understanding.

The Difference Between a Poison and a Medication

The noted sixteenth-century Swiss physician Paracelsus (see Paracelsus, 2004) is credited with having written that the difference between a poison and a medication is the dosage thereof. More accurately, however, one might add that it is the system's capacity—a function of its underlying resilience—to process, integrate, and ultimately adapt to the impact of the stressor that will actually make the difference.

So a poison is not always toxic, and nor is a medicine always therapeutic. If a depressed patient on 20 mg of fluoxetine is responding, but only suboptimally, perhaps, counterintuitively, 10 mg will be the more optimal dose and not ever-higher doses of the selective serotonin reuptake inhibitor. And whereas mild to moderate exercise will stimulate and energize the body, excessive or prolonged exercise may ultimately deplete the body of its nutrient and energetic reserves, thereby doing more harm than good. Stressful input, therefore, is inherently neither bad (poison) nor good (medication), which is to say that the therapist's interventions are inherently neither toxic (poison) nor therapeutic (medication).

Rather, the dosage of the stressor, the underlying resilience and adaptability of the system, and the intimate edge (Ehrenberg, 1992) between stressor and system will determine if the patient (reacting defensively to the therapist's interventions) devolves to greater disorganization or (responding adaptively to the therapist's interventions) evolves, by way of a series of healing cycles, to ever more complex levels of organization and dynamic balance.

In other words, if the interface between stressor and system is such that the stressor is able to provoke recovery within the system, then what would have been poison becomes medication, what would have constituted toxic input becomes therapeutic input, what would have been deemed traumatic stress (van der Kolk, 2006) becomes optimal stress, and what would have overwhelmed becomes transformative.

The Goldilocks Principle and Optimal Stress

In truth, the patient will find herself reacting/responding in any one of three ways to the therapist's stressful input. Too much challenge, too much anxiety, too much stress will be too overwhelming for the patient to process and integrate, triggering instead defensive collapse and at least temporary derailment of the therapeutic process: traumatic stress.

Too little challenge, too little anxiety, too little stress will provide too little impetus for transformation and growth because there will be nothing that needs to be mastered; too little challenge will serve simply to reinforce the (dysfunctional) status quo.

Although, admittedly, some theorists believe that it is the experience of gratification itself that is compensatory and ultimately healing, most believe that it is the experience of frustration against a backdrop of gratification, frustration (or disillusionment) properly grieved, that will promote structural growth and development of adaptive capacity. Such theorists (Kohut, 1984; Bacal, 1998); contend that if there is no thwarting of desire (no frustration), there will be nothing that needs to be processed and integrated and therefore little impetus for adaptive transmuting (i.e., structure-building) internationalizations. In other words, too much challenge will be traumatizing, but too little challenge will do nothing to advance the therapeutic endeavor.

Just the right amount of challenge, however, just the right amount of anxiety, just the right amount of stress—to which the father of stress, Hans Selye (1974, 1978), refers to as *eustress* and to which I (Stark, 2008, 2012, 2014) refer to as *optimal stress*—will offer just the right combination of challenge and support needed to optimize the potential for transformation and growth. Like the three bowls of porridge sampled by Goldilocks—one too hot, one too cold, but one just right (which is the one that worked best for her)—so too the dose of stress provided by the therapist's interventions will be either too much, too little, or just right (which will be the one that works best for the patient).

To highlight the clinical usefulness of optimal (nontraumatic) stress to provoke healing, the idea here is that if the patient is offered only gratification and support, then there will usually be insufficient impetus for transformation and growth, especially if the patient has longstanding, deeply entrenched psychological issues. Certainly direct support is necessary, but it is not always sufficient. In truth, direct support and optimal challenge work in concert. Whereas optimal challenge provokes recovery and revitalization by prompting the system to adapt, direct support facilitates transformation and growth by reinforcing the system's underlying resilience, thereby honing the system's ability to adapt to, and benefit from, ongoing stressful input. The successful working through of recursive cycles of disruption and repair will effectively create a positive (amplifying) feedback loop and, with each successive healing cycle, ever-greater adaptive capacity and functionality of the system.

The Sandpile Model and the Paradoxical Impact of Stress

Let us shift for a moment from the realm of the animate to the realm of the inanimate. Long intriguing to chaos theorists has been the sand-pile model (Bak, 1999), which is thought to offer a dramatic depiction of the cumulative impact, over time, of environmental impingement on open systems. Evolution of the sandpile is governed by some complex mathematical formulas and is well known in many scientific circles, but the sandpile model is rarely applied to living systems and has never been used to demonstrate either the adaptability and resilience of the living system or the paradoxical impact of stress on it. My contention, however, is that this simulation model provides an elegant visual metaphor for how we are continuously refashioning ourselves at ever- higher levels of complexity and integration—not just in spite of stressful input from the outside but by way of that input (Stark, 2012, 2014).

Amazingly enough, the grains of sand being steadily added to a gradually evolving sandpile are the occasion for both its disruption and its repair. Not only do the grains of sand being added precipitate par-tial collapse of the sandpile (a minor avalanche), but also they become the means by which the sandpile will be able to build itself back up—each time at a new level of homeostasis. The system will therefore have been able not only to manage the impact of the stressful input but also to benefit from that impact. And, as the sandpile evolves, an under-lying pattern will begin to emerge, characterized by iterative cycles of disruption and repair, destabilization and restabilization, defensive collapse and adaptive reconstitution at ever-higher levels of integration and dynamic balance.

Challenge to Provide Impetus and Support to Provide Opportunity

Just as the grains of sand being systematically added to the ever-changing sandpile will ultimately provide both impetus and opportunity for reconstruction at ever-higher levels of complex orderedness, so too the systematic use of psychotherapeutic interventions that alternately break down and then build up will ultimately provide both impetus and opportunity for reconstruction at ever-higher levels of complex orderedness.

As psychodynamic therapists intent upon facilitating deep and lasting change in our patients, we are constantly striving—against a backdrop of empathic attunement and authentic engagement—to formulate interventions that, like the grains of sand being added to the sandpile, will either challenge (thereby providing impetus for destabilization of the patient's dysfunctional defenses) or support (thereby providing opportunity for at least temporary restabilization of those self-protective mechanisms at a higher level of functionality and adaptive capacity). Based on our moment-by-moment assessment of what the patient can tolerate (Stark, 1994a, 1994b), we will therefore either challenge the patient by directing her attention to where she is not (but where we would want the patient to be) or support the patient by resonating with where she is (and where the patient would seem to need to be).

Again, ever attuned to the patient's capacity to process, integrate, and adapt to the impact of our optimally stressful interventions, we will either challenge, with anxiety-provoking interpretive statements that call into question defenses to which the patient has long clung in order to preserve her psychological equilibrium, or support, with anxiety-assuaging empathic statements that honor those self-protective defenses—a therapeutic stance often referred to as *going with the resistance.*

For example, we might first challenge by highlighting what the patient is coming to recognize as a disillusioning truth about the object of his desire, but then we might support by resonating empathically with the patient's investment in holding on to his hope that perhaps someday, somehow, some way, were he to be but good enough, try hard enough, be persuasive enough, persist long enough, or suffer deeply enough, he might yet be able to make his girl friend fall in love with him.

Or we might first challenge by reminding the patient of a sobering reality that she really does know although she would rather not, namely, that she will need to work through the pain of her grief about her father's emotional unavailability before she will be able to commit fully to a more appropriate partner. But we might then support by resonating empathically with the patient's fear that were she to let herself revisit the pain of that early heartbreak, she might never stop crying.

With our finger ever on the pulse of the patient's level of anxiety and capacity to tolerate further challenge, in order to expedite progression of the patient from dysfunctional defense to more functional adaptation, we will therefore strategically formulate optimally stressful interventions that alternately challenge the patient and then support her, all with an eye to jump-starting the patient's innate ability to self-repair in the face of environmental impingement.

It is indeed a delicate balancing act that we must perform between challenging (to precipitate rupture) and then supporting (to facilitate, at least temporarily, repair and reconstitution at a higher level). Sometimes we will first challenge and then support; sometimes we will first support and then challenge. But either way, it will all be done based on our sense of what the patient can tolerate in the moment and always with an eye to creating ever-increasing tension within the patient between her dawning awareness of sobering truths about either herself or her objects and her new-found understanding of just how invested she is in maintaining her self-protective (but ultimately self-sabotaging) defenses.

As we sit with our patients, there is always a dialectical tension within us as well, between, on the one hand, our vision of who we think the patient could be (were she but able to make healthier choices) and, on the other hand, our respect for the reality of who she is (and for the choices, no matter how unhealthy, that she is continuously making). We are therefore always struggling to find an optimal balance within ourselves between wanting the patient to change and accepting the reality of who the patient is.

Importantly, we must never lose sight of the fact that the patient has come to be as she is and to defend herself in the ways that she does because, at the time of the original privations, deprivations, and injuries, she was simply unable—for whatever complex mix of reasons—to process, integrate, and adapt to the impact of those traumatic stressors. She was forced instead to cobble together, in order to survive, whatever defenses she could—defenses that would become only more firmly entrenched over time and, eventually, would emerge as her characteristic (defensive and dysfunctional) posture in the world.

Optimally Stressful Psychotherapeutic Interventions

In an effort to make the fine line that we must walk a little easier to negotiate, as earlier noted, I have developed a particular kind of therapeutic intervention—an anxiety-provoking but ultimately growth-promoting intervention that juxtaposes challenge and support in the interest of creating an optimal level of destabilizing stress and incentivizing anxiety in the patient (Stark, 1999, 2008, 2012). In one fell swoop, these strategically formulated interventions, specifically designed to advance the psychotherapeutic endeavor by inducing healing cycles of disruption and repair, will first increase the patient's level of stress (by confronting her with her objective knowledge of a painful truth) and then decrease the patient's level of stress (by resonating empathically with her subjective experience of that painful truth).

More specifically, the therapist will challenge whenever possible (thereby increasing the patient's anxiety, destabilizing the underlying defensive structure, and effectively superimposing an acute injury on top of a chronic one) and support whenever necessary (thereby decreasing the patient's anxiety and creating the potential for adaptive restabilization of the system at a higher level of integration, functionality, and balance). To the point here is Clare Boothe Luce's description of Eleanor Roosevelt as someone who "comforted the distressed" but "distressed the comfortable" (quoted in Freedman, 1967), that is, as someone who appropriately supported whenever necessary, and challenged whenever possible.

Conflict statements are custom-made to create dissonance within the patient between, on the one hand, sobering realities that at least on some level she really does know and, on the other hand, the defenses that she, made anxious, will find herself unwittingly mobilizing in an effort to deny that knowledge—"you know . . . , but you find yourself thinking, feeling, doing . . . in order not to have to know."

> "You know that ultimately you will need to confront, and grieve, the reality that Jose is not available in the ways that you would have wanted him to be and that until you make your peace with that frustrating reality you will probably continue to nag him and make both of you miserable; but, in the moment, all you can think about is how angry you are that he does not tell you more often that he loves you."

"You know that you won't feel truly fulfilled until you are able to get your manuscript completed and are able to make yourself simply sit down to do that; but you continue to struggle, fearing that whatever you might write just wouldn't be good enough or capture well enough the essence of what you are wanting to convey."

"You know that if your relationship with Ellen is to survive, you will need to take at least some responsibility for the part you're playing in the incredibly abusive fights that you and she are having; but you tell yourself that it isn't really your fault because if she weren't so provocative, then you wouldn't have to be so vindictive!"

In essence, conflict statements encourage the patient to step back from the immediacy of the moment in order to focus on the underlying forces and counterforces within her that are tying up her energies and interfering with her forward momentum. They are designed to tease out, and articulate on the patient's behalf, the conflict within her between her voice of reality (which will be anxiety-provoking but ultimately insight-promoting) and the growth-obstructing defensive counterforces she mobilizes in an effort to ease her anxiety and silence that voice.

"You know that eventually you will need to face the reality that your mother was never really there for you and that you won't get better until you let go of your hope that maybe someday you'll be able to make her change; but you're not quite yet ready to deal with all that because you're afraid you might not survive the heartbreak and the despair you would feel were you to have to face that devastating truth."

"You know that your need for your children to understand your perspective might be a bit unrealistic; but you tell yourself that you have a right to their respect—and their forgiveness."

"You're coming to understand that your anger can put people off; but you tell yourself that you have a right to be as angry as you want because of how much you have had to suffer over the years."

In other words, the goal of these optimally stressful interventions is not only to give the patient sufficient space to experience whatever she might find herself feeling as a reaction to being confronted with anxiety-provoking realities that she can no longer deny but also to promote enough detachment that she will be able to bring to bear her self-reflective capacity, all with an eye to making her acutely aware of the struggle raging within her between what her head, albeit begrudgingly, knows and what her heart, in desperate protest, feels.

Importantly, by locating within the patient the conflict between her anxiety-provoking knowledge of a distressing reality and her anxiety-assuaging reactive experience of that reality, the therapist is deftly side-stepping the potential for conflict between patient and therapist. In other words, the therapist who is able to resist the temptation to get bossy by overzealously advocating for the patient to do the right thing will be able masterfully to avoid getting deadlocked in a power struggle with the patient, because such a struggle can easily enough ensue when the therapist takes it upon herself to represent the voice of reality, a stance that then leaves the patient no option but to become the voice of opposition.

In fact, when the therapist introduces the conflict statement with "you know . . . ," she is insisting that the patient take responsibility for what the patient does indeed know. But if the therapist, in a misguided attempt to urge the patient forward, resorts simply to telling the patient what the therapist knows, not only does the therapist run the risk of forcing the patient to become ever more entrenched in her defensive stance of protest but also the therapist will be robbing the patient of any incentive to take responsibility for her own desire to get better.

Although it happens all the time, it is an untenable situation for the therapist to be the one representing the healthy (adaptive) voice of *yes* and for the patient, made anxious, to be then stuck in the position of having to counter with the unhealthy (defensive) voice of *no*. And so it is that the therapist speaks (in the first part of a conflict statement) to what the patient, at least on some level, already knows:

> "You know that if you are ever to get on with your life, you will have to let go of your conviction that your childhood scarred you for life; but it's hard not to feel like damaged goods when you grew up with a horribly abusive father who was always calling you a loser."

> "You know that if you are really serious about finding yourself a partner, then you will need to put yourself out there in a way that you

don't ordinarily do; but you find yourself holding back because you have an underlying conviction that no matter what you might try, it wouldn't really make any difference anyway."

"You know that eventually, if you are ever to work through your fears of intimacy, you will have to let someone in; but right now you're feeling that you simply cannot afford to be that vulnerable. In the past, when you were vulnerable, especially with your mom, you always got hurt."

In sum, conflict statements, by locating the conflict squarely within the patient and not in the intersubjective field between patient and therapist, will force the patient to take ownership of both sides of her ambivalence about getting better—both the *yes* forces and the *no* counterforces mobilized in reaction to those *yes* forces.

Therapeutic Leveraging of Pain and Gain

By repeatedly formulating conflict statements that strategically juxtapose the patient's dawning awareness of just how steep a price she is paying for holding on to her defenses and her new-found appreciation for how they have served her, the therapist will be able to create galvanizing tension within the patient—growth-promoting dissonance that will ultimately become the fulcrum for therapeutic change. And so it is that the therapist goes back and forth between challenging and supporting in order incrementally to make the patient's ambivalently held dysfunctional defenses ever less ego-syntonic (i.e., ever less consonant with who she would want to be) and ever more ego-dystonic or ego alien (i.e., ever more dissonant with who she would want to be).

As long as the gain (i.e., the benefit) is greater than the pain (i.e., the cost), the patient will maintain the defense and remain entrenched. But once the pain becomes greater than the gain, the stress and strain thereby created will force the patient ultimately to relinquish her dysfunctionality in order to restore her psychological equilibrium. More specifically, once the pain (as a result of all that the patient is coming to recognize as the price she pays for silencing her inner voice of truth) becomes greater than the gain (which will become ever less compelling as the patient comes increasingly to understand the defensive nature of her maladaptive ways of being and doing), the stress and strain of the cognitive and affective dissonance thereby generated within the patient—between her ever-greater awareness of the cost and her ever-greater appreciation for the defensive nature of the benefit—will provide powerful leverage for the patient gradually to relinquish her attachment to her dysfunctional (increasingly ego-dystonic) defenses in favor of healthier (ever more ego-syntonic) adaptations.

Three Complementary Modes of Therapeutic Action

To this point, the focus of my chapter has been on the therapist's ongoing use of optimally stressful interventions to heighten the patient's awareness of not only how costly it is for her to remain so steadfastly entrenched in her dysfunctionality but also how invested she is, even so, in maintaining her attachment to it. Her ever-evolving insight into these conflictual dynamics will ultimately generate within her so much cognitive dissonance that, to resolve what has become an increasingly untenable endopsychic situation, she will eventually have almost no choice but to replace her dysfunctional defenses with more functional adaptations.

Admittedly this paradigm, with its highlighting of the patient's ever-expanding awareness of her internal landscape as she is forced to confront the reality of her ambivalent attachment to her dysfunctionality, is certainly more intrapersonal (1-person) than interpersonal (2-person). Although beyond the scope of this chapter, elsewhere I advance the more holistic idea that the therapeutic action of psychodynamic psychotherapy can best be conceptualized as involving not only knowledge (1-person) but also experience (1½-person) and relationship (2-person) (Stark, 1999, 2012, 2014). And even though, as conceived by me, each of these three modes of therapeutic action privileges a different facet of the healing process, what all three interdependent modes have in common is their advocacy of optimally stressful, anxiety-provoking but ultimately growth-promoting interventions, the working through and mastery of which will provoke graduated transformation of unhealthy, less-evolved defense into healthier, more-evolved adaptation.

My *Model 1, enhancement of knowledge*, is a derivative of the interpretive perspective of classical psychoanalysis. I use as a springboard Freud's premises of drive-defense conflict as the source of neurotic suffering and of the goal of treatment as therefore taming the id and strengthening the ego so that the ego's primitive defenses will no longer be necessary and the id-ego conflict can be resolved. But I have broadened Freud's conceptualization of neurotic conflict to encompass, more generally, growth-impeding tension between anxiety-provoking but ultimately health-promoting internal forces pressing *yes* and anxiety-assuaging defensive internal counterforces protesting *no*. These latter forces—to which the patient, as I have emphasized throughout this chapter, is ambivalently attached (inasmuch as they both serve her and cost her)—will interfere with her capacity to derive pleasure and fulfillment from her love, work, and play (Freud, 1990) and will therefore contribute to her psychic inertia and resistance to change.

But before these resistive counterforces can be surrendered, the patient must become aware first of their existence and then of what exactly fuels the tenacity with which she is unwittingly clinging to them. As has already been elaborated, this process of rendering conscious what had once been unconscious can best be facilitated through the use of optimally stressful conflict statements that alternately speak to the patient's adaptive (ego) capacity to know any number of anxiety-provoking realities and then resonate with her defensive (id) need to deny such knowledge. As a result of the working through process (which will tame the id and strengthen the ego), where once id and ego were in conflict, now the patient will be better able to harness the energy of the id to fuel forward momentum and actualization of potential.

In writing about the conflictual relationship that inherently exists between id and ego, Freud likens it to the tension-filled relationship that exists between a horse and its rider; he suggests that the horse represents the id and its rider the ego. But once the horse has become tamed and therefore more manageable and its rider has become stronger and therefore more adept at managing, horse and rider will be better able to coordinate their efforts to create a relationship that is no longer conflictual but collaborative. The defensive need to rein the horse in will have become transformed into the adaptive capacity to give the horse free rein.

My *Model 2, provision of corrective experience,* is a more contemporary perspective, one that focuses on the patient's psychological deficiencies, the psychic scars that result from early *absence of good* in the form of *parental deprivation and neglect.* This deficiency-compensation perspective is one that offers the patient an opportunity both to grieve the early parental failures and, in the context of the here and now relationship with her therapist, to experience symbolic restitution.

As the patient, over time, mourns the loss of her illusions—be they in relation to the infantile, a contemporary, or the transference object— and simultaneously works through the cumulative stress of these optimal (nontraumatic) disillusionments, transmuting (structure-building) microinternalizations will take place, which will enable her to master the loss. These adaptive internalizations will promote gradual accretion of internal structure, filling in of psychic deficit, and consolidation of self (Kohut, 1966). And as the patient, now more integrated, begins to make her peace with the reality that the people in her world were not, are not, and will never be all that she would have wanted them to be, she will relinquish her relentless pursuits and evolve to a place of greater acceptance and inner calm.

And my *Model 3, engagement in authentic relationship,* is another contemporary perspective, one that focuses on the patient's psychological toxicities, the psychic scars that result from early *presence of bad* in the form of *parental trauma and abuse.* This relational model of therapeutic action conceives of the treatment situation as offering the patient a stage upon which to play out symbolically her unresolved childhood dramas but ultimately to encounter a different response this time. The outcome will indeed be different, and better, because the patient will be negotiating at the intimate edge of authentic engagement with a therapist who will be able to facilitate resolution by bringing to bear her own more evolved capacity to process and integrate on behalf of the patient who truly does not know how.

Although initially the therapist may indeed fail the patient in much the same way that her parent had failed her, ultimately the therapist will be able to challenge the patient's projections by lending aspects of her otherness, or, as Donald W. Winnicott (1990) would have said, her "externality" to the interaction—such that the patient will have the experience of something that is "other than me" and can take that in.

In other words, because at the end of the day the therapist is not in fact as bad as the parent had been, there can be a better outcome. And this will happen again and again, repetition of the original trauma but with a much healthier resolution every time; the repetitions lead to incremental detoxification of the patient's internal world and integration on ever-higher levels of functionality and adaptive capacity. As the patient is confronted with, and forced to take ownership of, the dysfunctional scenarios that she has been compulsively and unwittingly choreographing on the stage of her life, she will eventually evolve to a place of greater accountability for her often misguided and provocative ways of being and doing.

In essence, in Model 1, the more classical model, the therapeutic action will involve working through the cumulative impact of all the stress resulting from the *cognitive dissonance* created by the experience of gain-become-pain (once benefit exceeds cost). The net result will be transformation of resistance into awareness and actualization of potential. In Model 2, the corrective-provision model, the therapeutic action will involve working through the cumulative impact of all the stress resulting from the *affective disillusionment* created by the experience of good-become-bad (once illusion—positive misperception—is superseded by disillusionment). The net result will be transformation of relentlessness and refusal to grieve into acceptance. In Model 3, the contemporary relational model, the therapeutic action will involve working through the cumulative impact of all the stress resulting from the *relational detoxification* created by the experience of bad-become-good (once distortion—negative misperception—is superseded by reality). The net result will be transformation of re-enactment into accountability.

In sum, the patient's resistances (Model 1), her relentless pursuits (Model 2), and her re- enactments (Model 3) are the dysfunctional defenses to which she clings in order not to have to know, not to have to feel, and not to have to take responsibility for what she plays out on the stage of her life. Cognitive dissonance (Model 1), affective disillusionment (Model 2), and relational detoxification (Model 3) are the anxiety-provoking but ultimately growth-promoting optimal stressors that will provoke transformation and growth. And awareness (Model 1), acceptance (Model 2), and accountability (Model 3) are the adaptations that will ultimately emerge from the chaotically disorganized depths of her unconscious.

The healing process in all three paradigms will involve the therapeutic induction of healing cycles of disruption and repair, recursive cycles triggered by the therapist's ongoing use of strategically formulated, optimally stressful interventions that will first precipitate destabilization and then, with enough support from the therapist and by tapping into the patient's underlying resilience and intrinsic ability to self-correct in the face of optimal stress, create opportunity for restabilization at ever-higher levels of awareness, acceptance, and accountability.

Conclusion

Let us return for a moment to our model of the self-organizing sandpile. As a result of the cumulative impact, over time, of the grains of sand being steadily added, the sandpile will evolve through cycles of destabilization (minor avalanche) followed by restabilization at ever-higher levels. Eventually, however, there will come a time when the sandpile reaches a tipping point, which will trigger a total collapse of the sandpile (major avalanche).

Now consider the impact of optimal stress on the patient's awareness of her internal conflictedness and resistance to change. Here, too, and as a result of the cumulative impact over time of the therapist's interventions, the patient will evolve through cycles of destabilization (minor avalanche) followed by restabilization at ever-higher levels—a series of small incremental changes that will produce ever more profound levels of insight and complex understanding. Once the patient has evolved to the point of being able to recognize (with not only her head but also her heart) that she really does lose more than she gains by remaining so obstinately attached to her dysfunctional defenses, then the galvanizing dissonance created by this new-found awareness will trigger a total collapse (major avalanche) of the patient's defensive structures, thereby forcing her to let go of her dysfunctional ways of being and doing so that she can re-equilibrate at a new, more evolved homeostatic set point—only to start all over again (but this time from a different, better baseline).

References

Bacal, H. (1998). *Optimal responsiveness: How therapists heal their patients.* Northvale, NJ: Jason Aronson.

Bak, P. (1999). *How nature works: The science of self-organized criticality.* New York, NY: Copernicus.

Bentov, I. (1988). *Stalking the wild pendulum: On the mechanics of consciousness.* Rochester, VT: Inner Traditions Bear.

Bland, J. (1999). *Genetic nutritioneering: How you can modify inherited traits and live a longer, healthier life.* New York, NY: McGraw-Hill.

Buchanan, M. (2000). *Ubiquity: Why catastrophes happen.* New York, NY: Three Rivers Press.

Cannon, W. B. (1932). *The wisdom of the body.* New York, NY: Norton.

Casement, P. (1992). *Learning from the patient.* New York, NY: Guilford.

Ehrenberg, D. (1992). *The intimate edge: Extending the reach of psychoanalytic interaction.* New York, NY: Norton.

Fairbairn, W. R. D. (1963). Synopsis of an object relations theory of personality. *International Journal of Psychoanalysis 44,* 224–255.

Freedman, M. (1967). *Roosevelt and Frankfurter: Their correspondence, 1928–1945.* Boston, MA: Little, Brown.

Freud, S. (1937). Analysis terminable and interminable. *International Journal of Psychoanalysis 18,* 373–405.

Freud, S. (1990). *The ego and the id.* New York, NY: Norton.

Kauffman, S. (1995). *At home in the universe: The search for the laws of self-organization and complexity.* New York, NY: Oxford University Press.

Kohut, H. (1966). Forms and transformations of narcissism. *Journal of the American Psychoanalytic Association, 14*(2), 243–272.

Kohut, H. (1984). *How does analysis cure?* Chicago, IL: University of Chicago Press.

McEwen, B. S. & Lasley, E. N. (1998). Stress, adaptation, and disease: Allostasis and allostatic load. *Annals of the New York Academy of Science, 840*(1), 33–44.

McEwen, B. S. (2002). *The end of stress as we know it.* New York, NY: The Dana Foundation.

Mitchell, S. (1988). *Relational concepts in psychoanalysis: An integration.* Cambridge, MA: Harvard University Press.

Paracelsus, T. (2004). *The archidoxes of magic.* Whitefish, MT: Kessinger Publishing.

Sapolsky, R. M. (1994). *Why zebras don't get ulcers.* New York, NY: W. H. Freeman.

Selye, H. (1974). *Stress without distress.* New York, NY: Harper & Row.

Selye, H. (1978). *The stress of life.* New York, NY: McGraw-Hill.

Stark, M. (1994a). *A primer on working with resistance.* Northvale, NJ: Jason Aronson.

Stark, M. (1994b). *Working with resistance.* Lanham, MD: The Rowman, Littlefield Publishing Group.

Stark, M. (1999). *Modes of therapeutic action: Enhancement of knowledge, provision of experience, and engagement in relationship.* Lanham, MD: The Rowman, Littlefield Publishing Group..

Stark, M. (2008). Hormesis, adaptation, and the sandpile model. *Critical Reviews in Toxicology, 38*(7), 641–644.

Stark, M. (2012). The sandpile model: Optimal stress and hormesis. *Dose Response, 10*(1), 66–74.

Stark, M. (2014). Optimal stress, psychological resilience, and the sandpile model. In S. Rattan and E. Le Bourg (Eds.), *Hormesis in health and disease* (pp. 199–222). Boca Raton, FL: CRC Press/Taylor & Francis.

Strogatz, S. (2001). *Nonlinear dynamics and chaos: With applications to physics, biology, chemistry, and engineering.* Boulder, CO: Westview Press.

van der Kolk, B., McFarlane, A. C., & Weisaeth, L. (2006). *Traumatic stress: The effects of overwhelming experience on mind, body, and society.* New York, NY: Guilford Press.

Winnicott, D. W. (1960). The theory of the parent-infant relationship. *The International Journal of Psychoanalysis, 41*, 585–595.

Winnicott, D. W. (1990). *The maturational processes and the facilitating environment.* London, UK: Karnac.

Zevon, W. (1996). *I'll sleep when I'm dead* [recording]. Burbank, CA: Elektra Records.

9

How Couples Change

A Psychobiological Approach to Couples Therapy (PACT)

Stan Tatkin

COUPLES THERAPY HAS a long history of ineffectiveness (Gurman, 1973), possibly because early approaches attempted to retrofit cognitive, behavioral, and psychoanalytic models to a *dyadic system* (the couple), and possibly due to lack of specialization in the field of dyadic systems. Systems theory seemed to promise a more appropriate model for family therapy; however, that too did not fully address the intersubjective, phenomenological problems of the two-person system (Olson, 1970). To meet the complexity of the couple system, an integrated psychobiological approach to couples therapy—one that addresses that system from a bottom-up, procedural memory perspective—is recommended. In essence, this approach combines the contributions of three key domains: attachment theory, arousal and affect regulation, and developmental neuroscience. The last of these dimensions encompasses social–emotional deficits and issues of brain integration along both the horizontal (right–left, left–right) and vertical (top–bottom, bottom–top) axes.

A psychobiological approach to couples therapy (PACT) is a capacity model. Instead of looking at conflict or at the content of conflict, we look at the psychobiological capacities of partners to remain self-regulated and to maintain safety and security through effective mutual regulation. I have proposed that partners in a primary dyadic system are only as successful as their ability to interactively regulate each other's autonomic nervous systems (Tatkin, 2003). One aspect of successful coupling is the combined ability of both partners to mutually generate positive high states of arousal (e.g., exciting love) and positive low states of arousal (e.g., quiet love), and to foreshorten and attenuate negative low and high states of arousal (e.g., threat, distress).

For instance, Sam and Max reveal during our initial therapy sessions that they are able to create high sympathetic states of exciting love (dopaminergic) through the use of direct eye gaze, joint attention (mutual joy from a third object), and conversion of self-excitement (e.g., exciting news for one partner) into something useable for mutually amplified exciting love (e.g., "I'm so lucky to be here with you"). These are all social–emotional skills in the co-generation of high positive states. However, both Max and Sam have great difficulty creating or managing quiet love (serotonergic) because the quiet but alert state makes Sam deeply anxious. More troubling, they have difficulty, as a regulatory team, foreshortening and attenuating distress. This functional deficit can easily create a pattern of mutual dysregulation, leading to increased threat and spiraling into avoidance or aggression that cascades toward dissolution of the relationship.

PACT takes into account each partner's psychobiological capacities in areas of interoception and somatic awareness (e.g., anterior insula); theory of mind (e.g., orbitofrontal cortex, anterior cingulate, and temporal–parietal junction); recognition of facial expression (right-hemisphere limbic structures); use of prosody (right-hemisphere speech structures); inhibitory systems (e.g., ventromedial bundle and ventral vagal system); and other mediators that allow individuals to remain friendly and deal quickly and effectively with distress. PACT views threat as one of the most troublesome and predictable factors influencing relationship dissatisfaction. Thus, the PACT process of change focuses on how partners deal with threat and the brain's tendency toward automation, and ultimately guides them toward the stance of secure functioning.

Threat in the Dyadic System

Arguably, the human brain is built more for war than it is for love (Solomon & Tatkin, 2011). This bias serves the human need for survival. We must remain alert to danger and threat in order to survive. However, this threat system, which is intended to keep the species alive, can work against safety and security in relationships because the brain is constantly ticking up threat cues in the form of visual, auditory, kinesthetic, and even olfactory cues. Thus, in attempting to move couples from war toward love—in short, toward desirable change—the PACT therapist is concerned not so much with threat in the large sense, but in the microscopic sense. PACT focuses on threat that is built into all transactions and interactions; in other words, the misattuned moments between individuals.

Threat and the Brain

Threat detection is fundamentally a subcortical operation and may be understood as noncognitive because it is informed by implicit memory systems (Joseph, 1996) and because its actions are deployed by the autonomic nervous system (Schore, 1994). Various subcortical structures and networks have been implicated in threat detection and management. For instance, activating hypothalamic centered systems, such as those driven by the amygdala, employ the motor thalamus, stratum, and periaqueductal grey, as well as neuroendocrine processes involving both the adrenal and pituitary glands (i.e., the limbic–hypothalamic–pituitary–adrenal [LHPA]). All these subcortical structures regulate the fight–flight–freeze response. Even the anterior insula, which is a primary center of the disgust response, is intimately involved in threat reaction (Herz, 2012; Rozin, Lowery, & Ebert, 1994; Wicker et al., 2003).

Also hooked into this system is the right hemisphere's predilection for recognizing threatening facial expressions, vocal intonations, gestures, movements, and postures. The left hemisphere's ability to recognize dangerous words and phrases leads back to the amygdala, subthalamic, and stratum axis via Wernicke's and the inferior parietal area (Ekman, 1993; Joseph, 1996; Schore, 1994). Deeply inhibitory reactions to life threat, wherein one cannot fight or flee, involve the reptilian branch of the 10th cranial nerve, often referred to as the dorsal–motor–vagal complex. An extreme reaction to internal and external threat cues leads to energy conservation withdrawal, stilling, and collapse (Porges, 2001). Somatic responses to internal and external threat stimuli have been elaborated on by somatically oriented trauma specialists (Levine, 1997; Ogden, Minton, & Pain, 2006; van der Kolk, 1984).

Hypothalamic-mediated threat states tend to compromise error correction ability and downregulate brain structures, leading to dissociative fear or rage. Dorsal–motor–vagal dominated life-threat states greatly compromise similar structures. Thus, partners who are dysregulated are unable to properly resequence or contextualize stressful interpersonal interactions. Mutual dysregulation in dyadic systems necessarily leads to a psychobiological threat response, which may in turn lead either to violence or to systemic avoidance.

Moreover, the brain has a negativity bias toward picking up internal cues as well as cues from the environment that it considers dangerous. Assuming this bias, there is a strong tendency to recall negative experiences over positive ones (Vaish, Grossmann, & Woodward, 2008). The unattended mind is negatively valenced, leaning toward aversive emotions, such as fear (Rozin & Royzman, 2001). This negative bias means that relationship security is easily threatened by often minuscule errors in the intersubjective back and forth between individuals.

Sam and Max are what PACT therapists term a *high-arousal couple*. Besides having frequent conflicts, their biological set points are biased toward the high-sympathetic end of the arousal spectrum; hence their ability to generate high positive states. They are able to create high negative states, as well. For example, Max finds Sam's eye rolling threatening enough that he launches a spate of threatening words and phrases. The amygdala seizes on these words, leading Sam to jut out her chin, bare her teeth, and strike back sparingly with a barely controlled, "I can't stand you!" These are just the macroscopic threat cues. During our sessions, I use video frame-by-frame analysis of their fights to reveal the micromovements, microexpressions, and microshifts in prosody that appear prior to obvious signs of heightened arousal. PACT therapists are particularly interested in the rapid microevents that take place in the couple's intersubjective field, and in sharing these observations with the partners as a means of training them to regulate their arousal states.

Threat Detection and Attachment Needs

The instinct to survive is based both on threat detection and on attachment needs. These two mechanisms can come into conflict when primary attachments offer hope alongside danger. Attachment formation creates bias in procedural memory for injuries suffered in primary attachment relationships. Attachment memories are state-dependent, and thus alter perception to collude with both memory and state. This is sometimes referred to as a "reweighting" of discrete neuropathways (Seung, 2012, p. 93; Shapiro, 2001). Partners are likely to make more errors in perception and appraisal when they feel under threat, which in turn leads to increased feelings of interpersonal danger.

Max and Sam continually trigger threat in one another. This state change not only compromises error-correcting brain structures, but also reweights neuropathways (procedural memory), which can occlude other contravening memories and greatly skew perception, especially visual and auditory. Additionally, Max and Sam encounter problems with language processing under threat—in either hyperaroused or hypoaroused states—which increases their rate of misappraisal considerably.

"You're angry with me!" declares Sam.

"I wasn't before, but now I'm getting very angry," replies Max, his face flushing, jaw set, and eyes glaring.

"If you don't stop giving me that look, I'm walking out," Sam says in a threatening, resolute tone.

"You're already out the door anyway. I can tell."

"No! Why are you twisting things?" says Sam, rolling her eyes. "You're the one who's angry, and I need to leave if you continue speaking to me that way."

"So leave! That's what you do. Just go!" Max shouts. He has now convinced himself of Sam's intentions and trajectory.

In particular, organized insecure models of attachment, such as those found in the distancing group (avoidant) and clinging group (angry resistant), are structurally more inclined toward threat perception and reaction than toward bonding, due to continuous relational trauma in the caregiver–infant intersubjective field. The avoidant individual's sensorium, for example, is on alert for threat related to engulfment, coercion, exploitation of the self, attack on the self, humiliation, and shame. Therefore, part of the avoidant individual's attachment structure is the psychobiological certainty and expectation of further injury matching or exceeding that experienced during childhood. Thus, the avoidant person operates in a manner that places the self above relationship, continuously guarding against threats to his or her autonomy, through distancing behaviors. Similarly, the angry resistant individual is inclined to anticipate rejection, withdrawal, punishment, and abandonment. Thus, this individual operates in a predictable fashion according to his or her psychobiological certainty and expectation that self-activation in a primary attachment relationship will lead to abandonment, and so employs predominantly clinging but also distancing behaviors.

Max's internal working model is oriented toward clinging and negativism. Sam's defensive structure is distancing. Because they possess little understanding about who each is (in terms of attachment orientation), their threatening behaviors remain unbridled and without any repair; thus, they become more predatory, perceptually speaking, to each other. A primary reason threat continues unabated between insecure partners is that their internal working models are one-person oriented. As such, their interactions are insensitive, unfair, and unjust too much of the time. They are neither collaborative nor cooperative. Theirs is a win–lose culture.

Individuals who are structurally disorganized often suffer from a psychotic core, making them, by definition, unpredictable (Cassidy & Mohr, 2001; Tatkin, 2014). These organizations are not synonymous with disorders of the self because individuals with a personality disorder are more predictable than are those who suffer an early, severe, and continuous relational trauma. In addition, a diathesis model of pathogenesis includes genetic and constitutional predilections toward developing various psychobiological disturbances.

Automation and Real-Time Interaction in the Dyadic System

Pair bonding is based on recognition of familiarity and familial familiarity. Partners generally do not pair-bond voluntarily if either experiences the other as too strange and unfamiliar. Therefore, a procedural memory and affective bias toward familiarity exists from the beginning of a relationship. All novel experiences that follow (processed by the neocortex) eventually become automated in procedural memory (processed by the subcortex) (Beaunieux et al., 2006). Thus, partners' focus and attention are replaced by automation, which is driven by a procedural memory system covering the lifespan of each individual to date. Notably, automation can become the enemy of successful long-term romantic relationships due to the fact that it gives partners the false impression of knowing one another when, in fact, they have switched over to a memory system that can increase misattunement, threat, and dysregulation. The only antidote to the problem of the automatic brain is *attention _and_ presence*—features that naturally existed during courtship when partners' experience of each other was still novel. One of the fundamentals of change in couples is the therapeutic reestablishment of attention and presence.

Sam and Max do not pay close attention to each other. They act and react automatically, according to memory. They *think* they know each other's intentions, motivations, thoughts, and feelings, which is why they are almost continually in trouble. When forced in therapy to pay close attention, moment by moment, to each other's face, eyes, voice, movements, and muscle tension, they begin to see their automatic reflexive actions, their misappraisals, and their partner's stranger-ness (novelty). As they develop presence, especially through the near-visual field (ventral visual system), they reintroduce novelty, love, and interest in the other in real time.

Because automation is non-conscious behavior by definition, declarative explanations offered by partners under stress are highly unreliable and given to confabulation. Moreover, partners experience real-time interactions as occurring too rapidly to fully process in the moment; therefore, especially when under threat, they tend to operate reflexively and automatically according to procedural memory. Conflict can accelerate as partners quickly become threatening to each other.

Increased arousal may also be correlated with increased perceptions of threat. As arousal increases, so does the number of errors people make in appraisal. Again, the automatic brain is involved in this calculus. In the heat of the moment, partners pull from state-dependent memory, causing them to misinterpret present events. They may employ low-level defenses, such as *denial, projection, projective identification, splitting,* and *transference acting out* (Masterson, 1981).

The Antidote of Coregulation

From a psychobiological point of view, the key to couple safety and security is not only the individual's capacity for social–emotional engagement on a rapid level using integrated systems, but also some modicum of hard-core cortical (i.e., frontal area, ventral vagus) engagement that is able to slow things down and to keep resources high enough to stay engaged. If the threat level rises too high, partners will become dysregulated and move into a state that Porges (2001) calls *danger.* Hypothalamic–amygdala propelled systems become fully engaged, and striated muscles in their faces, arms, and legs become ready for action. This sympathetic readiness for dealing with danger is expressed outwardly in subtle and not-so-subtle behaviors emanating through the face, skin color, pupils, voice, movement, and posture.

The higher cortical areas must be fully resourced with glucose and oxygen to operate properly; however, as arousal increases, these resources become less available. As a result, the automatic brain (i.e., subcortical processes) takes over the entire system. Of course, partners rarely do any of this purposely. Because they are driven by a procedural memory system, partners are unaware of what they are doing or why they are doing it. Most the time, this is the case with all of us during ordinary day-to-day life. Our automatic brain engages the environment according to memories and other rules of engagement, some of which are determined by personality structure. This process makes us predictable and also exacerbates our tendency to be rigid and maladaptive while under stress.

In the context of a primary attachment relationship, the only antidote to threat-related hyperaroused or hypoaroused states is unequivocal signals of friendliness. Whereas repeated interpersonal threats will likely overwhelm both partners' ability to self-regulate enough to sustain social engagement, removal of threat allows for the upregulation or downregulation of the autonomic nervous system. Therefore, the PACT therapist shows couples that downregulation of the threat process must be interactive and mutually achieved. This, again, is a neurobiological matter, much of which is subpsychological; that is, the recognition process for both friendly and unfriendly cues is automatic, primitive, and often subconscious. Partners in states of conflict or distress do not have time to engage the higher error-correcting cortical areas of their brains, such as the anterior cingulate and the orbital frontal cortex.

I could instruct Max how to regulate himself in the face of a threatening Sam, and do the same for Sam, but this one-person model would be minimally useful when Sam and Max go "live" in their relationship. In PACT, the goal is to help Sam learn how Max works, so she then knows how to help him shift his state. And vice versa. In other words, both Sam and Max must become experts on each other and know what to do in any and all cases of distress. To accomplish this, both partners must reorient to a two-person psychological system in which both are in each other's care, and not simply their own. This is challenging for the therapist to facilitate because insecure cultures inherently distrust this idea of cross-care.

Nevertheless, I postulate that a couple's capacity to change so the partners are able to effectively co-regulate, or to be a good co-regulatory team, determines the dyad's success over the long run. A dyadic system that is poor at co-regulation is likely to accrue threat, which negatively reinforces procedural memory and becomes increasingly amplified by further interactions. This process of accruing threat leads to hyperarousal and dysregulation of the couple system, and eventually results in either violence or systemic avoidance. Many couples react to threat by avoiding interaction in a manner similar to that seen in cases of untreated trauma or phobia.

Error Correction in Real Time

The psychobiological view of couple relationships is based on the no-fault principle. People are assumed to be doing the best they can, and rarely are there angels and devils in couple work. Even if behavior appears malicious, it often occurs automatically, through subpsychological, implicit mechanisms that keep partners from any awareness of what they are doing. This is especially true when partners are under stress. When pressed to explain what they are doing and why, partners will often make up a reason. We know from split-brain operations that the left hemisphere, when faced with a void, will make things up (Funnell, Corballis, & Gazzaniga, 2000); it will confabulate information. The left hemisphere may try to organize implicit experience by putting it into a declarative format. But that declarative format is at least partially, if not completely, flawed. Psychobiologically speaking, people make errors all the time. These errors typically are tolerated when people are in a good state of mind and feel friendly toward one another. However, as arousal or distress or physical pain or a feeling of threat increases within a relationship, these errors come into awareness as threatening. For instance, both Sam and Max can sound like they are making good sense when they argue their points, but I know not to automatically believe narratives, especially self-reports, due to error and the inability of patients to understand implicit drives and motivations. The PACT therapist instead looks to somatic markers, shifts and changes in states, and coherency issues in speech to discern a more accurate map of what's real and true.

The same dynamic is seen in the phenomenon of *one-mindedness*. One-mindedness, or the fusion of two minds, is commonly considered a pathological error in narcissistic states of mind (Masterson, 1981). Marion Solomon has written extensively on narcissism and romantic relationships (Solomon, 1985, 1989, 1991, 1998). The fused narcissistic mind feels threatened by the differences it sees in another mind, which has its own intentions, motivations, thoughts, and feelings. In narcissistic personality disorder, awareness of separate mindedness is threatening to the narcissistic individual. It is experienced as an attack on the self. On the other hand, nonpathological one-mindedness is often experienced in friendship or romantic situations. For example, during the initial phase of infatuation in their relationship, Sam and Max enjoyed a kind of fusion—albeit, in fantasy—that they were of one mind. The fact is that they were only approximating each other's minds. When they felt good about each other, this approximation was not troubling. However, as distress increased, the approximation of minds became painfully threatening.

In verbal communication, people use words in a highly subjective manner; as a result, their meaning is often incorrectly assumed by others. Romantic relationships aside, teaching or being a therapist should provide you with the humbling experience of being misunderstood more often than you might like. In the context of dyadic systems, time and duration of contact are essential to allow for error correction and repair. Short interactions in which misunderstandings occur are doomed if there is no time for error correction repair. It is essential to make time to fine-tune meanings and to engage in the back and forth of error correction needed for successful verbal communication.

Nonverbal communication is also fraught with errors. A tilt of the head, rolling of the eyes, or dipping of the voice can mean nothing to one individual, yet be quite threatening to another. An individual whose resting face naturally has downturned corners of the mouth and furrowed eyebrows may unwittingly send messages of unfriendliness to the outside world. However, this person's partner can error-correct and modify these perceptions by spending time with him or her and accumulating data that controvert initial impressions. Again, time is essential for error correction and repair. However, if partners continue to mistake verbal, vocal, and facial cues, perceived threats will amplify and their relationship can quickly spin out of control.

Secure Functioning in the Dyadic System

PACT focuses on secure functioning as the pinnacle of couple help and the cornerstone of change. The therapeutic goal is to facilitate secure functioning in the couple system, regardless of the individuals' personalities, pathologies, attachment styles, or other factors commonly used to evaluate couple prognosis. PACT therapists maintain that any partner can have a secure-functioning relationship, even if neither individual has a secure attachment style.

This principle is evident when witnessing homeless couples, couples in the military, and other dyads that are forced to collaborate in contexts of environmental danger. For example, cop-car partners must first and foremost protect each other, despite their respective personalities or attachment styles. Not only is it a cultural expectation in the police department that partners remain loyal, cooperative, collaborative, and dedicated to one another, but constant threats from the environment reinforce that solidarity. The same can be said for those in the military, particularly special forces units. Members of the special forces make the grade not only by virtue of their physical ability but their ability to form secure-functioning relationships within their group. Any special forces individual who fails in this respect may be viewed as dangerous by the rest of the group.

Dyadic Creatures

As attachment theory confirms, the human being is a dyadic creature. We are conceived as a single-cell organism, but then through mitosis, we divide into many cells and become a fetus. At birth, we are psychobiologically connected to our mother, and subsequently, if not to our mother, then to some other adult caregiver. Without any adult caregivers, we would not survive infancy.

In her work on the psychobiological development of the human infant, Margaret Mahler (1980) described several phases, beginning with autism and symbiosis—which both involve psychological fusion between infant and caregiver. It isn't until the differentiation phase that the baby begins to separate from his or her caregiver. At that point, the baby begins to have a sense of his or her body as separate from other bodies, and especially from the caregiver's body. In the hatching phase, the baby's sensorium comes fully online, and the infant begins to view the outside world as separate from the inside world. Increasing focus is put on the outside world as well as on differentiating between the mother and not-mother experiences. This separation phase is elaborated more fully in the practicing phase, as the infant becomes a dyad in the classic sense with the mother figure. This process develops in more complex ways during the rapprochement phase and throughout life, toward object constancy. Sigmund Freud (1949) similarly defined infancy as a period of fusion, followed by a period of separation, culminating in the oedipal complex. The process of going from dyads to triads has also been discussed at length by Melanie Klein (1957), Jean Piaget (1932), Eric Erikson (1950), Lawrence Kohlberg (1971), and others. Despite the fact that there is a developmental leap from dyads to triads—triads being symbolic for interacting with groups of people—we nevertheless continue to be dyadic creatures.

The mammalian drive to pair-bond is not only for procreation, but also for security and preservation of the species. Mammals who pair-bond protect each other from environmental dangers, including predators. In this respect, we are not that different from some other animals. For example, the dik-dik, a deer-like species found in the African landscape, pair-bonds for mutual protection from predators and is famous for appearing to be dedicated in partnership. They seem immutably bonded to one another throughout their lives, and when one partner of a dik-dik couple dies, the other dies shortly after. Obviously, this is not necessarily the case with human couples.

Whereas the animal kingdom has relatively limited resources for mutual support compared with humans, we can draw upon our higher reasoning and social skills to keep one another safe. By *secure functioning*, therefore, I mean the ability of that two-person relationship to function according to principles of true mutuality, justice, fairness, and sensitivity. Secure-functioning relationships, in sum, are relationships in which both parties have a mutual investment in providing safety and cover for one another in the face of a dangerous environment. The central idea is that two people band together, have each other's backs, see themselves as being in the foxhole together, and form a protective bubble around one another in order to survive and thrive.

Presenting the notion of being in a foxhole together often changes partners' views of their relationship purpose. For most couples, this idea is appealing because it makes sense. It grounds the purpose of being together in animal survival. PACT therapists commonly engage couples by questioning their purpose for being together:

"Why should you be together?"

"What purpose do you serve?"

"What do you do for each other that you couldn't pay someone else to do?"

Frequently heard responses include "We love each other" or "We have children" or "We have so much history together" or "We don't believe in divorce." These answers seem to disregard the more basic purpose of being in a foxhole together, which implies they that they must voluntarily position themselves as stewards of each other's safety and security.

In PACT therapy, partners enter into an agreement to protect each other from the harsh, unforgiving, and unpredictable environment, with all its dangers. They agree to be experts on each other because they must in order to survive and thrive. They agree to make good use of the resources they free up by taking off the table fears of abandonment, betrayal, and other threats to self and other. This they do simply because they *can*, and if they resonate with the foxhole image, they do it because they *must*. The notion of a foxhole changes partners' perspectives and focuses them away from personality, mood, and various internal and external forces that encourage them to view themselves as one-person psychological systems.

Theory of Mind

The early infant–caregiver relationship is one in which the adult is emotionally and physically primed to focus his or her attention on the infant. A secure environment requires that the caregiver be interested in focusing on the baby not just once but over and over again. The process of secure attachment is filled with interruptions and failures, but also with an interest in correcting those failures by making adjustments. Those adjustments can be considered corrections or repairs. Winnicott's (1953) concept of the "good-enough" mother assumes that the mother is imperfect and must be imperfect in order to fail and repair. Repair is what cultivates security and, ultimately, love. The care-giver repeatedly loses the baby and then finds the baby again. This process continues beyond infancy, as the caregiver is willing to find the small child, the adolescent, the young adult, over and over again as the growing individual's mind develops over time.

This process requires a flexible, interested, curious, and self-reflective mind. Caregivers who do not possess a *theory of mind*—that is, they cannot imagine their own mind let alone another's—cannot provide what Peter Fonagy calls *reflective functioning* (Fonagy & Target, 1998) or what Dan Siegel (2010) terms *mindsight*. The same can be said of the psychotherapist who is unable to find the baby in his or her patients. The therapist must be available and have the mental capacity for reflective function, intuition, and creative use of the self to attune and reattune to each patient. In adult coupling—whether it be friendships, sibling relationships, work relationships, or romantic relationships—the same principle applies. Partners in a dyad must be interested in finding the baby in the other person. This requires a process of attunement, misattunement, and reattunement. It is a process of making errors and correcting them, or creating injury and repairing it.

Sam and Max demonstrate poor theory of mind. Neither seems able to imagine the other's mind; they cannot put themselves in each other's shoes. The PACT therapist must determine if this perceived inability is due to defense, resistance, or deficit. A deficit can be a "software" (functional) or "hardware" (structural) problem, or both. In the case of Sam and Max, it is functional because they demonstrate theory of mind when pressed, and their continuously high threat levels and persistent defenses against self-injury explain their lack of empathy and understanding. In other words, their behavior is a purposeful means of protecting themselves and their interests. The therapist can feel this purposefulness in the countertransference. In structural cases, poor theory of mind is due to a neurological deficit going back to early childhood and is therefore neither a defense nor resistance. In cases involving these structural deficits, the therapist may begin to experience the countertransference of being cruel, akin to criticizing a paraplegic for not walking. Identification of structural deficits is important because the partner usually experiences them as purposeful, and the therapist may mistake the behavior as a defense.

Vertical Learning, Therapeutic Alliance, and Coregulation

We learn by repetition. We change through repetition, as well. Even our internal self–object representations are modified through experience and repetition. Horizontal learning can be described as the acquisition of factual knowledge across a wide range of areas; for example, memorization of the multiplication tables, the states of the union, and the elements in the periodic table. Vertical learning, on the other hand, allows us to gain complexity and to know ourselves and to understand ourselves through time.

Change in therapy is a process of vertical learning. Patients have an "_aha_" experience when they are able to connect ideas, memories, and feelings that drive their behaviors and interactions. In a secure-functioning relationship, partners inherently have the resources to handle complexity and to push development forward. In contrast, partners in an insecure or dysregulated dyad tend to squander those resources as they focus instead on defending against perceived or anticipated threat. Therefore, the PACT therapist provides insecure partners with a safe and secure therapeutic relationship in which to explore their own minds in a manner previously unavailable to them.

In terms of neural connectivity, vertical learning involves not so much the creation of new neural pathways as the reweighting and reconnecting of old ones. These neural pathways are like dirt roads: They are unused and therefore out of awareness. When they are reconnected, previously lost memories are regained.

In the therapeutic process, memories change as a patient moves toward complexity. Bad experiences are metabolized by the brain, which gains the capacity to manage these early experiences. Previously recalled two-dimensional figures become three-dimensional. Splitting is largely resolved. The individual is more inclined to experience him- or herself as simultaneously containing both good and bad, as well as to view others in this light. Memories as well as the states associated with them—both positive and negative—are modified through further understanding and through the co-regulatory process developed between patient and therapist. This involves vertical learning on the part of the patient as well as the therapist, who must have the ability to regulate him- or herself and be fully resourced, relaxed, and available to self-correct errors and engage in repair.

The PACT therapist's ability to regulate the relational field is essential for helping couples move toward secure functioning. The therapeutic relationship allows for the emergence of a therapeutic alliance wherein patient and therapist are fully collaborative and maintain a continuous focus on the task of psychotherapy. Whereas in individual therapy, that task creates an intersubjective third, which is the relational experience between patient and therapist, in couples therapy, partners work on themselves in the phenomenological intersubjective third that is their relationship. Thus, a therapeutic alliance assumes full collaboration between all parties with a shared interest in the task of therapy. Any deviation from these conditions is considered acting out by therapist, couple, or both.

To effect change, the PACT therapist must gain a therapeutic alliance with each partner regardless of attachment orientation. In fact, the manner in which the therapist gains a therapeutic alliance is critical to success. For instance, the therapist must find opportunities during the first session to "rescue" an avoidant partner who feels under attack by the other partner by cross-interpreting the avoidant to his or her partner. The therapist must also locate the avoidant partner's pain and amplify it to create interest in therapy. This must be done with great care due to the avoidantly attached individual's propensity for suspiciousness, devaluation, and dismissal. In contrast, an angry-resistant partner must be supported and not confronted during the first session due to his or her inclination to feel like the identified patient, yet the one who has "tried everything" or "given everything," and who has received nothing for those efforts. This too is accomplished through cross-interpretation to the other partner to serve as a supportive, regulatory function. Cross-interpretation allows the PACT therapist to accurately represent each partner's interests and concerns while getting useable material out on the table for future use and steering the couple toward secure-functioning behavior.

By expecting partners to behave in a secure-functioning manner, the PACT therapist not only encourages them to engage in vertical learning but also encourages them to be each other's therapist or healer. They must learn how to pay attention and be present with one another through close proximity and preferably with eye contact. Partners are expected to co-regulate all potential emotional states and especially those that are distressing. They are expected to mutually amplify positive states, such as exciting love, an addictive dopaminergic state that reignites novelty and pleasure in a relationship (Fisher, 2005; Schore, 2003). Partners are also expected to co-create quiet love similar to that of Winnicott's (1956) going-on-being, a more parasympathetic serotonergic system of being quiet but alert with one another. In particular, the PACT therapist expects partners to quickly attenuate and foreshorten negative experience or distress states.

Moving Toward Secure Functioning

Many years ago, during a group supervision session, James Masterson likened working with individuals with personality disorders to working in a very hot kitchen and said that if the therapist couldn't stand the heat, he or she should get out of the kitchen. In other words, that therapist should work with a different population or switch to another occupation. I subscribe to Masterson's (1983) belief that change occurs through the therapist's willingness to apply and tolerate sufficient therapeutic tension, in support of the self, by confronting or interpreting attempts to act out against therapy or the therapist and/or act out against self-activation.

Self-determination theory (Deci & Ryan, 1985) supports the notion that the level of patient motivation to engage in therapy successfully can be parsed through the Client Motivation for Therapy Scale (Deci & Ryan, 1985; Pelletier, Tuson, & Haddad, 1997). This scale has three overarching classifications of motivation: intrinsic, extrinsic, and amotivational. One of the main tasks for the PACT therapist is to move patients toward both intrinsic and extrinsically integrated forms of motivation. Pelletier et al. (1997) consider extrinsically integrated motivation the highest form of self-determined behavior. For example, partners who decide to continue therapy after resolving their issues so they can maintain their gains would show extrinsically integrated motivation. Because patients rarely come into therapy motivated in this fashion, the therapist must deal with the matter of acting out, an often pervasive attitude of noncollaboration and noncooperation.

The PACT therapist assumes the presence of a sufficient level of distress that can be relieved only by pressuring couples to go down the tube of secure functioning. The therapist thus takes a stand for secure-functioning principles. For insecure partners, this requires a big leap of faith. They do not have experiences in their historical record that can serve as proof that a secure-functioning model would be good for them. They may be attracted to the menu of secure-functioning principles, but should not be expected to know what the food tastes like or if they would like it. Because insecure partners are fundamentally unjust, unfair, and insensitive, and do not view relationships as coming first, they have no reason to accept the therapist's belief in secure functioning.

Long-Term Potentiation and Neuroplasticity

In PACT, change is congruent with basic understanding about the neurobiology of the mind, including neuronal action potential (AP) and long-term potentiation (LTP). AP is basically a charge that is sufficient to fire a neuron. LTP is a cellular mechanism related to learning and memory. LTP involves the building up of synaptic strength between neurons, whereby several weak synapses repeatedly fire simultaneously to create a new (or reinforce an old) neuropathway. In therapy, LTP can be associated with the "*aha*" experience of "getting it." In a manner of speaking, insecure individuals, like connecting neurons, must cross a synaptic cleft of unknowing to forge new neuropathways and acquire new knowledge. In systems theory, this is first-order change. In Piagetian terms, this is accommodation (Piaget, Cook, & Norton, 1952).

The PACT therapist creates neuroplasticity through LTP and AP in the insecure couple (or partner) by locating, amplifying, and leveraging pain and distress. He or she aims to convert lower social–emotional complexity into the higher social–emotional complexity of a secure-functioning model of relating, and maintains persistent pressure on the couple (or partner) to move in this direction. In this way, the therapist pushes insecure partners through the synaptic cleft (or off the cliff in a leap of faith) of unknowing to create a previously unexperienced knowing of secure function. The influence the PACT therapist can exert on partners may result in both neuroplastic and epigenetic first-order changes.

I postulate that effective change in couples therapy involves the following elements: (1) locate pain, (2) amplify pain, (3) maintain pressure, and (4) leverage pain to move toward secure functioning.

Locate Pain

Without pain, the therapist's tools are useless. No pain, no gain. Pain is a huge motivator because it opens the mind to influence. If one partner is without distress, both the therapist and the other partner are rendered helpless. In that case, the therapist must locate the pain of the seemingly nondistressed partner. The therapist accomplishes this by paying close attention to the patient's psychobiological cues and narrative "tells." I developed the Partner Attachment Inventory (PAI), based on the Adult Attachment Interview (AAI; Main & Hess, 1990), as a means to identify pain by delving into early memories with a primary caregiver. It is particularly good at locating pain in avoidant patients.

When working with Sam and Max, I used the PAI to establish how each was feeling distress. Max's pain centered on themes of abandonment, rejection, withdrawal, and feelings of being punished. Sam's pain included feeling misread by Max, sensitivity to feeling attacked, and loneliness—all features of her avoidant nature. Avoidant individuals tend to have difficulty remembering in detail one-on-one experiences with their early caregivers. They have ideas about themselves, their history, and their parents, but lack the autobiographical memory that places them emotionally in their recalled experiences. Sam believes she had a perfect childhood and therefore does not have anything to work on in therapy. For example, when asked, "Who hugged you, held you, kissed you, rocked you when you were a child?" she responded quickly, "Oh, both my parents were very loving." But when asked for a specific memory to back that up, she was unable to come up with one.

Amplify Pain

The PACT therapist has to get partners to hold the identified pain and sustain it so that its meaning becomes important to them. The sequence of questions is designed to stress the patient by requiring him or her to provide a specific autobiographical memory to support each claim. Because of Sam's strong avoidant nature, I suspected she would have great difficulty doing the PAI without becoming depressed. Indeed, she became increasingly troubled by her inability to support her claims that her childhood was perfect. At first she tried to blame her memory, a common defense when faced with this problem. However, during the course of the interview, she became increasingly aware that who she thought she was and who she thought her parents were could not be reconciled. As her pain was amplified in this manner, she became disequilibrated.

Toward the end of the interview I am able to cross-question Max about Sam as a means of amplifying Sam's pain.

THERAPIST: (to Max) Were you aware of how neglected Sam was in her family of origin?

MAX: I had no idea how much she had to be alone and take care of herself. That explains a lot.

THERAPIST: (to Sam) I'm so sorry you've had to take on so much. You weren't allowed to be needy. You were expected to be perfect, perform well for your parents, and put on a good face for everyone. No wonder you get angry when Max complains or needs your attention. How dare he do that when nobody ever allowed you to do the same, right?

SAM: (*head down, tears streaming down her cheeks, gently nodding in agreement*) I just wanted their approval. And I would never get it if I needed anything from them.

By the end of the session, I have a stronger therapeutic alliance with Sam, and she now has a reason to be in therapy. I also have gained her agreement with many of my interpretations and ideas, and can use these ideas as further leverage going forward.

Maintain Pressure

The PACT therapist applies continuous pressure on partners to perform in a secure-functioning manner. This pressure is like pushing partners down a tube that both focuses and limits behavior and attitude. The combination of pressure, focus, and limitation also forces feelings and emotions to arise. For instance, when the therapist expects partners to demonstrate developmental complexity, they will expose their limitations, along with the pain (e.g., fears of abandonment and engulfment) that underlies their developmental delays.

Take the example of a halved bagel with lots of cream cheese in the middle. If you squish the halves together, cheese will come out the sides and middle. In this analogy, the squeezing of the bagel is like the therapeutic pressure, and the oozing cheese is what the pressure exposes in the partners, with which the therapist can then work. Without this pressure, there is no discovery of who the partners are, their true agendas, and their developmental limitations. This pressure is expressed both implicitly and explicitly by the therapist.

Sam and Max keep secrets, especially Sam. To expose their secrets without drawing fire toward myself, I can ask what I call a *corralling question*. This kind of question is placed down the middle (between both partners) as a way of addressing them equally. I ask it knowing it will exert pressure that causes some measure of disturbance to the partners. I pay special attention to their pauses, movements, facial expressions, and flaws of narrative coherence (e.g., deflection).

THERAPIST: Do you guys tell each other everything?
MAX: (looks at Sam) Sure. (to Sam) Right?
SAM: (agrees but lowers her head)
THERAPIST: Wait. I'm not sure you both agree. You weren't together on this.
SAM: (to therapist) What do you mean by "everything?"
THERAPIST: (shrugging) I don't know. What do you mean? (long pause) OK, what wouldn't you tell each other?

Sam responds by revealing that she keeps secrets because she believes she should have more privacy in her life—a common concern for avoidant partners, in particular. This concern is highlighted as I strategically throw into the couple system a question that pressures the partners to take up the matter of what can and cannot be shared between them. Sam's secrets, it turns out, are not threatening to the relationship, but her wish to remain secretive with Max is experienced as threatening to him.

Leverage Pain to Move Toward Secure Functioning

The PACT therapist maintains a clear, focused, and coherent therapeutic stance of secure functioning. As the therapist points the couple away from insecure models of relating, he or she is careful to balance the amplification of pain with appropriate arousal regulation. In Sam's case, I use my body and face, and speak to the neglected child in her, bypassing her defenses. When Sam begins to sob, Max moves in to comfort her. Thus the couple is already moving toward secure functioning.

My stated expectation that Sam and Max conduct themselves in a secure-functioning manner helped shear off their maladaptive defenses. Max's ego-syntonic defenses (e.g., the use of negativism, rejection, resistance, and punishing behavior) soon became ego-dystonic. The same occurred for Sam's distancing, dismissiveness, avoidance, and denial.

Leveraging pain creates interest, which in turn creates AP in the brain. To create interest, the therapist places partners in a situation in which each is stressed, and holds them there. Only then can partners know what they cannot or will not do, which then creates an opportunity to work with the reaction. This is also the point at which the therapist begins to get accurate somatic reactions and pushback, exposing true feelings, wants, agendas, and developmental delays. Without locating and amplifying pain while maintaining pressure, the therapist cannot catch partners in the act of being themselves. This is difficult for many therapists who find holding their patients in distress as unhelpful or unkind. The PACT therapist views it quite differently: Without distress, there is little interest and no discovery worth interpreting.

Therapy, in essence, involves repetition, both in the patient's psychobiological response to inter- and intrarelational stress and in the therapist's therapeutic stance, which points the way forward on a path toward relief. Repetition is what contributes to LTP. In PACT, all roads lead to secure functioning. Substance abuse, lying, secrets, infidelity, and other one-person-oriented forms of self-regulation and autoregulation compete with secure functioning, and so the PACT therapist works to replace these behaviors with secure functioning.

Conclusion

In PACT, change is a work in progress for the couple. Since I began combining the many elements that contribute to a psychobiological approach, I have been encouraged to see change in the couples with whom I work, and now also in the couples with whom PACT-trained therapists work. Having available the tools described in this chapter increases the confidence of the therapist and ensures that couples have the best chance of finding love, not war, in their intimate relationships.

However, there is always more to be done. Future research should examine how the nonlinear process of therapeutic change manifests in specific couple behaviors and outcomes, and how it correlates with relationship satisfaction and other standard hallmarks of change. This is where the rubber meets the road. For example, I mentioned the importance of tension as a prerequisite for change. But how much tension is helpful, and how much tension is too much? Similarly, how much repetition is necessary, and at what point (if any) does it become counterproductive?

Finally, although I have emphasized dyadic systems in this chapter, the change model described here can be applied to individual psychotherapy as well as to larger systems involving three or more individuals (e.g., family therapy). Additionally, the term *couple* encompasses both romantic and nonromantic partners; thus, the ideas contained herein can apply to any dyadic system, and particularly to those that represent attachment associations such as parent–child, sibling–sibling, interdependent friendship, and workplace partners.

References

Beaunieux, H., Hubert, V., Witkowski, T., Pitel, A.-L., Rossi, S., Danion, J.-M., . . . Eustache, F. (2006). Which processes are involved in cognitive procedural learning? *Memory, 14*(5), 521–539.

Cassidy, J., & Mohr, J. (2001). Unsolvable fear, trauma, and psychopathology: Theory, research, and clinical considerations related to disorganized attachment across the life span. *Clinical Psychology: Science and Practice, 8*(3), 275–298.

Deci, E. L., & Ryan, R. M. (1985). The general causality orientations scale: Self-determination in personality. *Journal of Research in Personality, 19*(2), 109–134.

Ekman, P. (1993). Facial expression and emotion. *American Psychologist, 48*(4), 384–392.

Erikson, E. H. (1950). *Childhood and society* (1st ed.). New York, NY: Norton.

Fisher, H. (2005). *Why we love: The nature and chemistry of romantic love.* New York, NY: Owl Books.

Fonagy, P., & Target, M. (1998). Mentalization and the changing aims of child psychoanalysis. *Psychoanalytic Dialogues, 8*(1), 87–114.

Freud, A. (1949). Aggression in relation to emotional development: Normal and pathological. *Psychoanalytic Study of the Child, 3*(4), 37–42.

Funnell, M. G., Corballis, P. M., & Gazzaniga, M. S. (2000). Hemispheric interactions and specializations: Insights from the split brain. *Handbook of Neuropsychology, 1*, 103–120.

Gurman, A. S. (1973). The effects and effectiveness of marital therapy: A review of outcome research. *Family Process, 12*(2), 145–170.

Herz, R. (2012). *That's disgusting: Unraveling the mysteries of repulsion.* New York, NY: Norton.

Joseph, R. (1996). *Neuropsychiatry, neuropsychology, and clinical neuroscience: Emotion, evolution, cognition, language, memory, brain damage, and abnormal behavior* (2nd ed.). Baltimore, MD: Williams & Wilkins.

Klein, M. (1957). *Envy and gratitude: A study of unconscious sources.* New York, NY: Basic Books.

Kohlberg, L. (1971). From is to ought: How to commit the naturalistic fallacy and get away with it in the study of moral development. In T. Mischel (Ed.), *Cognitive development and epistemology* (pp. 151–235). New York, NY: Academic Press.

Levine, P. A. (1997). *Waking the tiger: Healing trauma: The innate capacity to transform overwhelming experiences.* Berkeley, CA: North Atlantic Books.

Mahler, M. S. (Director). (1980). *The psychological birth of the human infant* [Film].

In M. S. M. P. R. Foundation (Producer). United States: Margaret S. Mahler Psychiatric Research Foundation.

Main, M., & Hesse, E. (1990). Parents' unresolved traumatic experiences are related to infant disorganized attachment status: Is frightened and/or frightening parent behavior the linking mechanism? In M. Greenberg, D. Cicchetti, & E. Cummings (Eds.), *Attachment during the preschool years: Theory, research and intervention* (pp. 161–182). Chicago, IL: University of Chicago Press.

Masterson, J. F. (1981). *The narcissistic and borderline disorders: An integrated developmental approach.* New York, NY: Routledge.

Masterson, J. F. (1983). *Countertransference and psychotherapeutic technique: Teaching seminars on psychotherapy of the borderline adult.* New York, NY: Brunner/Mazel.

Ogden, P., Minton, K., & Pain, C. (2006). *Trauma and the body: A sensorimotor approach to psychotherapy.* New York, NY: Norton.

Olson, D. H. (1970). Marital and family therapy: Integrative review and critique. *Journal of Marriage and the Family, 32,* 501–538.

Pelletier, L. G., Tuson, K. M., & Haddad, N. K. (1997). Client motivation for therapy scale: A measure of intrinsic motivation, extrinsic motivation, and amotivation for therapy. *Journal of Personality Assessment, 68*(2), 414–435.

Piaget, J. (1932). *The moral development of the child.* London, UK: Kegan Paul.

Piaget, J. (1952). *The origins of intelligence in children* (Vol. 8). New York, NY: Norton

Porges, S. W. (2001). The polyvagal theory: Phylogenetic substrates of a social nervous system. *International Journal of Psychophysiology, 42*(2), 123–146.

Rozin, P., Lowery, L., & Ebert, R. (1994). Varieties of disgust faces and the structure of disgust. *Journal of Personality and Social Psychology, 66*(5), 870–881.

Rozin, P., & Royzman, E. B. (2001). Negativity bias, negativity dominance, and contagion. *Personality and Social Psychology Review, 5*(4), 296–320.

Schore, A. N. (1994). *Affect regulation and the origin of the self: The neurobiology of emotional development.* Hillsdale, NJ: Erlbaum.

Schore, A. N. (2003). *Affect regulation and repair of the self.* New York, NY: Norton.

Seung, S. (2012). *Connectome: How the brain's wiring makes us who we are.* New York, NY: Houghton Mifflin Harcourt.

Shapiro, F. (2001). Trauma and adaptive information-processing: EMDR's dynamic and behavioral interface. In M. F. Solomon et al. (Eds.), *Short-term therapy for long-term change* (pp. 112–129). New York, NY: Norton.

Siegel, D. (2010). *Mindsight: The new science of personal transformation.* New York, NY: Bantam.

Solomon, M. (1985). Treatment of narcissistic and borderline disorders in marital therapy: Suggestions toward an enhanced therapeutic approach. *Clinical Social Work Journal, 13*(2), 141–156.

Solomon, M. (1989). *Narcissism and intimacy: Love and marriage in an age of confusion.* New York, NY: Norton.

Solomon, M. (1991). Narcissistic vulnerability in marriage. *Journal of Couples Therapy, 1*(3–4), 25–38.

Solomon, M. (1998). Treating narcissistic and borderline couples. In J. Carlson & L. Sperry (Eds.), *The disordered couple* (pp. 239–258). Bristol, PA: Brunner/ Mazel.

Solomon, M., & Tatkin, S. (2011). *Love and war in intimate relationships: Connection, disconnection, and mutual regulation in couples therapy.* New York, NY: Norton.

Tatkin, S. (2003). *Marital therapy: The psychobiology of adult primary relationships: Part 1.* Unpublished manuscript.

Tatkin, S. (2014). Psychoneurobiological clinical challenges in working with disorganized partners in couples therapy: A PACT perspective. *The Therapist*, 8–17.

Vaish, A., Grossmann, T., & Woodward, A. (2008). Not all emotions are created equal: The negativity bias in social-emotional development. *Psychological Bulletin, 134*(3), 383–403.

van der Kolk, B. A. (1984). *Post-traumatic stress disorder: Psychological and biological sequelae.* Washington, DC: American Psychiatric Association.

Wicker, B., Keysers, C., Plailly, J., Royet, J.-P., Gallese, V., & Rizzolatti, G. (2003). Both of us disgusted in my insula: The common neural basis of seeing and feeling disgust. *Neuron, 40*(3), 655–664.

Winnicott, D. (1953). Transitional objects and transitional phenomena: A study of the first not-me possession. *International Journal of Psychoanalysis, 34*(2), 89–97.

Winnicott, D. (1956). Primary maternal preoccupation. In D. Winnicott (Ed.), *D. H. Winnicott collected papers: Through paediatrics to psychoanalysis* (pp. 300–305). London, UK: Tavistock.

10

How Couple Therapy Can Affect Long-Term Relationships and Change Each of The Partners

Marion Solomon

IN THE PAST few decades, neuroscience has overturned our conception of the adult brain as largely intransigent. Instead, we now recognize that one of the fundamental principles of brain function is change—the power of our brain is not in the billions of neurons that populate it but in the connections between them, forming and changing with our experiences. It should come as no surprise, then, that the presence of another person in our daily lives has a profound effect on our thoughts, emotions, behaviors and somatic responses. In fact, recent research has shown that even after we lose a spouse, that relationship continues to affect our quality of life (Bourassa, Knowles, Sbarra, & O'Connor, 2016).

The mechanisms by which our brains are shaped present a paradox: Despite the malleable nature of the connections among neurons, lifelong habits can make significant behavioral changes difficult. We develop like Russian nesting dolls—*matryoshkas*—with each doll representing a significant period in our lives and leaves an imprint on the wiring of our brains (Solomon, M. 1994)[1]. Despite our desire for change, we easily fall into thought patterns and behaviors that were laid down in our past. Our brains are the culmination of our genetic heritage and all of our experiences. To effect positive, permanent change in our behavior toward significant others, especially our most intimate partners, we need to understand what happens with the nesting dolls that make up our current personalities.

How Understanding the Brain Helps in Couples Therapy

Evolution has made the human brain social. The brains of our early ancestors grew exponentially in size around the time that we started living in larger social groups. Over time, the ability to connect and recognize what goes on in the minds of others determined survival success. Such "mindreading" underscores the privileged place that our significant relationships occupy in our brains (Dunbar, 2002). Neuroscience has also shown that while early patterns of relationships tend to be recreated throughout our lives, these tendencies are not rigidly fixed; it is possible to learn new ways of relating to one another with deliberate effort. Sometimes it means using the thinking part of our brains to override the instant reactions of the emotional part of the brain.

Because of the *matryoshka effect*, making a commitment in a new relationship often results in a surge of old responses. With little conscious awareness, a partner can bring up feelings and thoughts that originated in childhood relationships. There are two possible results; instant defenses against being hurt, causing a deterioration in the relationship, or, in a best case scenario, an opportunity to heal old wounds.

I have chosen to focus my work on how repair of primary relationships in adult lives result in healing of early life injuries. By working conjointly with couples, healing is possible while maintaining connection to our core self. In therapy, I focus on changing in how patients react when old memories come up. Patterns of defense and attack or stonewalling and criticizing (Gottman, 1996) can be changed to attuning and understanding each other. What we do in our sessions can translate into new neural wiring patterns and, ultimately, lasting change of the relationship and of the partners. Our new understanding of brain plasticity means that we can begin to grasp our own inner power to remake our minds, revise habitual and unproductive ways of being, and effectively relate with new patterns that far transcend what we were taught in dysfunctional families of origin. This is what I call the largely untapped "wonder of *we*" in a culture that has become unbalanced in its defense and magnification of *me*.

When memories, emotions, and defenses from old experiences are reactivated in new relationships, the possibility for change arises. What occurs in this process is the ability to see with a new perspective experiences reminiscent of past interactions. The essential ingredients of this change include (a) recurrence of the old memories in a new relationship, (b) engaging in the experience in a different way than in the past, (c) incorporating the new way of interacting into the repertoire of responses, and (d) reinforcing the integrated memory structure by practicing a new way of behaving and experiencing in relationships (Lane, Ryan, Nadel, & Greenberg, 2015). Rather than being replaced, memories are revised by incorporating new information through a corrective experience.

Just as in individual therapy, exploring the transference, recognizing when we are seeing old faces in new people, can change the way we perceive both current and past relationships. In a very real sense, that means that it is never too late to have a happy childhood.

Working With Two Brains Rather Than One

When a couple comes in for help, each member seems certain of what is wrong in the relationship: It is their partner. Each wants the therapist to fix the other such that they will learn to love properly. Sometimes the intention of a partner calling for couple therapy is to leave the other working with the therapist to heal their old unfinished business. Some therapists get "caught" in a collusion, believing that one of the mates is the cause of the relationship problem, while the other is a victim, suffering with a disturbed mate. This is rarely the case. Each partner enters the relationship with a history of interactions, and ways to protect themselves when hurt. The two come together, building a system, intertwining their individual patterns of relating. By the time the couple call for therapy, the system has become firmly entrenched.

The brain in love feels like a merger—two becoming one that produces a wonderful sense of timelessness and euphoria that involves little thought but intense emotion. Millions of neural networks, as well as microbes and bacteria are activated, and the brain centers that mediate emotions, sexuality, and the self begin to expand and reorganize (Solomon & Tatkin, 2011). Romantic love releases surges of the neurotransmitters dopamine and norepinephrine and activates brain regions that drive the reward system, similar to what happens when we take addictive drugs (Fisher, Aron, & Brown, 2006). New lovers talk endlessly, intertwine themselves incessantly (often to the discomfort of those around them), call each other baby names—and are convinced that this is a normal state that will continue forever.

New love is like magic: each partner has a fantasy that the other will fill in everything that is missing. The fantasy of each is that the other will recognize and meet important needs. It turns out that what is wished for replicates the bonds of early childhood attachments, to be lovingly held and touched, made comfortable by the presence of another, recognized, accepted, and loved as we are. This is the basis of developing secure attachments. There are inevitable ruptures in the secure connection. Parents and other caretakers must eat, sleep, work, and take care of their own needs. Learning to wait, trusting that needs will be responded to and ruptures repaired, is part of healthy development. And when the fit between parent and child is good enough, this is what tends to happen: secure attachment bonds are imprinted into the brain and affect adult relationships. When attachment is not secure, protective defenses develop, and these continue into adult relationships.

When people fall in love, the seeds of their later battles are already there. Each carries their personal history wired into their brains. It is no accident that of all the possible people to choose from, often the person selected to become the center of our world turns out to have an uncanny resemblance to a person who raised us. We recreate, in our intimate bonds, patterns of interaction that were scripted in our earliest life relationships—how often have we seen someone we know who divorces, only to marry someone just like the partner left behind— hoping that this time, we will feel safe, soothed, and comforted when our brain and body send signals of distress. Too often the partner, playing out his or her own scenario, does the opposite of what is needed. Each then defends or acts out against the other. Love turns to war.

We all have parts of ourselves that, at stressful times, regress to a place where we wish for a loving other who responds with care, understanding, and nurturing. Some partners who had a history of being securely attached find it easier to meet each other's needs at points of vulnerability. Others need to gain understanding and make new choices when vulnerability and pain emerge in the relationship.

In some relationships this occurs naturally. The needs, defenses, and fulfillment of needs are spontaneous, and each helps the other to grow. Home becomes understood not as a physical place but as the couple system itself—two friends celebrating profound companionship while maturing and growing together. This effect was described many years ago by Christopher Lasch (1995) as a "haven in a heartless world." The couple system becomes "home"—a sealed-off entity that interacts as a unit with the external world. The main danger in such relationships is that one individual grows while the other does not want change. Only occasionally does a couple come into therapy with a joint systemic dynamic in which both have a solid basis of mutual loving support and safety. Repair in such cases takes a relatively short time. A couple who married during college was offered jobs in different areas of the country upon graduation. Another couple married when she became pregnant; she miscarried in the third month. Their questions: Should they stay married? Should they try to become pregnant again quickly, or wait? A couple who have been married over twenty-five years felt alone when their children were all away in college.

It is important for the therapist working with partners who have been together over time to attune to what has gone wrong. The problem at the core is rarely the identified problem of money, work, sex, affairs, or other specific issues. The question is what made the primary love relationship not a haven but a danger zone, in which each partner calls on whatever protection they can against perceived emotional assaults by the other. Often, what couples therapists see are partners who, over a long period, have built up defenses against being invaded, attacked emotionally, and/or abandoned by the other. It is necessary then to point out that it is not by chance or malice that this is occurring. The defenses may be wired into each of the partners from early-life events. This kind of wiring is common and out of conscious awareness.

Often these experiences occurred at a time in life before the thinking capacities emerge, around eighteen months of age. It is the age when the left hemisphere comes online and the ability to think in words and produce speech emerges. It is a time when children learn new ways to protect themselves against the pain of disturbing experiences, including abuse or disconnection by the caretakers, who are supposed to provide them with safety and security. When the pain is too great during this early period, the defenses that emerge become wired into the developing brain and can reemerge again as the individuals navigate other significant relationships throughout life.

People have different internal capacities and strengths, degrees of resilience, and senses of connection with others. Some, who experienced early pain in the formative years, tend to regard their environment as dangerous and easily become terrified of abandonment. Others feel constantly intruded upon and put up walls to keep any invasion out. Some learn to fight; others, to flee or to detach from any reaction.

One thing is certain: Not one of us came into the world seeking autonomy. The process of separation and individuation (Mahler, Pine, & Bergman, 1975) does not emerge until the basic needs for belonging, security, and inclusion in a family or family-like system are satisfied. Autonomy requires a secure connection first. The core requirements for attachment bonds must be met before babies become capable of what Margaret Mahler describes as separation/individuation necessary for the psychological birth of the human individual (see Mahler et al., 1975).

Implications for Treatment

As a psychodynamic couples therapist, I repeatedly encounter partners whose complaints about each other turn out to be reenactments of early disappointments in the relationships that they had with their parents. My patients often enter therapy believing that they have left behind unmet infantile needs in childhood, but the imprint of the earliest and, in some ways, most formative relationships persists in our brains, and the minds that emerge from them.[2]

People resist letting go of their dysfunctional, self-protective defenses, despite the fact that their early, learned, traditional ways of being and doing have long since outlived their usefulness. Inevitably it comes up in work with couples. Since these defenses are constructed during a time of rapid brain growth, these primitive defenses are wired into the brain and pop up in adulthood even when we "know better." As far back as the beginning of psychoanalysis (Freud, 1927), the concept of the "repetition compulsion" has helped psychotherapists understand the tenacity of patients who hold on to patterns of interaction that fail to achieve a desired effect, an effect called *resistance* in the literature.

It is not that people do not want to change but, rather, that they lack the knowledge or the resources to behave in ways that differ from those that were learned and wired into their brains early on. What is more, they often fail to recognize that patterns of behavior that they wish to change were protective in childhood. As a result, the brain, driven by habit, reverts to what was reinforced long ago. To overcome these instinctive reactions, we need to help our patients first recognize them and then address their causes, gain insight into how early disappointments are playing out in the current relationship, and collaboratively readjust expectations and desires. Only then can we enable lasting change.

Like Russian *matryoshka* dolls that I mentioned earlier, one embedded in another, with tiny remnants of ourselves hidden inside layers of increasingly larger versions, importantly, the shape of each of our core selves does not change across our lifespan, even as we grow in size. This analogy is appropriate not only with respect to our physical shape—as we can all recognize our younger selves—but also regarding the shape of the emotional self. The way the brain registers events, evaluates others, and creates a repetitive pattern of social interactions remains consistent throughout our lives. For couples therapy, this means we have a tendency to regress to smaller, younger, less mature versions of our emotional selves whenever we are reminded of old relational experiences. That is why we need to understand what those younger selves learned in terms of relating to others before we can facilitate lasting change in the relationships we learned to navigate early. It is not necessary to take an extensive history to ascertain the learned attachment pattern. It unfolds as we observe a couple interacting with each other. Do they sit together or in chairs across the room? How do they respond to things the other says? How does the body react physically when hurt? Do they protect themselves by distancing, reacting in anger, saying, "It hurts me when you say that?" What happens in your body as a therapist as you are in a session with the couple? What thoughts and emotions arise as each partner interacts with the other and with you?

A major challenge for the couple therapist is to identify which defenses are emerging in the dynamics between the partners. Only then is it possible to see how they unconsciously use these defenses to protect themselves. As noted, the problem is that often these defenses were built during a time in which the infant was preverbal, or almost certainly when the brain was still in development. As a result, spoken language, which most couples rely most heavily on, can be an ineffective way of probing the deeper issues that are at the root of their problems. In difficult cases, a focus on the body and sensorimotor experiences—with a centering on memories, imagery, cognitions and emotions can help a person who has experienced developmental traumas. Couples come to therapy because they have not managed to solve their communication problems on their own, and that is because they try to use *adult* words, thoughts, and rationale to address their *infant* needs. In therapy, we need to get beyond the trappings of adult rationalizations and address the core feelings that have persisted for decades.

The interactions we see between partners in couples therapy is a mirror of their early world with their caretakers. If we attempt to help them with the problems they present, we are often pulled into the unconscious collusion between the partners. The unconscious of the therapist then comes into play. "Take my side," is the message of each.

For this reason, in my work, the couple system rather than the individual is the focus of attention. All couples develop their own unique systemic approach to protecting the vulnerable parts of each partner, even when there is a similarity of core needs. The needs are some version of our evolutionary mandate for connection.

To help us understand how these defenses manifest during therapy and how the therapist can help the couple recognize their interactive habits, I turn to three case studies from my practice. Each of these cases is designed to demonstrate a different step in the process and to give examples of the different tools I use to first trace the cracks in my patients' early attachment relationships, then discover the defenses that the patients have built to protect against these cracks, and finally, help the couple find new ways of interacting that are less toxic and more fulfilling.

I watch for signs of early attachment failures in the body language and other forms of communication between the two individuals. I often mirror their bodies to get visceral cues into what they are feeling and how they are defending their core self. I then provide opportunities for them to discover the shape and characteristics of their deepest *matryoshka* self and encourage each partner to discover and learn how to provide the security and love that the partner is requesting. "Why should I do that?" some partners ask. "There is no guarantee that you will get back something comparable when you give to the other what they need," I say. "But there is a guarantee that you *won't* get what you need if you don't give."

The Case of Jeremy and Sue: Discovering Defenses

Jeremy and Sue are two intelligent, creative people who have been married for almost twelve years and came to therapy on the verge of divorce. They have an eleven-year-old son, Ben. Both are professionals with advanced degrees, committed to coparenting their son whether or not they remain married. They are financially stable, own their own home, and see eye to eye in their liberal political ideas. The trouble, they say, begins when dealing with day-to-day issues with respect to their son.

I met them soon after Jeremy announced that he is moving out and was filing for a divorce. I learned in our first session that this was the third time Jeremy thought seriously about divorcing Sue and had already taken a one-year lease on an apartment. Sue said that she knows that their differences, especially the disagreements over raising their son, have caused many problems between them, and she worries that what has gone wrong may be unresolvable. But even if they get a divorce, they still have a son to raise, and she felt that therapy would be helpful whether they are raising Ben together or apart.

From the beginning, I shared with them my view of the work in couple therapy: the couple is my patient, and my goal is to help each of the individuals consider why two people who loved each other enough to commit to marriage now find living together too painful to bear. Both had also been seeing therapists individually.

I started the first session by asking them to describe their initial meeting and courtship. From the smiles they demonstrated as they described meeting and falling in love, as well as their description of the first year of marriage twelve years ago, it was clear that they each believed they had found the right person at the time. Both Jeremy and Sue felt loved in the relationship and demonstrated love to each other in return.

Then I turned to the core of the matter. "Something went wrong, and it is causing you both a lot of pain," I said. "When people experience pain in a relationship, their natural reaction is self-protection against further hurt. You might find yourself withdrawing from each other, or you might become enraged. Some people shield themselves in a tight bubble that is impenetrable, while others retreat and disconnect emotionally." I added that when we are hurting, we all use whatever protective defenses we developed early in our lives.

Jeremy indicated that he had a good childhood and continues to have a good relationship with his parents. To better understand what he meant by a "good" childhood, I explained my view of how partners each unconsciously bring their histories into their marriage relationships. A "good childhood," in my terminology, is one in which the normal hurts and disappointments that children experience do not last overly long before repair is made. The occasional small traumas of separation, sadness, fear, or anger are mostly matched with understanding, empathy, and compassion on the part of parents. "If there is emotional pain, the longer it lasts, the more deeply embedded are the protective measures," I told them. "Throughout our lives, the way we learned to relate to our primary caregivers early in life becomes locked in as the template for how we relate to people important to us."

I watched their bodies carefully to see if they were understanding and if they had any emotional reaction. I went on to give examples of how early-life occurrences make us react when experiences reminiscent of the past come up, and I saw them each nodding to what I was saying. Then I said, "If you are willing to work together with me, I will try to help you understand and change the old patterns of interaction that have been making you both so unhappy. Whatever you ultimately decide to do, divorce and coparent or develop better ways of sharing marriage, our goal is to make what is dysfunctional newly functional."

I wanted to be clear that my role was not to determine who is right and wrong in their disagreements. Nor was I concerned with who has more pathology in the relationship. I gave the example of the Addams Family, a television show depicting a family who may appear crazy, but their craziness fits well together and they are happy. "Something is happening in your relationship," I said. "You went from both being very happy twelve years ago to very unhappy now. Our work together will be to alleviate your current unhappiness." On this basis, we made an agreement to work together with weekly double sessions.

As therapists, we must recognize in our office that what is happening in the here and now is often a reemergence of the there and then. How do we, as therapists, help people recognize that they are re-experiencing an old scenario rather than the often inaccurate "truth" that they perceive, without making them feel blamed and shamed? Moreover, how do we do it with two people in the room who may be in the midst of what feels like a life-and-death struggle? Finally, how do we help them change the built-up pattern in which they collude unconsciously in distancing themselves from their vulnerable cores?

Early Sessions

Early in our therapeutic work, Sue's main concern was a fear each time we met that Jeremy was going to inform her that therapy is not working and that he has decided to proceed with a divorce. She always came into the sessions in a state of high anxiety. She was constantly leaving what she felt was her "safe space." When this happened, she was unable to contain her emotional reactions or slow down her flood of words. She recognized that this was a problem and asked me to help her control her anxiety before she takes up too much of the session constantly talking in her attempt to explain herself.

When she began her monologic descent, I observed that Jeremy had stopped talking and simply sat in my office with a blank expression on his face. Sue looked at me for help, saying that she knows it is happening but cannot stop herself. Meanwhile, she saw Jeremy looking at her with glazed-over eyes. Her anxiety level shot up, and she became even more talkative.

In this situation, I try to infer her internal feelings and uncover that shape of the nesting doll who was crying out to be heard. I interpreted her behavior as stemming from a fear of being cut off and abandoned, because she felt that she was misbehaving, as happened often in her childhood experiences with her mother. I told her that I will let her know when she is doing things that take us off track. While her behavior gave a clue as to what part she has played in the negative interactions with Jeremy, I had yet to discover what Jeremy's role in the dysfunctional dyad was.

At first, when I pointed out that she was veering off track, Sue stopped. But in later sessions, she seemed unable to stop herself even when I pointed out that her emotions were making it hard for her to think clearly. This is not unusual as old patterns tend to reassert themselves. When the sessions seemed to go out of control, she stopped herself and looked to Jeremy, asking for reassurance that he would still come back to the therapy sessions. Even when he said he would return the following week, she still felt that the relationship was very tenuous. In fact, of course it was.

In Jeremy's case, he needed to feel that either Sue or I was listening before he would open up. When that was the case, he revealed that he couldn't stand Sue telling him how to raise Ben. He felt that she was constantly criticizing him and telling him that he was doing it wrong. This was an important revelation. But instead of recognizing that his talking was a first step toward repairing their relations, Sue interpreted his comments as simply the precursor to his announcement that he was leaving the marriage. After her misinterpretation had happened several times, I helped her to refocus, asking about how she might feel the tension in her body. She talked about her anxiety, which led to her to talking about the sense of imminent abandonment. We slowed things down for self-reflection. In these moments, she spoke about what happens when she feels anxious and how she does things that she seems to know are not good for her or the relationship. She verbalized that a part of her knows what she should do, and another part of her goes into a state that is obstructive for getting what she wants.

Here, we see the struggle between our fast-thinking, intuitive, automatic, emotional reactions and our slower-thinking, deliberate, conscious, and rational mind. What we therapists have to remember is that, compared with the fast-reacting, emotionally driven limbic brain, this slower-reacting, cortex-driven thinking part of our brain is not inclined to work vas hard and easily regresses to old behaviors. It tries to find shortcuts and the easiest solution whenever possible, to avoid painful emotions. To reengage Sue's conscious, deliberate thinking, I pointed out that I saw a lot going on in her body as she was talking: her arms were tight across her chest, her right leg moving back and forth.

"I don't know how to do this—I need help," she said.

"I see that you are really frightened that you will say the wrong thing and Jeremy will give up and leave you." She nodded but said nothing for what seemed like an unbearable amount of time. I watched Jeremy for his reaction. He remained blank. I marked it for later discussion.

"You want to do it right, Sue, but are afraid whatever you say will cause the relationship to end," I prompted.

"I know what I need to do, but can't do it right," she said. "I look at Jeremy, and I see that he is wanting to leave me."

I was looking at Jeremy and saw the tension and pain under his almost blank expression. "He is in pain . . . as are you, Sue. Yet he is still here." I spoke to the part of her that could still think rationally.

"But every time we come in, I expect him to say, 'Enough, I want to go ahead with the divorce,'" she responded.

I turned to him and said, "Did you know, Jeremy, that Sue walks into every session in such a state of high anxiety because she is certain you are getting ready to announce the end of your marriage?"

He said he now recognizes it but can't do anything about it because he cannot assure her that their marriage won't end.

"So, Jeremy, her concern seems valid. Are the sessions leading you to the conclusion that it is time to get a divorce?"

"No. I wish we could find a way to make it better. I just know that I cannot live like this."

"Is that feeling, that you can't live like this, what you are experiencing right now as we are talking and you see Sue's reactions and know how upset Sue has gotten today?"

"Yes."

"And when you feel that you cannot live like this, what happens inside of you?"

"Something in me just wants to close up."

"You close up! I have noticed that your body seems to close down. I see it, and Sue sees it and can recognize your disconnect. Then she goes into a state where she just keeps trying to explain herself, over and over again, and can barely catch her breath for all the words that keep pouring out. I wonder if either of you have any idea of the root of this anxiety? When did Sue learn that she must talk her way out of this disconnection? Where did this need to explain, to use words to repair relations, come from?"

Neither had an answer.

I said, "It's important because, just as you had experiences that affect the way you relate now, Sue has a history that made her afraid that she will be abandoned if she doesn't do or say the right thing."

Going One Doll Deeper

In a later session, Sue said that she recognized that growing up in her family, she was taught that there is only one right way to do things. When she and Jeremy married, she was so happy and felt so loved that she made up her mind that she must become the perfect wife. She knew that there were things in Jeremy's family that didn't seem right. So she thought it was her job to teach Jeremy the things that he did not learn from his family. When their son, Ben, was born, she strove to make sure that Ben would feel good about himself. So when she sees things that either she or Jeremy does that might hurt Ben, she tries to make sure that Jeremy understands the right way to do it.

She realizes now that these corrections were creating a problem for Jeremy, and she has tried to stop telling him the "right way" to parent. But sometimes he does things that she thinks can be damaging to Ben, and she feels compelled to protect her son.

"So you learned in your family that there is only one right way to do things. And you see that this belief is causing a problem for you now," I reflected.

"Yes. I try not to say anything to Jeremy, but then something happens that forces me to say something." She gave an example of Ben getting out of the car and wanting to cross the street to go to store. "He could have gotten hit by a car. Jeremy didn't realize it was dangerous."

This time, Jeremy didn't glaze over and disconnect. "I knew it was safe," he said, "and I hate it when you criticize me in front of Ben." His words were slow and very modulated.

I commented on the way he was talking, and he said that he tries to be careful with his words when talking with Sue. Whereas Sue finds herself favoring her emotional reactions over her rational mind, Jeremy is the opposite: He silences his emotional, intuitive mind and focuses on the information processed by his cautiously-thinking, conscious mind.

"I always have to think about how to say things, so Sue won't get too upset at me," he admits.

"So when you are quite upset, you have to speak slowly and carefully and hold back any angry feelings," I commented. I asked if it was a familiar feeling.

He said, "Lots of times." But when I asked for any examples earlier in his life, he could only remember having these feelings with Sue. "It happens a lot when she contradicts me in front of Ben, or when she criticizes what I am doing as a parent." A bit later, he remembers that his father always seemed larger than life and was brilliant in business decisions. Jeremy wished his father listened to his ideas when he came into the family business.

I think of how the core issues become organized in a system that gets locked in. Jeremy becomes most upset when his ideas are disparaged or depreciated. Sue reacts strongly when she feels emotionally disconnected or abandoned. She attempts to correct what Jeremy does when she feels that his parenting choices might be harmful in the long term to their son.

The battles all seem on the surface to be over their parenting of their son. But in fact the problem lies in their inner core selves. On Jeremy's part, he seems to react when he feels denigrated by Sue's words. On Sue's part, she reacts to a sense of being abandoned if she disagrees with him. She is caught between needing to help Jeremy see what he is doing that might damage their son, and keeping quiet so as to not damage the marriage.

Overcoming the Compulsion to Repeat Dysfunctional Self-Protective Defenses

The fact is that these partners are reenacting scenarios that keep them both unhappy and could easily result in the thing that neither of them wants: the end of their relationship. Each came to therapy feeling helpless to change and hopeless when they see each other's repeated patterns. Sue recognizes that her own pattern isn't working and asks for help in changing herself. She goes to talk to her individual therapist but can't recall exactly what happened in our couple session.

When the stress in a relationship takes people out of their safe space, rising anxiety levels take them out of their area of competence. When Sue's limbic or emotional brain takes over, her carefully-thinking or deliberate brain closes down. The intensity of her emotion causes dysregulation. She loses her ability to think clearly and remembers little of what happens. Then her punitive superego punishes her and reinforces her greatest fear that she will be abandoned because she is unworthy of love.

The tendency toward high arousal results in emotional states over which the person has no control. The reaction may be with extremes of emotion or, in some cases, with flat affect. Not only is the person feeling emotion, but also the intensity of the emotion causes dysregulation. The surge of overly strong feeling may cause an emotional shutdown, or bursts of feeling that cannot be handled with equanimity.

Creating Lasting Change in Therapy

Both couples and individual therapy bring up core emotions and defenses that are reminiscent of early-life emotional injuries and scars; the work is creating change when this occurs. How do we accomplish this change? First comes an awareness of the pattern of relating that has become established in the dyad. Next, we help partners understand that their interactions result in the opposite of what they want. Along with this understanding is a clarification of what they have been doing: instead of changing something in themselves they have been trying to force change in their partner. "Why should I have to change myself?" is a question often asked at the beginning of therapy. "Because it's the only way to get what you want" is the answer to that question. There is no guarantee that making the changes will work, but not making the changes is a guarantee that the relationship will stay the same. Two years later Jeremy and Sue have gone through some painful emotional experiences. They are still together, and come back for occasional sessions as needed.

The Case of Rodney and Sheila: Disrupting Toxic Bonds Before Change Can Occur

I met Rodney and Sheila for the first time in consultation. Rodney had just told his therapist that they had both decided, after seven years of unhappiness, that they were ready to get a divorce. But, having previously made a appointment with me, they decided to come in anyway.

Rodney began by saying that he has done everything he can to give Sheila a great life. They have a beautiful home, two wonderful children, and many interesting people in their lives because of his very successful career. "Once," he added, "we even had a great sex life." Sheila said that when they decided to marry, Rodney asked her to give up her successful career, which she did willingly, to become a wife and mother. But he is so busy with his work that she gets nothing from him emotionally, she says. He responded, "When you told me that you have no interest in having sex with me, and are turned off to me no matter how many things I do for you, of course I pulled away."

Sheila then replied, "I turned off a year ago, and you know why." He responded, "I have no idea why." I listened to the two of them for a few minutes, and watched their facial expressions, body language, and breathing, making note of who begins, who listens, and whether they respond to what is said or hear something entirely different.

Sheila reported that a year ago Rodney and his business partner were going on a trip to Europe on business. The partner decided to take his wife. "Rodney did not want to take me…. He said that this was a working trip for him, but I pleaded with him to go, and he agreed." She then decided that she would make this trip like a second honeymoon. She bought several negligees and was determined to make the marriage better.

But he ignored her the whole time they were in Europe, and even told her that they had to leave early because he had an unexpected business event come up in New York. She finished her story saying, "I turned myself off completely after that, and have not been present in this relationship since." I asked what she meant when she said that she turned herself off. Rodney responded, "This is something she has always done and it makes me very upset."

They continued saying the same thing in different ways. "Look at all I do for you," he says. "Look at how you are never there for me," she counters. I told the couple that their problem has nothing to do with the trip to Europe or even the lack of sex. "You are fighting a battle in a whole different arena," I say. "And it is at a level below your ability to think about, or at this point to do anything about. This is not about Sheila's disinterest in sex," I told Rodney, "nor," turning toward Sheila, "is it about Rodney's preoccupation with work. . . . It is not about anything you are thinking," I said. "In fact, there are no thoughts involved in the pain that either of you are experiencing."

Even if partners listen to each other's distress at the surface level, they are not getting to the recognition and repair of core needs and feelings that could open the channels necessary to establish a secure attachment between them. Furthermore, arguing repeatedly about the identified problems produces real toxicity portending a rupture in the relationship. In fact, it almost did with this couple, and still might if they succeed in avoiding what they experience as shameful or terrifying issues.

What is needed is an intervention that is emotionally accessible and a welcome outreach to the part of the self of each that has hidden away for almost a lifetime. I point to my collection of Russian nesting dolls and say, "We are all made up of many parts. There is a 'you' that is a functioning adult, and a 'you' that is a little kid, a 'you' that is an infant who needs caretaking, and many other parts of you that come out at different times. We all learn to cope with things that we didn't get emotionally from important others as we go through various phases of life. The earliest months and years are almost impossible to recall because it is a time before words or thoughts. So we do the best we can, depending on the resources with which we came into the world. Some infants get very angry with people who didn't respond to them, and the angry wiring is imprinted in their memory banks. Some infants protect themselves with a thick shield, and learn to close the world out when they are upset. Yet others learn, as soon as they can think, that they must be in control at all times, because no one in their young life seems strong enough to take charge and make things safe. There are many ways a growing young child learns to avoid pain caused by interactions with important others."

Rodney and Sheila each learned ways to shield themselves with protective defenses at times when they believe the other is doing things that cause them pain. Sadly, based on their own history, they are prone to interpreting their partner's behavior as intentionally harmful when no harm is intended. It is in their memory banks. They each read the other's emotional defense of disconnection as an intention to inflict pain.

TREATMENT GOALS

As I described previously, the first step in the therapy is to treat the couple as the patient rather than focus separately on problems of one or both of the individuals. The next goal is to find ways to remain equidistant in the space between the partners, thus allowing the relationship to be at the center. This focus makes it possible to open the channels to the deeper core issues, exploring the relationship in a way that is not shaming or blaming.

Goals with Rodney and Sheila include pointing out each time they begin using the relationship's identified problems—sexual ambivalence and workaholism—when in fact the primitive, chaotic, or frightening feelings of their early attachment failures start to emerge. When these feelings come up, the work of the therapist is to point out the natural tendency to turn away from painful emotions. The partner is called on to collude in protecting the self from these frightening reactions. This collusion results in a disruption of the bonds of intimacy. Each individual then can spend time being upset with the other or cut off from the other rather than acknowledging the reality of the dissociated self state.

Repair, when it happens, generally follows just such disruption of intimate bonds. In fact, in my experience, it sometimes requires a disruption initiated by the therapist. Change takes place over time, peeling off layer upon layer of defenses erected to protect against deep wounds long buried. Each healing experience makes the next one easier.

Still, where there have been early attachment wounds, partners are predisposed to expect pain in the face of perceived injury, regardless of whether or not the mate has intended to cause either pain or injury. Couples must recognize each other's vulnerability to such encounters. At the beginning of the conjoint work, they must be helped by the therapist, accepting responses to feel safe in the presence of the other's dissociated states.

In the second session, when Sheila went into her dissociated place,

I felt a physical reaction in my own body, which was mirroring hers. I pointed my hand toward my chest and said, "Something feels painful here. I'm not sure where the pain is coming from." I watched Sheila as I talked and saw her nodding. Rodney said nothing, but I could see that he was listening. I asked them if they could both take a moment and a few deep breaths.

At this point, I knew it was better if none of us filled the room with words, but I used my breath as a tool to encourage their bodies to mirror what I was doing, and I carefully watched their breathing. After a couple of minutes, I asked them to just pay attention and notice what is happening in their bodies. Sheila began talking about a "black hole" in her chest. Keeping my hand on my own chest, I asked if she remembered feeling this black hole before. She then began a description of a childhood experience in which she talked back to her mother, and her mother, in return, stopped talking to her for days. From this experience, she learned to keep quiet when she was upset and withdraw into silence. In fact, she explicitly remembers disconnecting. "You put a tight shield around yourself and didn't let anyone in," I said. She agreed, and said that she really wanted to break out of the shell she was in but didn't know how.

We stayed with her feelings in the room for a while longer. I then said that it was not hard to understand why Rodney would interpret this behavior as unloving. "When you are hurting, the part of your brain that is designed to deal with emotions takes over to protect you from unbearable pain. You need him to recognize that you are hurting and just be with you emotionally. But he is dealing with how awful it feels to be alone and unloved. He needs you to want to be loving. But at those moments, you just can't. And he can't be there for you."

I asked them to face each other and reach a hand toward the other. When they did, I asked them to look into each other's eyes. "Look at the pupils...... then the whites of the eyes. Then try to picture what is beyond the eyes. It may feel uncomfortable at first, but just stay in that pose until you feel yourself relaxing." This was a beginning exercise for connecting core-to-core.

As the work proceeded in the weeks that followed, they became more capable of responding to that deeper level of the other and were able to follow the therapist's model of knowing what to do to create a healing experience. As time went on, they began to understand each other's learned behaviors. With the therapist's help, they gained the ability to remain present while the partner joins with the therapist in visiting previously dissociated or cutoff parts of themselves. As each became better at remaining present for the other, they both became more willing and adept at knowing what to do to advance the other's sense of security, both personally and in the relationship. Things that once might have torn the couple apart became opportunities for growth.

The Case of Barry and Mandy: Slowing Down Communication

I got a message from Mandy on a Saturday night requesting an appointment. Early Sunday morning I got a similar call from Barry. Their sense of urgency was palpable. I found a time to see them early Monday morning.

They had been separated for three weeks. They were miserable together but also suffering greatly when apart. Barry, unable to tolerate being alone, went on a dating site looking to meet someone. Barry said he made a mistake and used his true name. A single friend of Mandy's called her and said she had seen Barry's profile on the site. Mandy immediately called Barry and was very upset. Barry came over to their home, and the two immediately began to hug. Barry never left the house. He said in therapy that he did this because he was so concerned about Mandy's mental state. I knew this was not just due to his benevolence but waited to hear more.

When they came in for our first session, Mandy said she was filled with anger about the way Barry has treated her for the past twenty years. I could see from Barry's body that he was ready to defend himself. This is a couple who needs lessons in listening, I thought. Sitting with them, even before they began talking, I could feel the race horse wanting to get out the gate. They knew how to fight and hurt each other.

I asked each of them to say what has gone wrong and whether it is a recent problem or one that has persisted for a while. "And," I added, "tell me if you have any idea what started it."

Barry said, "I want to start."

"Is that OK with you, Mandy?" I asked. She said yes.

"If so," I said to Mandy, "please listen carefully, because when Barry finishes, I'm going to ask you to look at Barry and tell him what you heard him say. Is that OK?" I asked. She agreed.

Barry began crying as soon as he began. "I know I left, but it was a mistake. I want us to work out our problems and live together as a happily married couple."

Mandy repeated what he said correctly, and I taught her to ask Barry, "Did I get it right?* Is there anything more that you said that I missed?" She repeated Barry's works very accurately.[3]

Mandy then said, "We've had problems for so many years. You left. I've been working on living by myself now. I'm not sure that I can stand the pain of trying to talk with you about it."

I asked Barry to repeat what he heard Mandy say. He started to repeat but then said, "We're going to get through this. We will be together."

I asked him to go back, to repeat what Mandy said about the pain she felt when they talk about the problems that went back so many years. Barry clearly had difficulty speaking directly to his wife about her pain. But eventually he did say it. Once again, he reassured her that they would get through it.

I asked Mandy to repeat what Barry said. She asked why they had to do this. "I don't like talking this way," she said.

I explained the reason: "You two have been talking to each other for years. But you respond to what is said so quickly that it doesn't look as though either of you feels heard, or feels felt when you talk about your feelings." Behavioral change is hard. Even when we understand the rationale behind the change, in times of heightened emotion, old habits take over. Therefore, we need to retrain behaviors in safe spaces. By this point, twenty minutes into the session, I felt a need to be very gentle with both. They felt to me like very young, wounded babies.

After that first session, we met twice a week for two weeks. Mandy repeatedly went back over how she had been abandoned by Barry. She spent weeks learning how to live her life when he left, because she'd always adapted to being alone. "I was just finding a way to live with what had happened when Barry came back home. How can I trust that this will last? How do I know that he won't leave again?" she asked repeatedly.

Barry continued to argue that leaving was a mistake and that he

---

* This exercise comes from the work of Harville Hendrix and Helen Hunt (2004). Receiving Love: Transforming Your Relationahip And Letting Yourself Be Loved.

was committed to making their relationship work. Mandy only wanted to talk about how upset she was about what he did. Barry repeatedly reached out to her, putting his hand on her arm and shoulder. Mandy was mostly unresponsive. Barry indicated that he was reassuring Mandy because he hates to see the pain he caused her by leaving. But he was also doing it because of his own inability to tolerate being alone away from home, knowing that his grown children were upset about his leaving.

In the fourth session, as Barry reached out to hold her hand, Mandy pulled away. I asked Barry if he could tolerate listening to Mandy's upset feelings, and even be able to hear what she is saying enough to tell her exactly what he heard her say. Barry said that he could do that.

Mandy said that he never wants to listen to her talk about it. "Let's see what happens now, in this room," I suggested. After only a little hesitation, she agreed.

Mandy began talking about how she loved Barry so much when they married and how she truly felt safe when they were together at the beginning. Then she went on to talk about their past. She related that once she had her first child, Barry seemed to disconnect. She has been alone in the marriage from the time her children were born. So she knew early on that if Barry wasn't going to be there, she had to find a way to make everything work for the children and for her. She has been a really good wife and mother, very organized about everything at home, she says. She has lots of friends and is active in tennis and golf. She has friends at the golf club they belong to, and she has learned not to need Barry.

When it was his turn to reflect back what he heard, each time he repeated her words and thoughts I coached him to say, "So, did I get that right? Is there more?" When she finally agreed that he was hearing her correctly, I asked Barry to respond.

He then talked about how he had no idea how to give her what she needed. His family was not a warm or giving group. He spoke of issues with his father and his anger with his dad for being mean to his mom. He learned not to say very much, to keep his mouth shut so his dad wouldn't turn on him. He said that his brother fought back and got a lot of beatings from his dad.

When I asked Mandy to repeat what Barry said, her first response was that she knew all of these things already. "Just tell Barry what you heard him say today, as you are together right now in my office," I replied.

With some help, Mandy was able to reflect to Barry what she heard about his difficult upbringing. When he told her "You got it right," I then offered Mandy a turn. As they each talked and reflected back what they heard from the other, Mandy's earlier anxiety seemed to have calmed down a bit. She no longer had her arms crossed in front of her chest. I could see both of their bodies relaxing.

Then I asked them if they would be willing to try another exercise. Both agreed. I told them that I had an exercise called the lover's pose, which I learned from the PACT model of Stan Tatkin. It is also called the child's pose because one partner is asked to put his or her head on the lap or shoulder of the other, as an infant with a mother. Most couples prefer I call it a lover's pose, because it avoids the fear of being seen as a baby.

"Who would like to start?" I asked. Mandy volunteered, and I gave her directions to begin by leaning against Barry's shoulder and finding a place where it felt comfortable.

She leaned her head against Barry's shoulder but seemed to have difficulty finding a comfortable position. I asked Barry to put his arms around her shoulder to make it easier for her.

Mandy soon said that she remembered her mother telling her that it was hard to hold her when she was a baby. "My mother told me that I kept sliding off."

"So you and your mom never found a comfortable position for her to hold you," I said. "That must have been hard for both of you." But I added, "Babies need to be held and rocked, so whatever your mother was experiencing, it was not what you needed."

Barry's abandonment fears stemming from the early loss of his mother and father were a good fit for Mandy's sense of never being held or seen by a mother who was present but depressed from the time Mandy was born. Neither had any idea how to give the other the very connection that was needed. It was only after their separation that they each came to recognize the pain and terror that they had been warding off for years. Rather than pointing out their defensive ways of disconnecting from emotions that frightened them, it was important to teach each of them behaviors that helped both feel held and seen. Only after a period of months were we able to visit the deeply emotionally painful areas at the core of each.

Final Thoughts

As therapists, it is not enough for us to focus only on the relationship between our patient couple—we must acknowledge that, with each session, we also play a role in the shaping of interpersonal interactions with our patients. Therapists with training in psychodynamic treatment track the transference patterns that emerge in the therapist-patient dyad. We have long known that patients come to experience emotional responses to their therapists that are reminiscent of the bonds they created with their parents. As a result, there are important clues into a patient's early experiences and what defenses they have built up, if we examine how they interact with the therapist. They have similar transference responses to their mate.

In addition, patients may behave in sessions such that they elicit reactions in their therapist that confirm their worst expectations: they may amuse, bore, frustrate, anger, or lead therapists to reject them through a process of projective identification. Analysis is not a one-way process, of course—therapists have their own early childhood residuals as well. What we do with the tendency to interact with another in an intimate relationship is the subject of several chapters in this volume. But when the dyad is not the therapeutic pair but an intimate couple, and the therapist is a third partner in the transference-countertransference process, the resulting transference is both similar and quite different from a two-person dyadic treatment.

What makes change so hard? Ways of interacting were first learned and embedded in the brain and mind at a very early age, sometimes before words. Failure to have needs met at the most vulnerable times in life creates a sense of abandonment, fear, anger, and danger. The pain that goes with feelings of loss, rejection, terror, and rage brings up protective defenses. Future experiences of similar feelings in encounters with others are reminders of the original incidents. Patterns of defenses surge forward in encounters with significant others. This pattern may not happen in work relationships or even in friendships. It is the vulnerability of connecting with an intimate other that recreates the dependency needs and sets in motion the cascade of needs and feelings on both sides that create unhappy relationships.

The cases presented in this chapter illustrate the foundational principles on which I rely in my couples practice. First, it is the job of the couples therapist to treat the couple, not each individual. Second, many of the problems that couples face stem from the unhelpful modes of communication that each individual learned during early life. To change these habitual behaviors, we must first discover the core attachment failure and the defenses that were built up to protect the self from harm. We do that not by examining their history, but by watching the here-and-now interactions in the couple session. It is then necessary to recognize how these patterns fit together like pieces of a puzzle. Unconsciously, partners try to find what they are used to and reinforce patterns that they learned earlier. This process of discovery and recreation is often the biggest challenge, as spoken communication is often inadequate. After all, when the child was building these defenses (at early times when needs were not met), the brain was undergoing a process of rapid development and change.

A useful tool to discover these defenses is to physically mirror a patient's body language so that the therapist can empathize and feel what the patient might be experiencing. Then, these defensive behaviors need to be made explicit, in a way that does not shame or blame to avoid sending the patient into a retreat. Finally, the therapist begins the difficult work of shaping and modeling new healing interactions between the two partners, so that old toxic behaviors are replaced with deep understanding, empathy, and love. The goals include changing the destructive ways partners treat each other and also helping each of the individuals to heal and grow.

Notes

1. I described the *matryoshkas* in my book *Lean on Me: The Power of Positive Dependency in Intimate Relationships* (Solomon, 1994).
2. Psychotherapists have long known that when failures occur in the very earliest relationships with caretakers, the result is an emergence of primitive defenses that protect the nascent self from obliteration. John Bowlby (1958) and Harry Harlow (see Harlow and Zimmermann, 1958) demonstrated decades ago that

we have a primary need for physical and emotional touch: we cannot develop healthfully if our emotional needs are not met, even if we are kept clean and have sufficient food to eat. Harlow's research with primate babies confirmed the need to experience provisions of safety and nurturing and that primates will choose to spend time with the soft cloth mother over the wiry provider of nutrition.

3. This is an exercise I learned from Harville Hendrix, developer of Imago therapy.

References

Bourassa, K. J., Knowles, L. M., Sbarra, D. A., & O'Connor, M. F. (2016). Absent but not gone: Interdependence in couples' quality of life persists after a partner's death. *Psychological Science, 27*(2), 270–281.

Bowlby, J. (1958). The nature of the child's tie to his mother. *International Journal of Psychoanalysis, 39*, 350–371.

Dunbar, R. I. (2002). The social brain hypothesis. *Foundations in Social Neuroscience, 5*(71), 69.

Fisher, H. E., Aron, A., & Brown, L. L. (2006). Romantic love: A mammalian brain system for mate choice. *Philosophical Transactions of the Royal Society of London: Biological Sciences, 361*(1476), 2173–2186.

Freud, S. (1927). *The ego and the id*. London: Hogarth Press.

Gottman, J. (1995). *Why marriages succeed or fail*. New York: Simon and Schuster.

Harlow, H. F., & Zimmermann, R. R. (1958). The development of affective responsiveness in infant monkeys. *Proceedings of the American Philosophical Society, 102*, 501–509.

Hendrix, H. and Hunt, H. L. (2004). Receiving Love: Transforming Your Relationship and Letting Yourself Be Loved. New York: Atria Books.

Lane, R. D., Ryan, L., Nadel, L., & Greenberg, L. (2015). Memory reconsolidation, emotional arousal, and the process of change in psychotherapy: New insights from brain science. *Behavioral and Brain Sciences, 38*.

Lasch, C. (1995) *Haven in a heartless world—the family besieged*. New York, NY: Norton.

Mahler, M. S., Pine, F., & Bergman, A. (1975) *Psychological birth of the human infant*. Basic Books.

Solomon, M. (1994) *Lean on me: The power of positive dependency in intimate relationships*. Simon & Schuster.

Solomon, M., & Tatkin, S. (2011) *Love and war in intimate relationships: Connection, disconnection, and mutual regulation in couples therapy*. New York, NY: Norton.

Tatkin, S. *What is PACT?* Retrieved from http://stantatkin.com/threecolpagex/what-is-pact/

11

Feeling Felt

Cocreating an Emergent Experience of Connection, Safety, and Awareness in Individual and Group Psychotherapy

Bonnie Goldstein and Daniel J. Siegel

THE UNDERSTANDING OF mental health and wellness is evolving, like life itself, to embrace wider and more interdisciplinary perspectives. Through the lens of individual and group therapy we explore the nature of the human mind, the experience of consciousness, the impact of culture on mental health, how our social brains influence our connections with others and with ourselves, and how we provide the kinds of experiences that promote well-being, cultivate resilience, and foster integrative neurological growth.

One aspect of mental life is the process of being aware—that is, the ways in which we know, and have a sense of the known, within our subjective experience of being alive. When we combine a deep view of consciousness and information processing with emerging findings from the study of the social brain, we realize that harnessing the power of these states of consciousness is essential for relational health, equanimity, and contentment and for cultivating a healthy mind overall. The term and the process called *mind* includes consciousness, information processing, and a regulatory function called *self-organization*, which is an emergent process of the mind that is both embodied—it is within our bodies, including our brains—and in our relationships with others (described in detail in Siegel, 2012a, 2012b, 2016). This chapter explores in depth how consciousness itself may relate to this self-organizing function and offers clinically relevant information and practices to cultivate a healthy mind.

Cultivating awareness can be facilitated through the group experience, as we are socialized to come together to speak, share thoughts, exchange insights, and connect through words. In addition, the powerful experience of co-creating stillness, at moments, throughout the group experience can offer a powerful opportunity for individual members and for the group as a whole. T. S. Eliot's line, "Not known, because not looked for. But heard, half-heard, in the stillness" (1968) illuminates the idea that the group psychotherapy format offers an experiential immersion that fosters awareness and exploration of the ways we know and have a sense of the known within our subjective experience of being alive. Applying the lens of interpersonal neurobiology to combine a deep view of consciousness with emerging findings from the study of the social brain, we will see that the goal of the group experience to promote mental health can be greatly enhanced with these new insights and practical applications.

Awareness is fundamental to human change processes. In this chapter we explore ways to cultivate the kinds of conscious experiences that promote change leading to well-being and relational health. In addition, using the lens of sensorimotor psychotherapy, we consider the somatic correlations to this sense of awareness, as well as explore the ways that consciousness itself may relate to this self-organizing function to cultivate health and well-being. This somatic focus is particularly significant because so many of us have been raised in a disembodied world—increasingly focused on technology, sitting endless hours at our desks predominantly emphasizing learning through our intellect, being "human *doings*" rather than "human *beings*." The pace of life has become untenable for many of us. When asked, "How are you?" often the response is "Busy!" There is a complicated duality wherein, on the one hand, to be busy means that we are productive, important, needed, and wanted. Our societal "currency" of accomplishment with the accompanying multitasking may generate positive feelings based on achievement, recognition, and validation. Yet this societal norm comes at an expense: increased stress, anxiety, and depression; less time for taking care of ourselves; and a pressing need for affirmation and recognition from others to validate ourselves. Moreover, a prevalent cultural phenomenon is FoMO, or fear of missing out, which perhaps best captures, in four letters, the underbelly of our currency of accomplishment.

Jordana, a young adult who was the youngest of four girls, described growing up feeling left out throughout her childhood. As a teen she would dress up, preparing to look older, with the ever-present hope that at the last minute she might be told, "You can come too"—though she never was invited. She wore a mask of confidence, hoping to erase her self-doubt through actions of bold self-assertion, presenting the "false self" that the British analyst/therapist D. W. Winnicott (1965) proposed so eloquently in the last century. Jordana's experiences with her peers perpetuated this sense of feeling left behind, this fear of missing out, and over time she seemed to feel alive only when things were in precarious balance, worried that if she didn't jump over ascending hoops she would be left behind, miss out, and fail to live life. Lou Cozolino uses the term *social status schema* to explain the origins of the kind of experience Jordana described: "What is seldom directly addressed in psychotherapy (or the research) is the significance of social status schema, or the role played by early experience in the shaping of how we behave in social groups. Like an attachment schema, a social status schema is a form of implicit memory that shapes how we relate to others and the role we take on in groups" (2015).

With her particular social status schema dictating her behavior, slowing down was impossible for Jordana. She became a human *doing*, rather than a human being, as collaborative work by Goldstein and colleagues has recognized. When she was twenty-four years old, she developed an autoimmune illness. Her awareness of her body was only as "a machine," running both literally (jogging 10Ks and minimarathons) and figuratively (pushing her limits, saying, "I can do anything, go anywhere, face any challenge!"). Her body was merely the vehicle she needed to maintain to live in this way, yet she had little awareness of how she felt, at any present moment, nor was she fully engaged in living a life of embodied meaning that would include feeling authentic, connected, safe, and able to navigate the vicissitudes of life's challenges.

As we worked together, Jordana developed a sense of safety over time that allowed her to add the concept of stillness to her life, while also cultivating a newfound body-based awareness that accompanied her new understanding of both the genetic markers of and the mind–body correlations contributing to her autoimmune illness. She became aware of the fallibility of her body and grew curious about her connection with it within the environments that she created for herself (e.g., How much did she listen to her body's signals as she pushed herself through her work week? Was she aware of her body's response—tension headaches, tightness in her back?) and within her community (e.g., Was she trying to use her body's athletic accomplishments to gain status at any cost to her body?). Together we identified the need for a personal reframe of the societal "glorification of busy" as the foundation upon which our co-created safe space would increase her general well-being and aid her in managing her struggles. As we worked together, prioritizing consciousness as a collaborative goal included the following aspirations: enjoying times of play and calm, experiencing moments of insight, gaining validation from within rather than from achievement and recognition, and noticing and finding meaning within joyful moments. Thus began a journey to expand Jordana's conscious awareness of her body's intelligence—awareness of the ongoing communication the nervous system provides, of the moments of appreciation after movement/exercise as the exertion of muscles leads to chemical releases in the brain (oxytocin, endorphins). Such pleasure is self-reinforcing, leading her to seek out those same healthy sources of pleasure, such as the exquisite sensitivity of her skin as she immersed herself in baths, pools, even oceans.

Therapeutic orientations that include a central focus on the body have burgeoned over the past half-century and include Reichian therapy, bioenergetics, Rolfing, the Alexander technique, Hakomi, Sensorimotor Psychotherapy, and Somatic Experiencing. Sensorimotor Psychotherapy is the approach described below for clients such as Jordana because it prioritizes a body-oriented approach as an adjunct to traditional psychodynamic psychotherapy's verbal narrative—the client's story. Pat Ogden's lifelong work integrates body-based therapeutic interventions with the concepts of embedded relational mindfulness and interpersonal neurology.

Ogden, Goldstein, and Fisher (2012) explain the value of including a somatic perspective:

> Adding a body-oriented approach to traditional narrative therapies does not rely on language for its efficacy and can directly target the non-verbal legacy of childhood trauma. Underscoring the role of unresolved trauma on affect regulation, procedural learning, and sensory processing, this [technique] focuses on the centrality of these phenomena in the treatment of children and adolescents. Moreover, a bottom-up approach that targets the body, in addition to the verbal narrative when available, can produce changes that will influence resolution of symptoms and increase the capacity for relatedness and adaptive behavior (Bakal, 1999; Ogden & Minton 2000; Ogden, Minton, & Pain, 2006; Fisher et al., 1992). We will prioritize the non-verbal "somatic narrative" that is beyond words and cannot be articulated but continuously anticipates the future and powerfully determines behavior. (p. xxx)

Ogden and Fisher (2015) offer clinicians a deep understanding of Sensorimotor Psychotherapy with practical exercises that can help clients learn to notice their internal experience, heighten their consciousness, and develop awareness of their body sensations, movements, perceptions, and cognitions. In this way, by prioritizing present-moment experience rather than the past or future, Sensorimotor Psychotherapy capitalizes on the brain's capacity for neuroplasticity by creating new experiences of awareness.

The importance of body-based forms of intelligence such as proprioception was first introduced to me (Goldstein) by Howard Gardner, one of my professors at the Graduate School of Education at Harvard University. Gardner has spent his entire academic career expanding the evaluation of frames of intelligence. Gardner (1983, 2004, 2011) proposes that we possess a range of capacities and intelligences extending beyond the traditional measurement tools, leading to expanded ways of identifying a fuller spectrum of intelligence. His concept of *bodily kinesthetic intelligence*, which stresses the powerful correlation between the body's natural, deep wisdom and our ability to use this wisdom to positively influence ourselves and the world around us, impacted the way in which I viewed the younger clients that I worked with individually, as well through the group experience. Sharing Gardner's concepts with group members—using everyday language to convey the scientific basis of the nonverbal somatic component of our work—had an impact that was amplified by the group context. A deep awareness is heightened collaboratively with the emergent experience of understanding and becoming connected to our bodies, and as appreciation for the body's intelligence evolves for both members and leaders.

Similarly, adding neuroscience and somatic components to the traditional group therapy models that emphasize the cognitive-based verbal narrative can shift the emphasis from primarily dialogue and cognitive tasks by also inviting an exploration of present-moment awareness, practicing sensory intelligence, and welcoming experiences of consciousness into the group process. For example, as group members engage with one another in new ways, developing mindful awareness leads to powerful insights, practical skills, and expanded awareness of the body as a source of important insight and information. More significant, the group format offers an authentic experience in which members "feel felt." Siegel describes this experience as "an eloquent way of expressing the connections we have with another person when we are felt, understood, and connected" (2016, p. 182). For example, just by holding someone's hand, one can quiet anger, fury, or fear, all through soothing touch. Even more, one's sense of the presence of another person whom one trusts can soothe distress in anticipated pain from a shock

Feeling felt can be viewed as the way in which two people become linked so that they resonate as they are influenced by the other but do not become the other, as in the symbiotic process. As we'll see soon, this state has two fundamental elements: differentiation and then linkage. This is the state of integration in which the whole is greater than the sum of its parts. From the point of view of interpersonal neurobiology, integration is the basis of health. When integration is blocked, chaos and rigidity are more likely to arise. We think of *integration* as an active rather than static state—meaning that we are in a state of becoming, not a fixed accomplishment. And so we can see how any process of becoming can nurture differentiation and then the linkages of those unique individuals in a system that becomes a "we." This is the underlying mechanism beneath the subjective sense of feeling felt.

An example of feeling felt in the group milieu comes from a case that addressed the social isolation of having your friends stop being your friends, feelings that are often buried—as was the case with Sophie, who was more successful in middle school than were her friends and was promoted to a private, high-achieving high school that launched a trajectory of success and left her friends behind.

Sophie, a group therapy member for the past six months, found that the gradual support of her peers in the group offered insight to the part of her that felt guilty for leaving her friends. Even more painful, she was then excluded by her former friends—they reportedly neglected her, not including her on weekends. She was fiercely determined to rekindle these friendships, with no success. Nor did she develop close friendships at her new school. Sophie buried her feelings so very deeply within that she couldn't access them in individual therapy. Only through observing others share similar experiences in group sessions and realizing that she was not alone could Sophie reframe these social dynamics as inherent in peer relationships and feel a shift toward self-compassion and self-acceptance. Hence, through listening to her peers, Sophie had an experience of "feeling felt." This means that she experienced being respected for her individual subjective world—she was able to differentiate, and then to link with respectful, accepting, compassionate peers. This is how an isolated "me" becomes an integral part of an interconnected "we."

This shift in perception of self, through the interconnectedness of feeling felt, is described in *Mind* (Siegel, 2016), with the following excerpt:

So at the end of treatment I said to her that we would have an "exit interview" when we review what had been most helpful and what could be improved. "Great idea," she said. So, I asked her, what was most helpful to you? "Oh, that's obvious" she replied. Yes, I said, I know, but if you had to put words to it, what would you say? She paused for a moment, looking at me with moist eyes, and she said, "You know, I've never had this experience before. I've never had this experience of feeling felt by anyone. That's what helped me get better." (p. 182)

Feeling felt describes the connections we form with another person when our experiences and emotions are empathically received and understood. In individual therapy, this process occurs through the therapist's focus on the client's inner subjective experience of mind, wherein the therapist is attuned to the client's inner world and offers a sense of trust in it, as in the following example from *Mind* (Siegel, 2016):

> And with that trust, she and I could explore the inner world of her mind that was troubling her so deeply. The mind that emerged in her as we worked closely together, the resolution of her traumas from a painful past with her family, her feelings of helplessness in the present with the death of her colleague, her experience of hopelessness for the future that gave her a sense of despair, these were now resolved. Trust was the gateway to our journey to heal those wounds. What was the healing action? Feeling felt. I could be present for her, attuning to her inner life—her inner subjective reality—and then resonate with that reality. I might even attune to that inner world and connect with information processing that she was not in touch with herself, aspects of her non-conscious mind. And that, too, could shape my internal world even if it was not in her awareness. I was changed because of our connection too. This is the experience of resonance. (p. 183)

Sometimes that resonance can be consciously recognized and we are overtly aware of feeling felt, as we sense this way in which we have become connected as a "we." I (Siegel) like to remember the importance of both differentiation as a "me" with the connection and membership of a "we" with the odd and funny neologism *mwe*. Mwe is how we can have both a "me" and a "we" in one integrated identity. With this term, too, we can recall that either one—*me* or *we*—by itself is missing the differentiation and linkage of an integrated life. *Mwe* is what mwe can feel in therapy when it goes well and our client feels felt by us, as his or her mind is experienced as existing within ours, and each of us is changed by the experience.

One way of considering the fundamental stance in therapy is the important *PART*—presence, attunement, resonance, and trust—we play in the growth of our clients, our patients, as well as our fellow travelers along this journey of life (Siegel, 2010). *Presence* is a state of receptive awareness the enables an openness to let into our consciousness anything that emerges in an experience with minimal filtering from expectation and judgment. *Attunement* is the focus of attention—that process that directs the flow of energy and information—on the internal world of self and of others. The term *interpersonal attunement* means that as therapists we focus beneath surface behaviors for the underlying mental experience driving those externally visible actions. With attunement, we focus on the inner experiences of feelings, thoughts, and memories. This is how we *SIFT*—sensations, images, feelings, and thoughts—the mind for its internal subjective contents.

Resonance is how we enable ourselves to be influenced by another, to be changed by the interaction without losing our identity. When we resonate with someone else and enable those changes to be revealed, the other person can feel felt by us. *Trust* is what develops with presence, attunement, and resonance, enabling what Stephen Porges's (2011) polyvagal theory suggests is the turning on of a social engagement system. This is the receptive state that facilitates not only interpersonal connection but likely also internal attunement and growth (Siegel, 2007). Both conscious and nonconscious experiences of our connection with clients can create trust between us, and that trust facilitates learning as it harnesses neuroplasticity—the ways the brain changes in response to experience.

One possible mechanism in the brain that may mediate such experiences of feeling felt can be hypothesized as the following sequence. When we have the repeated experience of others in the PART of someone with whom we feel felt, an implicit engram may be laid down in our own brain—that is, a neural net profile of activation that would include a set of neural firings that, with repetition, would become structural changes in the brain itself. In this way, a certain experience fires a set of neurons, and, as Dan Siegel has paraphrased the physician and psychologist Donald Hebb, "Neurons that fire together, wire together." *Firing* occurs in the moment of neural activation with feeling felt experiences; *wiring* is the synaptic, neuronal, and perhaps myelin growth associated with repeated experiences. This is how we learn. And what feeling felt may teach us is that we are not alone. How exactly that might influence brain anatomy, no one knows exactly, but it could involve any or all of a number of possibilities. One is that a client's window of tolerance for experiencing interactions that could be interpreted as isolating or rejecting would be widened, so that he or she could maintain equilibrium even in the face of such nonsupportive experiences. Another possibility is that the limbic appraisal processes would downregulate the tendency to experience dependency on nonsignificant others' actions as powerfully shaping a sense of self in the moment. Such a change might be enhanced by having a neural net profile of a sense of self that is more resilient, something that we might describe as "I am a loved and am a lovable person." When interactions happen, such a feeling-felt mental model of the self would serve as a source of inner resilience. Yet another possibility is the implicit memory that "my self in connection with others in the group was deeply rewarding," and with this implicit memory of a past actual experience, the prospective memory—the implicit memory of the future—would be shifted so a client could now imagine a future of connection as a realistic possibility, not just a fantasy, which would soothe current distress of isolation and support constructive behaviors to make such imagined future outcomes an actual reality.

The group experience offers the opportunity, cocreated by group members, for spontaneously arising moments of mindful awareness, thereby liberating expression through the emergent experience—both group experience and individual members' experiences—without interfering with the integrity of their narrative processing and spontaneously emerging experiences. These ongoing experiences likely shape the neural firing, wiring, and architecture of each member's brain—and these changes can positively reinforce the ongoing relational interactions that can then recursively support the continued experience of feeling felt in the group, infusing the group process with an atmosphere of enduring trust and exploration. Having an individual or a group experience wherein the focus is on attuning to a person's story—attuning not just to the external events described but especially to his or her inner subjective experience, as well as to the intersubjective cocreated experience of the group—offers a powerful and unique opportunity for feeling felt. Such opportunities expand consciousness, harness attention, and amplify present-moment awareness of transformations large and small, as they emerge and are cocreated.

Part of the mindful awareness nurtured here is captured by the acronym *COAL*—curiosity, openness, acceptance, and love (Siegel, 2007)—that we bring to our awareness and our interactions. In this way, mindfulness is not only a state of being aware but also a way of being. In a group setting, it is a relational way of approaching others with these COAL qualities. Such a group experience then models how individuals can use that same kind regard toward their own inner experiences when away from the direct support of the here-and-now group. The group's mindful awareness becomes an innate stance each individual carries with him or her both within the group experience and as each moves out into the world. As we noted previously, "Introducing mindfulness training in group therapy does not necessarily change the elements in the outside lives of group members, but it invariably changes the way they *react to* those elements. Because groups provide the opportunity to reexperience old patterns with new people, it is within such groups that members can repair old wounds and develop new ways in which to interact as they move more robustly into the overall growth process" (Mark-Goldstein & Siegel, 2013. p. 225).

Over the past three decades of working in the mental health field, we have explored mind–body processes through a multitude of perspectives, practices, and theories, including interpersonal neurobiology, mindfulness practices, Sensorimotor Psychotherapy, and other mind–body orientations toward healing. Each of these modalities has strengths and unique influences, depending on what clients need at a given point in their journeys. Harnessing movement and stillness, playful touch (as clinically appropriate), and awareness of sensations, breath, connection to self, and connection to other mental health practitioners provides a plethora of tools with which to engage clients in healing processes tailored to their particular circumstances.

Over the years, there has been an emphasis on identifying with schools of therapy, an emphasis on lineage—who has studied with whom, which therapeutic orientation is best. One benefit of the integrative model of interpersonal neurobiology is that it offers a scientifically grounded approach that prioritizes the relationship between therapist and client and incorporates awareness of somatic (embodied), intuitive, and emotional explorations of our life stories. Hence, the experience of sharing one's story ultimately takes place in those precious and deeply personal moments of connection that occur when we feel safe enough to share ourselves and listen to others. Inviting curiosity allows us to look for relational connections in which feeling felt can bring our consciousness toward cocreated safety. Through this safety, we can combat our anxiety about the novel experiences, particularly when relationships feel frightening. It is these new experiences that engage our minds actively, thereby expanding our brains. This attitude of wonder, interest, and investigation can facilitate the novelty of change that emerges when members feel safe to share.

Large and small group experiences offer opportunities for members to gather lots of useful information—about themselves, other people, the world—simply by their participation. Part of the challenge in group therapy (and in any context intended to facilitate change) is the inevitable uncertainty that arises with the new experience. The brain is often said to be an "anticipation machine," meaning that it filters experience through the lens of prior events embedded within memory. This is how "top-down" processing—what we have learned in the past—shapes our "bottom-up" experience of the sensory-rich present moment. Indeed, this top-down facility is one of the challenges of expertise, in that the more we know, the less we perceive. We have a propensity to view what is occurring in the present moment through the lens of what we are certain about, what we know, what we are an expert in. And one area we may even have a nonconscious expertise in is *who we are*—"I know myself." What this means, then, is that anything that invites me—or challenges me—to consider becoming different challenges my self-expertise. Moreover, nonconscious expertise is likely to block experiences of feeling felt because the expertise is not a present-moment expression but, rather, a fixed belief structure. Whether in verbal form or behavioral enacted form, our lived narrative reveals that model of self in need of change.

Becoming comfortable with uncertainty is a component of the journey of psychotherapy. Learning to thrive with uncertainty is part of the mastery of therapeutic change. We are all lifelong learners, and when we embrace the reality that the brain changes throughout the lifespan, we can go for the ride of our lives, open to the excitement of this unfolding change, this continual emergence of uncertainty to disrupt the complacency of a seeming expertise of who we thought we were.

In reality, the self is both a constructor and a conduit of experience (Siegel, 2016). In this way, our narratives arise as we construct a self; being open and learning to thrive with uncertainty is embracing the equally important but distinct role of conduit in our experience of self in the world. Being with others—with a therapist and other group members—is a way of embracing the conduit function of our self as it emerges, moment by moment.

Participants also begin to see the larger context and thus become less affected by any single thing in itself: not so driven to get more of what they like, and not so stressed and unsettled by what they don't like. Developing curiosity about others helps group members understand the inner workings of their own psyches. Curiosity is a great asset for healing, growth, and awakening, while also fostering awareness and engagement with the world and others. This is how the group process supports the ongoing development of a COAL state of mind, within the individual and relationally among the members. Such a process likely reinforces the neuroplastic changes in the brains of the members, which in turn support a mindful way of being with self and with others.

In working with trauma through the group experience, soothing and calming the nervous system of each member are paramount. We cannot explore and dare to take risks when our nervous systems are in a state of fearful physiological reactivity. The perception of being unsafe can be as covert as perceiving other members casting sidelong glances that are vague but slightly threatening. The cocreated safety in the therapeutic milieu helps offset discomfort by offering opportunities for mindful awareness of the present-moment experience, both implicit and explicit. Use of yoga-type breath work, mindfulness-based stress reduction techniques, and/or other somatic interventions are taught to aid members in calming their own nervous systems and increasing their social engagement systems; they are especially useful in this format, as group experiences are often novel and therefore anxiety provoking. This is how the therapeutic process can move members from the reactive state to the receptive state in which each member's social engagement system is activated.

Feeling unsafe can lead to *deactivation* of the autonomic nervous system, identified by avoidant behavior, numbness, deadness, and disconnection, or to *overactivation* of the nervous system, experienced as hyperarousal, impulsive movement, incessant talking, and intrusive interactions that are not mindful. Therefore, providing a sense of safety as fundamental to our clients' experiences is a foundational therapeutic goal that can be fostered through collaboration and the coconstruction of embodied relational safety—mwe emerges with a sense of trust. Porges (2011) proposes that only when we experience safety can we forge ahead in the environment. Safety is the prerequisite for activating the social engagement system, which is a key agent in healing. Ogden et al. (2012) write about strengthening the social engagement system as well as prosocial behaviors through the group therapy experience:

> Group provides an opportunity to revisit early attachment issues, and group members often take on a particular role in the simulated group "family." These roles, visible in the procedural tendencies of the body, are strongly influenced by early attachment relationships and the family milieu, which shapes posture, gestures, and movements in ways designed to adapt to the particular family environment.
>
> The microcosm of the world that group therapy creates makes it a profound therapeutic setting in which to observe and amend relational problems, examining interpersonal experience as lived in the present moment, as it unfolds, including the physical elements that both reflect and sustain relational dynamics. The group creates a natural, authentic, organic opportunity for members' issues and their physical manifestations to arise in real time: their own life experience recreated on the landscape of a group. The sensations, gestures, tensions, movement patterns, that go along with emotions, thoughts, and perceptions are happening live. The sensorimotor psychotherapist uses "bottom-up" approaches and interventions, teaching group members to observe, follow, and work through issues and relational dynamics starting with the physical experience. Sensorimotor psychotherapy also integrates bottom-up approaches that directly address the effects of trauma and relational issues on the body and on emotions with "top-down" approaches that focus on insight and understanding. Bodily experience becomes a primary entry point for intervention, while meaning-making arises out of the subsequent somatic reorganization of habitual responses. (pp. 124–125)

The conduit function of the mind (Siegel, 2016) is how we get as close to something as it is sensorily possible. *Pre-sense*, a way of thinking about presence, is limited by the fact that we live in a body. But once sensory inputs arise in our embodied realities, we then move to the level of perception. *Perception* often involves cognitive processes of input from sensory systems, with top-down memory filtering those bottom-up inputs.

Porges (2004, 2011) describes a perceptual system, *neuroception*, designed to scan for danger and alert us when a threat is present. This neural process of neuroception is outside the realm of awareness but can influence our conscious experience. Neurobiological mechanisms allow us to *neurocept* features in the environment that indicate degrees of safety, danger, and threat. These features include behavioral and nonverbal cues from others that incline us to move toward, away from, or ignore the source. Ogden et al. describe a child's ability to appraise the safety or threat of an environment through neuroception: "The nervous system evaluates risk in the environment and regulates the expression of adaptive behavior to match the neuroception" (2012, p. 17)

Overall, group and individual therapy aim to bring into awareness these many layers of often nonconscious neural, subjective, and relational processes. The chaos or rigidity that often characterizes the distress of individuals coming to therapy for relief of their suffering can be seen as the product of obstructed self-organizational flow, which innately tends to move us toward integration. In this way, a therapist detects chaos or rigidity as a sign of a blockage to health, a blockage to integration. Then the areas of a person's life that are not differentiated and/or linked are determined, and the facilitation of those areas is the focus of therapy (Siegel, 2010b). What we have described here is the powerful ways in which the relational integration of feeling felt can be seen as a crucial domain in the therapeutic journey. Other domains of integration—such as those of consciousness, verticality, bilaterality, memory, narrative, state, temporality, and identity—all interface with this important domain of interpersonal integration. With the creation of safety within the therapeutic setting, we come to the experience as therapists with our presence, attunement, resonance, and the facilitation of trust. Knowing these components of the PART we serve in helping others to experience feeling felt, which is at the heart of interpersonal integration, can guide us in establishing the important foundations of change across many modalities of psychotherapy. Together, mwe in the field of mental health can work to use these interdisciplinary ideas to find powerful and effective ways of helping others create more integration in their lives. With the ever-increasing pressures facing each of us in this deeply challenged world, the field of mental health is in an important position to play a key PART in cultivating resilience and supporting the growth of well-being for all we care for so deeply.

References

Cozolino, L. (2015). *Why therapy works: Using our minds to change our brains*. New York, NY: Norton.

Eliot, T. S. (1968). "Little Gidding." In *Four quartets* (section 5). New York, NY: Mariner Books.

Gardner, H. (1983). *Frames of mind: The theory of multiple intelligences*. New York, NY: Basic Books.

Gardner, H. (2004). *Frames of mind: The theory of multiple intelligences* (2nd ed.). New York, NY: Basic Books.

Gardner, H. (2011). *Frames of mind: The theory of multiple intelligences* (3rd ed.). New York, NY: Basic Books.

Mark-Goldstein, B., & Siegel, D. J. (2013). The mindful group: Using mind–body–brain interactions in group therapy to foster resilience and integration. In D. J. Siegel & M. Solomon (Eds.), *Healing moments in psychotherapy*. New York, NY: Norton.

Ogden, P., & Fisher, J. (2015). *Sensorimotor psychotherapy: Interventions for trauma and attachment*. New York, NY: Norton.

Ogden, P., Goldstein, B., & Fisher, J. (2012). Brain-to-brain, body-to-body: A sensorimotor psychotherapy approach for the treatment of children and adolescents. In R. Longo, D. Prescott, J. Bergman, & K. Creeden (Eds.), *Current perspectives and applications in neurobiology: Working with young people who are victims and perpetrators of sexual abuse* (pp. 229–255). Mount Holyoke, MA: Neari Press.

Porges, S. (2004) Neuroception: A subconscious system for detecting threats and safety. *Zero to Three, 24*(5), 19-24

Porges, S. (2011). *The polyvagal theory: Neurophysiological foundations of emotions, attachment, communication, and self-regulation*. New York, NY: Norton.

Siegel, D. J. (2007) *The mindful brain: reflection and attunement in the cultivation of well-being*. New York, NY: Norton

Siegel, D. J. (2010). *The mindful therapist: A clinician's guide to mindsight and neural integration*. New York, NY: Norton.

Siegel, D. J. (2012a). *The developing mind: How relationships and the brain interact to shape who we are* (2nd ed.). New York, NY: Guilford Press.

Siegel, D. J. (2012b). *Pocket guide to interpersonal neurobiology: An integrative handbook of the mind*. New York, NY: Norton.

Siegel, D. J. (2016). *Mind: A journey to the heart of being human*. New York, NY: Norton.

Winnicott, D. W. (1965) *The maturational Process and the facilitating environment: Studies in the theory of emotional development*. New York: International Universities Press.

List of Contributors

Daniel J. Siegel, MD is a clinical professor of psychiatry at the UCLA School of Medicine, founding co-director of UCLA's Mindful Awareness Research Center, founding co-investigator at the UCLA Center for Culture, Brain, and Development, and executive director of the Mindsight Institute. Dr. Siegel's books include *Pocket Guide to Interpersonal Neurobiology*, *The Mindful Therapist*, *The Mindful Brain*, and four *New York Times* bestsellers: *Brainstorm*, *The Whole-Brain Child* (with Tina Payne Bryson, PhD), *No-Drama Discipline* (with Tina Payne Bryson, PhD), and *Mind: A Journey to the Heart of Being Human*.

Marion Solomon, PhD, is in private practice in West Los Angeles, specializing in treating issues that are disruptive to her patients' relationships. She is on the faculty at the David Geffen School of Medicine, Department of Psychiatry at UCLA, and Senior Extension faculty at the Department of Humanities, Sciences and Social Sciences at UCLA. She is the Director of Clinical Training at the Lifespan Learning Institute in Los Angeles, author of *Lean on Me: The Power of Positive Dependency in Intimate Relationships; Narcissism and Intimacy: Love and Marriage in an Age of Confusion*, co-author of *Love and War in Intimate Relationships*, and co-editor of *Healing Trauma* and *The Healing Power of Emotion*.

Philip Bromberg, PhD, is a Training and Supervising Analyst and faculty member at the William Alanson White Psychoanalytic Institute, and Adjunct Clinical Professor of Psychology at the New York University Postdoctoral Program in Psychotherapy and Psychoanalysis. He is the author of *Standing in the Spaces: Essays on Clinical Process, Trauma, and Dissociation; Awakening the Dreamer: Clinical Journeys; The Shadow of the Tsunami; and The Growth of the Relational Mind*.

Louis Cozolino, PhD, is a writer, professor, and practicing psychologist in Los Angeles, California. He is the author of *The Making of a Therapist, The Neuroscience of Human Relationships 2e, The Healthy Aging Brain, The Social Neuroscience of Education, Attachment-Based Teaching, Why Therapy Works*, and *The Neuroscience of Psychotherapy 3e*.

Vanessa Davis is a graduate of the University of California, Davis and of Pepperdine University. She earned a Masters degree in Clinical Psychology and a lifetime membership into the Psi Chi International Honor Society. She works as a research and teaching assistant for Dr. Cozolino, and volunteers as a marriage and family therapist intern at a drug and alcohol treatment center. Her clinical interests also include multiculturalism and working with children and adolescents.

Margaret Wilkinson is a Jungian Analyst and professional member of the Society of Analytical Psychology in London, England. She is the Assistant Editor for the *Journal of Psychology* and author of *Coming into Mind: The Mind-Brain Relationship: A Jungian Clinical Perspective*.

Pat Ogden, PhD, is the Founder and Director of the Sensorimotor Psychotherapy Institute; Co-Founder of the Hakomi Institute, and faculty at Naropa University. She is the author of several books including *Trauma and the Body: A Sensorimotor Approach to Psychotherapy* and *Sensorimotor Psychotherapy: Interventions for Trauma and Attachment*.

Peter Levine, PhD, is a renowned therapist and educator who specializes in the understanding and treatment of Post Traumatic Stress Disorder (PTSD). He is author of *Waking the Tiger: Healing Trauma*.

Russell Meares, MD, is Emeritus Professor of Psychiatry at the University of Sydney and the director of Mental Health Sciences at Westmead Hospital. He is the founder of the Academic Department of Psychiatry at the University of Melbourne and author of *The Metaphor of Play*.

Dan Hughes, PhD, is a clinical psychologist who provides training and consultations throughout the US, Canada, the UK, and Australia. He is the author of *Building the Bonds of Attachment, Brain-Based Parenting: The Neuroscience of Caregiving for Healthy Attachment*, and *The Neurobiology of Attachment-Focused Therapy: Enhancing Connection and Trust in the Treatment of Children and Adolescents*.

Martha Stark, MD, has been on the faculty at Harvard Medical School for the past 36 years, is co-director of the Center for Psychoanalytic Studies at William James College, and has numerous teaching affiliations (as Adjunct Faculty) with local, regional, and national psychodynamic / psychoanalytic training programs. She is the author of *Working with Resistance, A Primer on Working with Resistance*, and *Modes of Therapeutic Action*.

Stan Tatkin, PsyD, MFT, is an Assistant Clinical Professor at the David Geffen School of Medicine, UCLA and Clinical Director of the Outpatient Drug and Alcohol Program at Charter Hospital. He is the author of *Love and War in Intimate Relationships* and *Wired For Love*.

Bonnie Goldstein, PhD, is a licensed clinical psychologist and social worker who works as an individual, family, and group psychotherapist in Los Angeles, and is Clinical Faculty at the USC School of Social Work. She is the author of *I'll Know What to Do* and co-editor of *The Handbook of Infant, Child, and Adolescent Psychotherapy: A Guide to Diagnosis and Treatment, Vols. I and II*.

Index